UNITED NATIONS CONFERENCE ON TRADE AND DEVELOPMENT

Economic Development in Africa Report 2020

Tackling Illicit Financial Flows for Sustainable Development in Africa

UNITED NATIONS
Geneva, 2020

United Nations publication issued by the United Nations
Conference on Trade and Development.

UNCTAD/ALDC/AFRICA/2020

ISBN: 978-92-1-112982-3
eISBN: 978-92-1-005044-9
ISSN: 1990-5114
eISSN: 1990-5122
Sales No. E.20.II.D.21

Acknowledgements

The *Economic Development in Africa Report 2020: Tackling Illicit Financial Flows for Sustainable Development in Africa* was prepared by Junior Davis (team leader), Milasoa Chérel-Robson, Claudia Roethlisberger (until 31 December 2019), Carlotta Schuster and Anja Slany, with the assistance of Héléna Diffo, Léo Picard and Gang Zhang. Specific background papers were prepared for the report by Alexander Ezenagu (Hamad Bin Khalifa University), Samuel Gayi (international consultant), Martin Hearson (International Centre for Tax and Development, Institute of Development Studies, University of Sussex) and Detlef Kotte (Hochschule für Technik und Wirtschaft Berlin – University of Applied Sciences). The work was completed under the overall supervision of Paul Akiwumi, Director of the UNCTAD Division for Africa, Least Developed Countries and Special Programmes.

An ad hoc expert group meeting on tackling illicit financial flows for sustainable economic development in Africa was held in Geneva on 11 and 12 December 2019 to conduct a peer review of the report. It brought together specialists in African tax, trade, finance and the modelling of illicit financial flows. The following people participated in the meeting and/or contributed to the report with comments: Laila Abdul Latif (University of Nairobi), Elisabeth Bürgi Bonanomi (Centre for Development and Environment , University of Bern), Gilles Carbonnier (professor, the Graduate Institute of International and Development Studies, Geneva), Rebecca Engebretsen (Organization for Economic Cooperation and Development), Uzumma Marilyn Erume (United Nations Economic Commission for Africa), Alexander Ezenagu (Hamad Bin Khalifa University), Gang Zhang (Graduate Institute of International and Development Studies, Geneva), Martin Hearson (International Centre for Tax and Development, Institute of Development Studies), Rahul Mehrota (Graduate Institute of International and Development Studies, Geneva), Markie Muryawan (United Nations Department of Economic and Social Affairs), Irene Musselli (Centre for Development and Environment, University of Bern), Léonce Ndikumana (professor, University of Massachusetts-Amherst), Joy Ndubai (Vienna University of Economics and Business) and Kathy Nicolaou-Manias (management consultant, Argent Econ Consult). Members of the *Economic Development in Africa Report* team also attended the meeting.

The following UNCTAD staff members took part in the meeting and/or made comments on the draft report: Celine Bacrot, Lisa Borgatti, Fernando Cantu-Bazaldua, Stefanie Garry, Janvier Nkurunziza, Patrick Osakwe, Matfobhi Riba, Yvan Rwananga, Antipas Touatam, Rolf Traeger, Elisabeth Tuerk, Giovanni Valensisi and Anida Yupari.

Rostand Ngadjie Siani provided administrative support; the Intergovernmental Support Service of UNCTAD designed the cover and infographics; Carlos Bragunde and Juan Carlos Korol were responsible for the layout and desktop publishing.

The report's analysis draws on insights from institutional collaboration with: the Swiss Consortium on Curbing Illicit Financial Flows from Resource-rich Developing Countries; the International Centre for Tax and Development coordinated by the Institute of Development Studies at the University of Sussex; and the UNCTAD–United Nations Office on Drugs and Crime Task Force on Statistical Methodologies for Measuring Illicit Financial Flows. We would also like to thank the International Investment Agreements Section of the UNCTAD Division on Investment and Enterprise for inputs provided to the report and Homi Kharas, John McArthur and Selen Özdoğan of the Brookings Institution for help with data on Sustainable Development Goal financing.

Note

Country-level detailed figures are available on request to the UNCTAD secretariat.

Any references to dollars ($) are to United States dollars.

Contents

FIGURES

TABLES

BOXES

BOXES FIGURES

Foreword

Worldwide, a loss of trust in multilateralism is weakening the capacity of globalization to deliver a more sustainable and fairer world. Growing awareness of the scale, scope and cost of illicit financial flows is stoking growing scepticism about the power of collective action versus unilateral measures. It is against this backdrop that the United Nations Conference on Trade and Development (UNCTAD) *Economic Development in Africa Report 2020* tackles the relationship between illicit financial flows and sustainable development in Africa. Illicit financial flows – cross border exchanges of value, monetary or otherwise, which are illegally earned, transferred or used – cost African countries around $50 billion per year, dwarfing the amount of official development assistance the continent receives annually. Illicit financial flows are a shared problem and a shared responsibility for developed and developing countries; their economic impacts are a major development issue across the globe, even more so for African economies whose sustainable development prospects critically pivot on massive investments.

This year's *Economic Development in Africa Report* adopts a multidisciplinary methodological approach, encompasses a gender lens throughout the analysis and includes environmental sustainability in its conceptualization of sustainable development. Although this report primarily provides substantive and analytical contributions on how to tackle illicit financial flows in Africa, the breadth of issues and topical debates around this subject are applicable to any country. They range from trade-specific illicit flows to international taxation issues, from international investment agreements to the institutional roots of illicit financial flows.

Illicit financial flows strip government treasuries of needed resources for development expenditure. The report's findings confirm that such financial flows are high in Africa and have been increasing over time. Curbing illicit financial flows is therefore an avenue for providing African countries with additional funds towards achieving Agenda 2063 and the Sustainable Development Goals. Our focus is on how to accomplish this by fighting the financial haemorrhage that these illicit flows generate, through stronger national policies, regulatory frameworks, data infrastructure and institutional and human resources capacity. African countries also need to engage much more in the international arena, including in the reforms of the international taxation system, to make it more relevant to the challenges Africa faces in the twenty-first century.

Multilateralism has a key role to play in reducing harmful illicit financial flows and encouraging stronger participation of African countries in global governance. Beyond the multiple United Nations resolutions on such illicit flows, recent initiatives such as the establishment of a joint High-level Panel on Financial Accountability, Transparency and Integrity provide hope towards more concrete action to amplify attention to illicit financial flows and to enhance the capacity of local revenue authorities in Africa. Building on these and other initiatives, such as the landmark Mbeki report (2015), the *Economic Development in Africa Report 2020* situates its recommendations within the broader context of the African Continental Free Trade Area, a new beacon for the continent and an opportunity to rewrite history.

As countries scramble to respond to the global health emergency due to the coronavirus disease 2019 outbreak, African economies that are already weakened by illicit financial flows face a difficult path ahead as the global pandemic stifles demand for exports from Africa, risking a major slowdown. In the lead-up to the fifteenth session of the United Nations Conference on Trade and Development in Barbados, it is our hope that the evidence and recommendations presented in this report will improve policy approaches to tackling the incidence and impact of illicit financial flows, laying the foundations for a stronger, more resilient Africa that can overcome this and future challenges.

Mukhisa Kituyi
Secretary-General of UNCTAD

Abbreviations

AfCFTA	African Continental Free Trade Area
AfDB	African Development Bank
AMV	African Mining Vision
ATAF	African Tax Administration Forum
BEPS	Base erosion and profit shifting
c.i.f.	Cost, insurance, freight
CPIA	Country Policy and Institutional Assessment
DOTS	Direction of trade statistics (method)
EITI	Extractive Industries Transparency Initiative
FDI	Foreign direct investment
GDP	Gross domestic product
GER	Gross excluding reversal (method)
ICTD	International Centre for Tax and Development
IFF	Illicit financial flow
IMF	International Monetary Fund
MNE	Multinational enterprise
ODA	Official development assistance
OECD	Organization for Economic Cooperation and Development
OEEC	Organization for European Economic Cooperation
OFC	Offshore financial centre
StAR	Stolen Asset Recovery Initiative
UN-Women	United Nations Entity for Gender Equality and the Empowerment of Women
UNDP	United Nations Development Programme

UNECA	United Nations Economic Commission for Africa
UNESCO	United Nations Educational, Scientific and Cultural Organization
UNFCCC	United Nations Framework Convention on Climate Change
UNODC	United Nations Office on Drugs and Crime
UNSD	United Nations Statistics Division
UNU-WIDER	United Nations University World Institute for Development Economics Research
WCO	World Customs Organization
WTO	World Trade Organization

Introduction
Illicit financial flows are a shared problem between developed and developing countries

The year 2020 is a milestone for Africa and for multilateralism. As many African countries celebrate their sixtieth anniversary of gaining independence from colonial rulers, the continent is making a significant stride towards transforming the promises of the 1960s into a reality as the African Continental Free Trade Area (AfCFTA) was due to open for trading on 1 July 2020, but had to be postponed due to the coronavirus disease 2019 outbreak. AfCFTA is a landmark achievement on the continent's journey towards greater integration and prosperity. The year 2020 also marks the celebration of the seventy-fifth anniversary of the United Nations, the twenty-fifth anniversary of the Beijing Declaration and Platform for Action, and the beginning of the decade of action towards achieving the 2030 Agenda for Sustainable Development. Finally, the fifteenth session of the United Nations Conference on Trade and Development will be held in Barbados.

ILLICIT FINANCIAL FLOWS (IFFs)
are a shared problem between
developed and **developing** countries

4 BROAD CATEGORIES OF IFFs

Tax and commercial
practices

Illegal markets

Theft-type and terrorism
financing

Corruption

Curbing
annual capital flight of
US$88.6 billion →
from Africa could bridge
half of its SDG financing gap

Beyond the milestones of 2020, the examination of illicit financial flows (IFFs) is motivated by growing concerns over its perceived effects on the world's economic, social and political stability. At dinner parties in capital cities around the world, the world's cosmopolitan elite compare notes on the best schools, the least-polluted cities, the alarming spread of insecurity, the threat of populism, and the latest on tax havens. In a parallel reality, when educated men and women from the world's disillusioned middle class meet, from the suburbs of industrialized countries to the compounds of African cities, they share common concerns about the future of their children, deep misgivings about inequality, injustice and a growing resentment towards the prosperous elite. The rhetoric is often the same: complaints about how the wealthiest individuals and the largest corporations are able to avoid paying taxes, how the poor cannot pay, and how those in the middle are increasingly squeezed. In mineral-resource-rich developing countries, including in Africa, these conversations sometimes allude to the latest press reports on unfair contract deals in the mining sector and the prevalence of IFFs, a term that has made global media headlines for the past 10 years.

This report provides an analysis of IFFs and sustainable development in Africa. It does so by considering the three dimensions of sustainable development: economic, social and environmental. As discussed in chapter 1, the report uses the definition endorsed by the Inter-Agency and Expert Group on Sustainable Development Goal Indicators as the basis for the measurement of progress towards Goal 16, target 16.4. The definition is as follows: "Illicit financial flows are financial flows that are illicit in origin, transfer or use; that reflect an exchange of value (instead of a pure money transaction); and that cross country borders" (UNCTAD and United Nations Office on Drugs and Crime (UNODC) (forthcoming)).[1]

This introduction is structured as follows: section I reviews the use of the term "illicit financial flows" in multilateral discourse, drawing on the economic and legal literature on the definitions of the term; section II highlights the key principles of the report's conceptual approach to IFFs; section III presents the objectives, overall approach and organization of the report.

I. Illicit financial flows in multilateral discourse

The plethora of studies and forums on IFFs shows that the definitions and measurement reflect tensions between polarized views of the world embedded in a set of values,

---

[1]   Further details on the components of this definition are presented in chapter 1.

historical legacy, legal frameworks and economic ideology. For the World Bank, for example, "the term 'illicit financial flows' began to appear in the 1990s to describe a number of cross-border activities. The term was initially associated with capital flight" (World Bank, 2016:1). The concern for capital flight in the least developed countries was at the time motivated by the need for capital funds from foreign loans, foreign equity and domestic sources to cater for the servicing of external debt and to provide capital for domestic investments. In a context of structural adjustment policies in most African countries, a sudden or prolonged outflow of domestic capital was likely to affect a country's macroeconomic performance, leading to these surges being labelled "capital flight" rather than "normal" flows (Cumby and Levich, 1987; Ajayi and Khan, 2000). By the mid-2000s, studies from leading civil society organizations popularized the use of the term illicit financial flows by shedding light on the potentially significant magnitude of such hidden flows due to either the illicit origin of the capital or the illicit nature of the transactions. This strand of the literature focused on commercial tax evasion and the manipulation of trade prices as accounting for most IFFs (Baker, 2005). As a sign of the term's legitimization, most leading multilateral institutions such as the United Nations, the World Bank, the International Monetary Fund (IMF) and the African Union now use the term illicit financial flows.

By 2015, the prominence of the coalition of stakeholders combating IFFs was such that the issue was included in the 2030 Agenda for Sustainable Development, in Goal 16 with target 16.4 specifically focusing on significantly reducing illicit financial and arms flows by 2030. Building on the 2015 historic step, the indicator framework for the monitoring of progress towards the Sustainable Development Goals adopted by the United Nations General Assembly in July 2017 includes indicator 16.4.1 on total value of inward and outward IFFs.[2] Considering these significant milestones, evidence-based policy responses and regulatory measures to curb IFFs are urgently needed. However, IFFs remain a contested field characterized by broad agreements on the criminal sources and use of such financial flows but a lack of consensus on the commercial components.

The diversity of approaches in the literature reveals that estimates of the magnitude of IFFs are shaped at the nexus of dominant economic principles and legal frameworks. On one hand, without an established theoretical model on IFFs, economists rely on a combination of economic ideology and rigorous analytical methods. On the other hand, variance across jurisdictions, layers of international and domestic laws, and evolving legal frameworks problematize "distinctions between the 'letter' and 'spirit' of the law,

---

[2] United Nations, General Assembly, 2017, Work of the Statistical Commission pertaining to the 2030 Agenda for Sustainable Development, A/RES/71/313, New York, 10 July.

on which the illegal/illicit distinction largely rests" (Musseli and Bürgi Bonanomi, 2020:1). In effect, considering such a distinction is blurry given the primacy of the intention of the law in its interpretation. Furthermore, as will be apparent throughout this report, institutional and administrative capacities play a central role in shaping the measurement of IFFs, their regulation and the enforcement of existing laws and regulations.

In what Musseli and Bürgi Bonanomi (2020:17) termed the "common denominator definition", IFFs are "cross-border transfers of money or assets connected with some illegal activity". Multiple definitions of IFFs refer to elements of the following: movement of money and assets across borders that are illegal in their source, transfer or use. Sources are generally classified in three categories: criminal activities, commercial activities and corruption. While the illegality of corruption and most criminal activities related to different types of trafficking and smuggling gathers consensus, the legal versus illegal lens for commercial activities such as trade mispricing, tax evasion, aggressive transfer pricing and tax avoidance has been subject to an intense debate (see, for example, Cobham and Janský, 2019; Forstater, 2017). Most disagreements centre on the treatment of tax evasion and avoidance. Tax evasion involves breaking the law, whereas tax avoidance involves the exploitation of national and international tax rules to gain advantages not intended by countries when they were adopted.

On one hand, most civil society organizations push for a broad definition of IFFs, beyond the legal and illegal divide, emphasizing their harmful impact on development. These views are echoed by the Independent Commission for Reform of International Corporate Taxation, which, in a letter to the United Nations Secretary-General, states as follows (cited in Forstater, 2018:3):

"We understand that some actors within the United Nations system are lobbying for a redefinition of the term 'illicit financial flows' in order retrospectively to exclude tax avoidance by multinational companies from the definition. Such a course of action represents a clear threat to the [Sustainable Development Goals] contribution of domestic resource mobilization, and will also undermine confidence in the [United Nations'] ability to deliver honestly on what member States have previously agreed upon."

For supporters of this view, an additional emphasis is placed on behaviours that are unethical or undesirable that result in unlawful and lawful (successful) avoidance (Picciotto, 2018).

On the other hand, multilateral organizations address the tax-related dimensions of IFFs with varying degrees of caution. Such caution is motivated by fluctuating interpretations of the term across the legal, illegal, lawful and unlawful continuum. The prevalence of the presumption of innocence in most jurisdictions implies that in practical terms, conceptualizing illicit to be equivalent to illegal would mean that activities cannot legally be construed as illicit/illegal unless they have been declared to be so by a court or competent authority. It infers that such characterization would ultimately depend on the legal challenge of reaching a verdict (Quentin, 2017). Doing so would be problematic because of differences in perceptions of standards in law-making and legal interpretation (Musseli and Bürgi Bonanomi, 2020). In addition, confining tax-avoidance practices to rigid legalistic examinations does not hold in light of the context-specific, fact-intensive assessment of corporate tax filing (Picciotto, 2018). Preliminary assessments of the validity of tax claims in turn depend on the institutional capacity, including that of the revenue authority, to conduct the associated tasks.

Reflecting these challenges, elements of IFFs appear in the 2000 United Nations Convention against Transnational Organized Crime with a focus on the criminal dimensions of the transfer and concealment of assets of illicit origin. The related resolution of the United Nations Economic and Social Council in 2001 further underlines the need for stronger international cooperation in preventing and combating the transfer of funds originating in acts of corruption, whereas the 2005 United Nations Convention against Corruption includes commitments on returning stolen assets. Within the main organs of the United Nations, a close synonym of the term appears in the 2010 Salvador Declaration on Comprehensive Strategies for Global Challenges calling for "developing strategies or policies to combat illicit capital flows and to curb the harmful effects of jurisdictions and territories uncooperative in tax matters" (United Nations, General Assembly, 2011:8). By 2015, IFFs were included in the Sustainable Development Goals, amid debates on the treatment of tax-avoidance issues. In 2016, a joint UNODC–Organization for Economic Cooperation and Development (OECD) issue brief stated, in a footnote, that "the term 'illicit financial flows' is not defined in the international normative framework" (UNODC and OECD, 2016). In the same vein, the report also states in a footnote that "for the purposes of this paper, IFFs are defined broadly as all cross-border financial transfers, which contravene national or international laws. This wide category encompasses several different types of financial transfers".

United Nations research reports take a pragmatic approach to IFFs. The UNCTAD *Trade and Development Report, 2014: Global Governance and Policy Space for Development*, for example, states that "this Report refers to tax-motivated IFFs whenever the international structuring of transactions or asset portfolios has little or no economic substance, and their express purpose is to reduce tax liabilities" (UNCTAD, 2014:174). The *World Investment Report 2015* does not use the term illicit financial flows. Rather, it emphasizes, as a starting point, the critical importance of the need for greater financing for development. To this end, the report builds on the assessment by the *World Investment Report 2014* of missing funds to cover the estimated $2.5 trillion annual investment gap needed to build productive capacity, infrastructure and other sectors in developing countries. The 2015 report then provides a detailed and rigorous examination of tax avoidance by multinational enterprises (MNEs) by addressing the "key question" as follows: "how can policymakers take action against tax avoidance to ensure that MNEs pay 'the right amount of tax, at the right time, and in the right place' without resorting to measures that might have a negative impact on investment?" (UNCTAD, 2015a:176). As discussed in section II, and further developed in chapter 1, tax avoidance is considered by many constituencies as a critical component of IFFs.

Notwithstanding these conceptual variations, in December 2018, the United Nations General Assembly adopted a resolution on "Promotion of international cooperation to combat illicit financial flows and strengthen good practices on assets return to foster sustainable development". The resolution places emphasis on the development dimension by "reiterating its deep concern about the impact of illicit financial flows, in particular those caused by tax evasion, corruption and transnational organized crime, on the economic, social and political stability and development of societies, and especially on developing countries" (United Nations, General Assembly, 2019:2). In addition, the second International Expert Meeting on the Return of Stolen Assets was held in Addis Ababa in May 2019. More recently, IFFs featured prominently in the President's summary of the High-level Dialogue on Financing for Development held by the General Assembly on 26 September 2019.[3]

The IFFs discourse in the intergovernmental African context is shaped by the High-level Panel on Illicit Financial Flows from Africa, commissioned by the African Union and the United Nations Economic Commission for Africa (UNECA) Conference of African Ministers of Finance, Planning and Economic Development. Marking a departure from the ambivalent treatment of IFFs by most multilateral institutions, the ensuing 2015 report, also known as the Mbeki Report, states that "the various means by which IFFs take place in Africa include abusive transfer pricing, trade mispricing, misinvoicing of services and intangibles and using unequal contracts, all for purposes of tax evasion, aggressive tax avoidance and illegal export of foreign exchange" (UNECA, 2015:24). Some of these concerns are shared by OECD as reiterated in a 2016 joint statement issued by the Secretary-General of OECD and the chair of the High-level Panel:

[3]   United Nations, General Assembly, 2019, Summary by the President of the General Assembly of the High-level Dialogue on Financing for Development (New York, 26 September 2019), A/74/559, New York, 21 November.

"The issue of illicit financial flows is at the forefront of the international agenda".[4] The joint statement calls on the international community to come together as "money-laundering, tax evasion and international bribery which form the bulk of illicit financial flows, affect all countries". The statement does not mention tax avoidance, aggressive or otherwise.

With regard to the treatment of IFFs in Bretton Woods institutions, in a factsheet, "The IMF and the Fight against Illicit Financial Flows", IMF lists combating tax-avoidance activities as part of its mandate to ensure the stability of the international monetary system. This role includes helping member countries guard against "base erosion and profit shifting" (BEPS).[5] The World Bank recognizes that in the international development community, the term illicit financial flows has become "a powerful and constructive umbrella to bring together previously disconnected issues" (World Bank, 2017a). It considers that cross-border movements of financial assets are illicit only when they are associated with activities that are deemed to be illegal in the local jurisdiction (World Bank, 2016). It specifies that "tax avoidance activities, such as legal tax planning and optimization, do not belong to illicit financial flows" (World Bank, 2016:2) while adding, in a footnote, that "the clarity of these distinctions is easier to maintain conceptually than in real life". It further acknowledges that it is the nature of tax crimes that determines the degree of level of "opaqueness" in defining IFFs and states that the differences between legal tax avoidance and illegal tax evasion can only be ascertained further to a legal ruling. Despite conceptual difficulties, the institution acknowledges dealing with tax avoidance in multiple ways through its work on international tax policy and its country-level support for improved tax administration and preventive measures for tackling abusive transfer pricing.

II. Conceptual contours of illicit financial flows in the *Economic Development in Africa Report 2020*

The report builds on the increasing engagement on IFFs in multilateral circles, sensitivities associated with the use of the term and the new body of work on the legal and illegal divide on tax-related matters. As elaborated on in chapter 1, the report considers the developmental impact of IFFs, reviews existing evidence on selected criminal

---

[4] See www.oecd.org/g20/topics/international-taxation/joint-statement-on-the-fight-against-illicit-financial-flows-by-angel-gurria-and-thabo-mbeki.htm.
Note: All websites referred to in footnotes were accesses in April 2020.

[5] See https://www.imf.org/en/About/Factsheets/Sheets/2018/10/07/imf-and-the-fight-against-illicit-financial-flows.

activities associated with such flows, addresses trade-related commercial activities, and considers corruption as a cross-cutting issue. It also investigates channels of IFFs through the global network of actors and analyses the roots of IFFs in the international legal and economic order.

As a starting point, the report takes note of the indications of the Mbeki Report, including its treatment of IFFs originating in commercial activities, as cited previously in section I. This definition has led to findings that show that 65 per cent of IFFs in Africa originate in commercial activities (UNECA, 2015). The magnitude of this estimate illustrates the central role that definitions play in the measurement of such flows and ultimately in the design of appropriate regulations. In addition, the political legitimacy of the High-level Panel in the African context has established this definition as the basis for Africa-based intergovernmental meetings. However, a full account of the Mbeki Report definition would imply a consideration of the capacity of domestic legal systems in Africa to address aggressive and developmentally harmful tax avoidance. In this regard, regulators' ability to play cat and mouse with businesses has resulted in what has become known as the "balloon effect", that is, filling a regulatory gap in one place merely leads to new loopholes elsewhere (Musseli and Bürgi Bonanomi, 2020). This feeds into a never-ending game that constantly requires alertness and regulatory adjustments, even in countries with well-developed legal systems.

The present report posits that a definition of IFFs for analytical purposes should acknowledge the evolving nature of the concept in a changing global environment on international corporate taxation. These developments happen concurrently with progress in the conceptualization of tax avoidance in the legal literature as shown in the latest research conducted by Musseli and Bürgi Bonanomi (2020) as part of the project Curbing Illicit Financial Flows from Resource-rich Developing Countries. These authors argue, for instance, that the evolving nature of regulatory reform of tax law, including the OECD-led BEPS agenda, further challenges the distinction between illegal and legal tax schemes. They contend that the BEPS general anti-abuse rules contribute to making this distinction increasingly irrelevant as they enable previously lawful practices based on the exploitation of loopholes to be turned into unlawful ones. The pragmatic inclusion of anti-tax-avoidance activities in the technical assistance programmes of major multilateral organizations somehow echoes Musseli and Bürgi Bonanomi's deconstruction of the illusion of a clear dichotomy between legal and illegal.

Finally, the present report takes the view that the measurement and monitoring of IFFs, and the definition of appropriate policy and regulatory measures to curb them, depends on the consideration of both sets of commercial and criminal activities. In this regard, the dominant emphasis on tax-related IFFs should not divert attention away from criminal activities, illicit trade and corruption, as these compromise the international financial system for money-laundering purposes and negatively impact prospects for achieving all 17 Sustainable Development Goals.

III. Objectives and organization of the *Economic Development in Africa Report 2020*

The report aims to equip African Governments and their partners with renewed arguments to address IFFs and sustainable development in international forums. In so doing, the report adds to the extensive literature on IFFs by deepening knowledge on its Africa-specific characteristics. Chapter 1 presents the report's conceptual framework.

The report's core analytical chapters aim to provide answers to the following questions:

(a) What is the state of play of the measurement of trade-related IFFs in the context of the Sustainable Development Goals? What is the magnitude of specific components of trade-related intracontinental and extracontinental IFFs in Africa? (chapter 2);

(b) What are the financial institutional mechanisms and regulatory loopholes behind the engineering of IFFs, including in the mining sector in Africa? (chapter 3);

(c) What are the root causes of IFFs in the international legal and economic order? What is the place of Africa in multilateral engagement related to IFFs? (chapter 4);

(d) To what extent are IFFs associated with missed opportunities for sustainable economic, social and environmental development in Africa? (chapter 5);

(e) How do IFFs feature in the landscape of domestic resource mobilization in Africa? What would it mean to reclaim IFFs for financing the Sustainable Development Goals at the regional level, or within a country, for example in Nigeria? (chapter 6);

(f) What should be done at the multilateral, continental and national level to fast track the curbing of IFFs? (chapter 7).

The report adopts an interdisciplinary approach that blends traditional economic tools with insights from international law, international relations and political economy perspectives and sets out to add value in the following ways. First, it seeks to revisit current estimates of the magnitude of trade-related commodity-based IFFs in Africa, accounting for new methodological and data insights (chapter 2). Second, it integrates gender-based and environmental considerations related to climate change in the analysis of the relationship between IFFs and sustainable socioeconomic development in Africa (chapter 5). Third, it adopts a balanced approach to a topic that has been subject to polarized views. The overall approach seeks to be inclusive of the vantage points of different actors across the spectrum of IFFs (chapter 3). It investigates the global web of actors involved in the facilitation and regulation of IFFs while also identifying policy and institutional loopholes in Africa (chapter 3). Fourth, the analysis sheds light on the historical and geopolitical foundations of some of the drivers of IFFs (chapter 4). The report brings these issues to life by examining the implications of curbing IFFs at the local level in Nigeria (chapter 6). Finally, in chapter 7, the report reviews existing initiatives to curb IFFs including ongoing efforts on the reform of the global corporate taxation system. This final chapter then offers new recommendations for tackling IFFs, drawing on two narrative threads: (a) IFFs are a shared responsibility between developed and developing countries; and (b) Africa should take its responsibility to new heights at the international, continental and national levels.

Chapter 1

Illicit financial flows and sustainable development: Definitions and conceptual framework

This chapter aims to provide a background to the report and a narrative thread of the rationale behind the focus of its analytical chapters. It is structured as follows. Section 1.1 underlines the report's anchoring in the development approach to IFFs. Section 1.1 also aims to provide a better understanding of the state of play on the measurement of IFFs for the monitoring of Sustainable Development Goal indicator 16.4.1. Section 1.2 examines a selected set of sources of IFFs that are of particular relevance to the study. Section 1.3 discusses some of the main enablers of IFFs. Section 1.4 follows with an exposé of the report's approach to the analysis of the relationship between IFFs and the economic, social and environmental dimensions of sustainable development. The overall conceptual framework of the report is summarized in figure 1.

EACH YEAR ON
THE AFRICAN CONTINENT

trade misinvoicing between

$30 and $52 billion

contributes to

capital flight

$88.6 billion

CURBING IFFs
is part of SDG target 16.4

in support of peace, justice and strong institutions

Figure 1

Conceptual framework of the *Economic Development in Africa 2020*

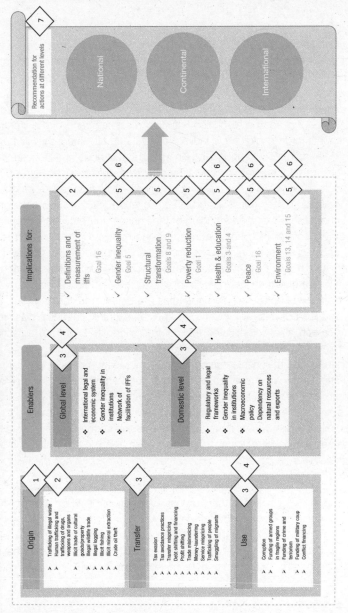

Source: UNCTAD secretariat.

1.1 Illicit financial flows in the report

The development approach to illicit financial flows

The present report adopts a development approach to IFFs, informed by insights from the legal literature highlighted in the introductory chapter. The development approach to IFFs is explicit in the concern expressed in General Assembly resolution 71/213 for the impact of such flows on "economic, social and political stability and development of societies".[6] In doing so, the resolution is in line with the strand of the literature on IFFs that accounts for their direct and indirect effects, and ultimately, their net negative impact on development (Blankenburg and Khan, 2012; Myandazi and Ronceray, 2018). In these studies, developmentally harmful IFFs include lawful transactions ("until proven unlawful"), such as aggressive tax planning and profit-shifting schemes, that result in government revenue losses (Musseli and Bürgi Bonanomi, 2020). This categorization comes with nuances on the understanding of the impact of IFFs on development. The use of bribes or profit shifting, for instance, can be motivated by the need to make investment viable and as such are not considered to be developmentally harmful (Blankenburg and Khan, 2012). When further elaborated upon, Musseli and Bürgi Bonanomi (2020) argue that this purposive approach also implies that all practices that erode the tax base of developing countries are developmentally harmful. The list would then include business tax incentives and tax-related contract provisions. The purposive approach also complicates the consideration of flows from artisanal and small-scale mining. In addition to formal small-scale and artisanal commercial mining entities, artisanal and small-scale mining includes individual miners operating outside formal legal and economic structures and who depend on the sector for their survival (Intergovernmental Forum on Mining, Minerals, Metals and Sustainable Development, 2017). However, the overall economic, social and environmental impacts of artisanal and small-scale mining are likely to be more nuanced. In Sierra Leone, for example, although estimated to generate substantial economic value, small-scale gold mining is a major source of money-laundering and IFFs with little taxation revenue for the Government (Hunter and Smith, 2017).

Given these layers of complexity, a purposive definition of IFFs risks making the assessment of their effects on development even more difficult. Instead, for policy purposes, this report subscribes to the contention that a better anchoring of the definition of IFFs in law is needed, in addition to striving for "granularity", "spelling out what is or is not within scope in terms of actors, transfer mechanisms, or origin" (Musseli and Bürgi

---

[6] United Nations, General Assembly, 2017, Promotion of international cooperation to combat illicit financial flows in order to foster sustainable development, A/RES/71/213, New York, 18 January.

Bonanomi, 2020:15) while also building on the literature on economic transformation and social development.

Multilateral efforts in the measurement of illicit financial flows

The large array of literature on estimating IFFs from commercial activities showcases major differences in methods, sample sizes and data sets. Main findings from these studies are presented in the annex to this chapter. These studies have played a critical role in raising awareness about the scale of IFFs. However, such estimates are not comparable and there is a lack of consensus. With regard to trade misinvoicing in particular, there are variants across analytical traditions on the treatment of inward IFFs. Some researchers, for instance, measure IFFs at a regional level and subtract outflows from inflows to determine net IFFs (Reuter, 2012). Others estimate the total sum of inflows and outflows. This latter approach is based on the belief that inflows and outflows cause development harm and hence must be added together to gauge the full impact (Global Financial Integrity, 2019).

By 2017, further to the adoption of indicator 16.4.1 on "Total value of inward and outward illicit financial flows", considering the complexity of the multiple dimensions of IFFs, development of the measurement of the indicator had been entrusted to two custodians: UNODC on crime-related IFFs and UNCTAD on the tax and trade components. Subsequently, an international Task Force on Statistical Methodologies for Measuring Illicit Financial Flows was established composed of country representatives and experts from international organizations such as IMF, OECD, the United Nations Department of Economic and Social Affairs, UNECA and Eurostat. The exercise has encountered a number of difficulties. First, efforts are constrained by the lack of statistics due to the hidden nature of IFFs and the diversity of what they mean across countries and regions. Second, many of the activities that lead to IFFs are intertwined, further compounding challenges in disaggregating between the different categories. Trade misinvoicing practices, for example, can hide tax-avoidance schemes, and while a stand-alone category, bribery and corruption also permeate most illicit and illegal activities. Third, innovation by perpetrators of illicit activities and facilitators of illicit financial transfers results in a constantly evolving field that is difficult to capture in statistics. Fourth, the treatment of the informal economy and how it relates to IFFs differs across countries. Fifth, statistical definitions of IFFs should be comparable across countries to allow for the ranking of their prevalence and for the design of a common set of solutions at the multilateral level.

In addition to these preliminary challenges, the international statistical Task Force underlined the need for the statistical definitions to be separated from legal definitions.

According to the Task Force, differences in legal frameworks across jurisdictions imply that it is empirically infeasible to separate illegal (for example, tax evasion) from illicit and licit practices (for example, aggressive tax avoidance) and lawful tax planning. The Task Force findings further show that this has implications for the development of Sustainable Development Goal indicator 16.4.1 by underlining the need to move away from a legal/illegal split in the definition (UNCTAD and UNODC, forthcoming). The Task Force states that the primary objective of the statistical exercise is to measure certain behaviours and activities and indicate the size of the phenomenon and steer away from definitions of what is illegal. This approach resonates with the findings from the legal strand of research on IFFs discussed in the introduction.

Expert meetings held during 2017–2019 further underscored difficulties in gathering data for the measurement of IFFs, given that such information is scattered across a range of institutions at the country level: from national accounts and balance of payments data from central banks; information from financial intelligence units and ministries of justice; tax-related data from national revenue authorities; and merchandise trade data from customs. Furthermore, although trade in services is a main conveyor of aggressive tax-avoidance practices mostly through the relocation of financial service flows and intellectual property, there is no single data source from which to derive relevant statistics.

By July 2019, the efforts of the UNCTAD–UNODC Task Force had led to a consensus on an agreed statistical definition of IFFs for indicator 16.4.1 as well as on a typology and methodology to measure them. By October 2019, the Inter-agency and Expert Group on Sustainable Development Goal Indicators had upgraded the classification of the methodology for classifying indicator 16.4.1 from tier III to tier II, thereby underlining that "the indicator is conceptually clear and has an internationally established methodology and standards are available, but data are not regularly produced by countries".[7] Core elements of the definition of IFFs, for statistical purposes, were underscored as follows:

- Illicit in origin, transfer or use;
- Exchange of a value (rather than purely financial flows);
- A flow of value over time (as opposed to a stock measure);
- Flows that cross a border.

[7] For further information on the classification of global Sustainable Development Goal indicators, see https://unstats.un.org/sdgs/iaeg-sdgs/tier-classification/.

Figure 2 and box 1 present a more detailed account of the categories of IFFs as endorsed by the Inter-Agency and Expert Group on Sustainable Development Goal Indicators. Data collection in a sample of pilot countries is under way to test the methodology. In this regard, the Task Force acknowledges at the outset that data related to corruption or commercial and tax-related IFFs will be more difficult to obtain due to the variety of channels used by MNEs across a number of related activities: transfer pricing, the relocation of intangible assets, royalty payments, and the like.

Figure 2
Categories of illicit financial flows

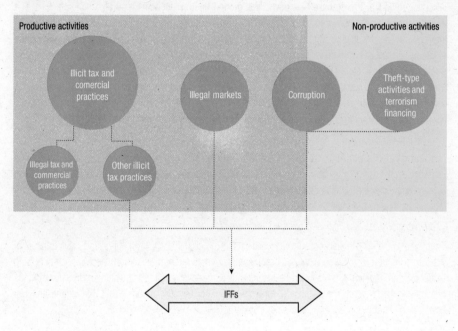

Source: UNCTAD and UNODC (forthcoming).

Box 1
The measurement of illicit financial flows for Sustainable Development Goal indicator 16.4.1

The UNCTAD–UNODC Task Force identified four main categories of activities that can lead to IFFs.

Tax and commercial IFFs

These include illegal practices such as tariff, duty and revenue offences, tax evasion, corporate offences, market manipulation and other selected practices. Some activities that are non-observed, hidden or informal, or part of the so-called shadow, underground or grey economy may also generate IFFs. The practices are typically motivated by increasing profits and avoiding taxes. Related activities included in the International Classification of Crime for Statistical Purposes comprise tax evasion, tariff, duty and revenue offences, competition offences, import/export offences, acts against trade regulations, restrictions or embargoes and investment or stock/shares offences. Also included are tax-avoidance practices, including transfer mispricing, debt shifting, relocation of intellectual property, tax treaty shopping, tax deferral, changes in corporate structure or economic residence and other profit-shifting schemes. When these activities directly or indirectly generate flows crossing country borders, they generate IFFs.

IFFs from corruption

The United Nations Convention against Corruption defines acts considered as corruption and these are consistently defined in the International Classification of Crime for Statistical Purposes. They include bribery, embezzlement, abuse of functions, trading in influence, illicit enrichment and other acts. When these acts, directly or indirectly, generate cross-border flows, they are counted as IFFs.

Theft-type activities and financing of crime and terrorism

Theft-type activities are non-productive activities that entail a forced, involuntary and illicit transfer of economic resources between two actors. Examples include theft, extortion, illicit enrichment and kidnapping. In addition, the financing of terrorism or crime involves the illicit, voluntary transfer of funds between two actors with the purpose of funding criminal or terrorist actions. When the related financial flows cross country borders, these activities constitute IFFs.

IFFs from illegal markets

These include domestic and international trade in illicit goods and services. Such processes often involve a degree of criminal organization and are aimed at creating profit. They include any type of illegal trafficking of goods, such as drugs and firearms, or services, such as smuggling of migrants. IFFs are generated by the flows related to the international trade of illicit goods and services, as well as by cross-border flows from managing the illicit income from such activities.

Sources: UNCTAD and UNODC (forthcoming).

The present report abides by the definitions issued by the UNCTAD–UNODC Task Force as highlighted in box 1. It further asserts that differences in patterns of intra-African and extracontinental trade and changing trade dynamics due to rising trade volumes between Africa and large emerging developing countries warrants a new examination of IFFs in Africa along these lines (chapter 2).

1.2 Selected sources of illicit financial flows

As per the definition of IFFs used in this report, illicitness comes from the activities from which flows originate and from the cross-border characteristic of the movements. Although an exhaustive review of the sources of IFFs is beyond the scope of the report, some of these activities are discussed below.

Tax avoidance

Tax avoidance is a global problem that affects both developed and developing countries. Estimates of revenue losses related to global corporate taxation range from $500 billion to $650 billion annually depending on the variables under study (Crivelli et al., 2015; Cobham and Janský, 2018). Calculations of corporate tax avoidance in the European Union, for instance, vary from €50 billion to €190 billion per year (Murphy, 2019). Analyses of recent data show that all European Union member States have tax gaps that might considerably exceed their health-care spending, with Italy, France and Germany topping the list in absolute terms.

In developing countries, losses due to global corporate taxation are estimated to range from 6 to 13 per cent of total tax revenue, versus 2 to 3 per cent in OECD countries (Crivelli et al., 2015). Research findings for India, for example, show losses of an average of $16 billion per year during 2002–2006 (Kar and Cartwright-Smith, 2009). The 2008 global financial crisis played a role in raising awareness of the scale of tax evasion and other commercial dimensions of IFFs. The political urgency of addressing global corporate taxation led to the establishment of the BEPS initiative at OECD (the Inclusive Framework on BEPS is discussed in chapter 3). Estimates by UNCTAD show that the magnitude of revenue losses due to MNE tax avoidance in developing countries was approximately $100 billion annually in 2012, comparable to the total annual amount of official development assistance (ODA) to developing countries computed at $115 billion the same year (UNCTAD, 2015a).

With regard to Africa, one sixth of the continent's aggregate government revenue comes from corporate taxation ($67 billion in 2015) and most estimates suggest that the cost of tax avoidance is of the order of a tenth of this figure (Hearson, 2018). Corporate taxation is a more important share of government revenue in African countries than in OECD countries, mainly because African countries are unable to raise as much revenue from payroll taxes.

Corruption and offshore accounts

Estimates from the African Development Bank (AfDB) show that Africa loses about $148 billion to corruption every year (AfDB, 2015). Conservative estimates by the Stolen Asset Recovery Initiative (StAR) based on 2007 data also show that between $20 billion and $40 billion per year are stolen by public officials from jurisdictions in developing countries and countries with economies in transition (van der Does de Willebois et al., 2011). More recently, publications by investigative journalists have uncovered the magnitude of African private wealth in offshore accounts. In 2015, for example, an investigation provided details on almost 5,000 individuals from 41 African countries with assets of about $6.5 billion (Moore et al., 2018).

Global-level analyses show that from 20 to 30 per cent of private wealth in many African countries is held in tax havens (Global Financial Integrity, 2017; Zucman, 2014; Johannesen et al., 2016). This is higher than the global country average of 8 per cent (Zucman, 2013).

Illicit flows from other criminal activities

Recent estimates suggest that, on a global scale, revenues generated from *11 crimes* (trafficking in drugs, weapons, humans, human organs and cultural property; counterfeiting; illegal wildlife trade, fishing trade, logging and mining; and crude oil theft) range from $1.6 trillion to $2.2 trillion per year (May, 2017). However, these estimates must be treated with caution as they cannot always be equated with IFFs, given the difficulty of determining the value that moves across borders. Human trafficking contributes to a significant part of these flows. Aggregating information on what is known and reported, UNODC (2018), for example, found that in 2016 along selected routes, 2.5 million migrants worldwide were smuggled for an economic return of at least $5.5 billion to $7 billion.

Most of these illegal activities have an impact on prospects for achieving economic, social and environmental goals and account for the findings detailed in chapters 5 and 6 of the present report on the relationship between IFFs and social and environmental sustainability. With regard to the illegal trade of counterfeit products, for instance, according to the World Economic Forum, substandard malaria medicines were responsible for the deaths of over 100,000 children in sub-Saharan Africa in 2013 alone. Further, the global numbers associated with counterfeit malaria and tuberculosis medicines are significantly higher (World Economic Forum, 2015).

Similarly, illegal waste trafficking is a little-known source of illicit flows that has significant consequences for human health and the environment. Waste trade is regulated by a number of international environmental agreements some of which, such as the Basel Convention on the Control of Transboundary Movements of Hazardous Waste and their Disposal, the Bamako Convention on the Ban of the Import into Africa and the Control of Transboundary Movement and Management of Hazardous Wastes within Africa (Bamako Convention) and the Convention to Ban the Importation into Forum Island Countries of Hazardous and Radioactive Wastes and to Control the Transboundary Movement and Management of Hazardous Wastes within the South Pacific Region (Waigani Convention), define an illegal activity under these Conventions as a crime (World Customs Organization (WCO), 2018). Although a lack of appropriate data makes it difficult to measure the actual extent of the problem, a recent study shows that, globally, the volume of waste traded grew by more than 500 per cent, from 45.6 million to 222.6 million tons during 1992–2012 (WCO, 2018). As part of this trend, the share of the world's waste being exported to developing countries grew by 40 per cent during the period 1998–2009. Africa and the Asia and Pacific regions are among the world's key destinations for large shipments of electronic waste, plastics and various scrap metals. In addition to the official data being recorded, illegal activities are thriving through different means. The most prominent channels are the sale of waste on the black market, the fraudulent declaration of hazardous waste as non-hazardous and the classification of waste as second-hand goods in order to avoid abiding by international waste regulations and allowing them to be traded with developing countries.

Globally, the trafficking of cultural property from all origins contributes to money-laundering and the funding of terrorism (United Nations Educational, Scientific and Cultural Organization (UNESCO), 2018). With regard to Africa, it is estimated that about 90 per cent of sub-Saharan African historical items are to be found in major world museums, private collections or missionary museums (Godonou, 2007).[8] Most of these items have been either the result of pillaging or unfair acquisitions during wars and colonial domination, and as such have been sources of illicit flows. The resulting paucity

---

[8] "From the British Museum (69,000 objects from sub-Saharan Africa) to the Weltmuseum of Vienna (37,000), to the Musée Royal de l'Afrique Centrale in Belgium (180,000) to the Future Humboldt Forum (75,000) to the Vatican Museums and those of the Musee du quai Branly-Jacques Chirac (70,000): the history of the African collections is a European history that has indeed been a shared history" (Sarr and Savoy, 2018:15).

of remaining historical cultural items across the continent is developmentally harmful for two main reasons. First, cultural goods shape historical narratives and collective values that contribute to the education and social culture of society. The trafficking of cultural goods robs people of their identity, of their place in the world and affects their ability to build a collective future (see foreword by Lehoundou Assomo, UNESCO, 2018). Second, past and contemporary trafficking of cultural goods represents missed opportunities for Africa to benefit from greater revenue from tourism. Indeed, cultural heritage represents "a basic prerequisite" for a thriving tourist industry.[9] The present report is published in a context of renewed impetus for the restitution of African cultural heritage held abroad. This trend and the dynamism of pan-Africanism has led many scholars working on Africa to argue that "the decolonizing project is back on the agenda worldwide" (Mbembe, 2015:18). For many African countries celebrating their sixtieth year of independence in 2020, the agenda for reclaiming IFFs is likely to be situated within this wider project.

1.3 Enablers of illicit financial flows

Studies on IFFs have identified a number of drivers at the domestic level. They include inadequate regulation of the financial system and capital account; trade openness in the context of weak regulation and poor governance; and poor institutional quality and excessive dependence on commodity exports (Ndikumana et al., 2014). These drivers act as channels for the economic, institutional, environmental and social harm caused by IFFs. In addition to these, the discussion that follows is based on a selected set of enablers of IFFs.

Capital account liberalization
Following the dissolution of communist rule in the 1980s, diminishing levels of ODA and large investment needs across African countries exposed the limited role that domestic savings were able to play in addressing such gaps. The expansion of global capital markets further contributed to policy choices in favour of a more open capital account to access much needed resources. Capital account liberalization and heavy reliance on foreign savings became the norm across African countries. Such liberalization was expected to promote growth through financial deepening and better allocation of resources (Kose et al., 2009).

[9] See http://archives.icom.museum/cultural_tourism.html.

Policymakers often consider financial liberalization as part of financial resource mobilization, a key part of the engine for economic growth and development (Cardoso and Dornbusch, 1989). However, part of the economic literature argues that the continent's struggle with substantial outflows of capital originates in macroeconomic reforms initiated in the 1980s and intensified in the 1990s in most African countries (Ndikumana, 2003). This led many Governments to move towards greater capital account openness by abolishing or relaxing existing capital controls. Liberalization measures also generally included a relaxation or an abolition of restrictions on non-residents' ability to repatriate dividends, interest income, and proceeds of sales or liquidation of investments. Similarly, the lack of restrictions meant that by the late 1990s, for the group of severely indebted low-income countries, private assets held abroad, as measured by capital flight, exceeded total liabilities, as measured by the stock of debt, thus leading to the continent being labelled a "net creditor to the world" (Ndikumana, 2003). The capital flight to gross domestic product (GDP) ratio even exceeded 200 per cent for nine countries in the group. As a result of these trends, capital account liberalization coupled with severe macroeconomic imbalances has been associated with the provision of "legal" channels of capital flight (Ariyoshi et al., 2000), including for transfers associated with IFFs.

Annual capital flight from Africa of

$88.6 billion

outstrips inflows of, respectively

ODA
$48 billion
FDI
$54 billion

Though African economies are generally credited to have opted for capital account liberalization, a study by AfDB researchers (Bicaba et al., 2015) shows that there is an important gap between the desire of policymakers for capital openness and the level actually observed. As of 2012, 18 African countries had liberalized their capital accounts. These countries are also those that are among the most integrated into global financial markets. The speed of liberalization also varied across countries: Mauritius and Zambia fully liberalized their capital accounts in the early 1990s; and Angola, Tunisia and the United Republic of Tanzania, for example, had major restrictions in place until 2005. Similarly, members of the West African Economic and Monetary Union eliminated capital controls on inward foreign direct investment (FDI) as well as foreign borrowing by residents in 1999, but kept controls on capital outflows to non-member countries (IMF, 2008).

The international legal and economic system

The distribution of taxation rights between countries of establishment and source countries has deep historical roots. These, in turn, have shaped contemporary patterns of opportunities and gains across global value chains. This report takes stock of the theoretical and empirical literature on the tax-motivated behaviour of MNEs. The latter is limited and is characterized by several "unresolved puzzles and blind spots" (IMF, 2020). Such limitations are mostly due to the highly technical nature of international taxation issues, to the paucity of suitable data partly for technical reasons, as well as the result of confidentiality clauses and lack of transparency. Despite these limitations, there is evidence of aggressive forms of tax-optimization strategies (Wei, 2015; IMF, 2020). This report examines risk factors along value chains that may be conducive to IFFs (chapter 3).

Countries with a high level of dependency on oil are more prone to higher levels of IFFs (UNECA, 2015). Yet, during the period 2013–2017, two out of five commodity-dependent countries were in sub-Saharan Africa and 89 per cent and 65 per cent of all countries in the Middle East and North Africa, respectively, were commodity dependent (UNCTAD, 2019a). In light of the persistent prevalence of commodity dependence in Africa, the present report examines the roots of international law and the historical configuration of the global governance of commodities and how these causes of IFFs contribute to creating distortions in market incentives (chapter 4).

Domestic institutions

The negative implications of IFFs for development are channelled through two main streams. On one hand, IFFs originating in commercial activities reduce government revenue. Enabling factors include policy and regulatory inconsistencies, limited oversight, entrenched vested interests and limited transparency in economic and financial processes. On the other hand, IFFs contribute to the weakening of governance and institutional systems, including the rule of law, hinder transparency and accountability, and ultimately undermine the foundations of democracy and progress.

The primacy of institutions is highlighted in Goal 16 ("Peace, justice and strong institutions") on promoting peaceful and inclusive societies for sustainable development, as well as providing accountable and inclusive institutions at all levels. The inclusion of IFFs in Goal 16 illustrates the relevance of institutions as a critical channel in their occurrence. Building on this, the present report posits that institutions are the primary channel through which IFFs negatively impact prospects for social and environmental sustainability (chapters 5 and 6).

Global actors

IFFs are enabled by transfers facilitated by global-level financial mechanisms. Covering major cases of corruption across different jurisdictions, the World Bank and UNODC publication *The Puppet Masters: How the Corrupt Use Legal Structures to Hide Stolen Assets and What to Do About It* (van der Does de Willebois et al., 2011) reveals the mechanics through which money-laundering operates. It uncovers billions in corrupt assets, shell companies and other spurious legal structures that constitute the complex web of subterfuge in corruption cases. The study also acknowledges that linking the beneficial owner to the proceeds of corruption is difficult because of the transnational constructions used, due to their sizeable wealth and resources; all rely on corporate vehicles – legal structures such as companies, foundations and trusts – to hide the ownership and control of "tainted assets".

The present report provides an overview of the role of global actors in facilitating IFFs (chapter 3). It also critically examines policy and regulatory loopholes at the international level and the extent to which they increase risks of exposure to IFFs (chapter 4).

1.4 Illicit financial flows and the 2030 Agenda for Sustainable Development

In the absence of an established theoretical literature for conducting such an analysis, the conceptual framework of this report draws on the guiding principles of the 2030 Agenda for Sustainable Development, and different strands of the literature on structural transformation and economic and social development. The report's operationalization of the relationship between IFFs and sustainable development is inspired by the capabilities framework (Sen, 1992). The report's joint analysis of structural transformation and social development as the foundation of the analysis of economic and social sustainability aligns with Sen's assertion that economic prosperity must go hand in hand with social development. Production and prosperity are merely the means, whereas the ultimate objective is people's well-being. As Sen contends, lack of education or good health limits a person's ability to make the most of opportunities offered by a well-functioning market, whereas the right human capital endowments would be of little use without access to economic opportunities.

This report is also aligned with the emphasis of General Assembly resolution 71/313 on associating the target related to combating IFFs with the indivisibility of the Sustainable Development Goals (United Nations, 2017a:2). Chapters 5 and 6 analyse the relationship between IFFs and the economic, social and environmental dimensions of sustainable development. It derives its working hypotheses from the conceptual framework of the 2030 Agenda for Sustainable Development, that is, that curbing IFFs in Africa will contribute to the achievement of the following:

(a)   Greater benefits for people through poverty reduction;

(b)   More protection for the planet thanks to more protection from degradation and sustainable management of natural resources;

(c)   Higher levels of investment for prosperity;

(d)   Contribution to peace through just and inclusive societies;

(e)   More solidarity-based partnership thanks to a revitalized Global Partnership for Sustainable Development, based on a spirit of strengthened global solidarity.

The report underlines that curbing IFFs is not a panacea for achieving the Sustainable Development Goals. However, considering their significant magnitude by all accounts, efforts in curbing them and in the recovery of stolen assets are likely to contribute to much additional financing for the Goals.

For people: Poverty reduction and gender equality

Far from being mere exaggerations, the perceptions of unfairness referred to in the introductory paragraphs of this report are validated by research findings (OECD, 2019a). The findings also underline the specific vulnerability of women and children to the detrimental effects of limited financing for development. In OECD countries, for example, strong feelings of unfairness and injustice prevail from low-income to high-income groups, with women and older people among the most dissatisfied with government social policy. In some countries, these feelings have fuelled street politics, the rise of national populist movements and an increasing share of voters drawn to the political far right. In countries in other parts of the world, for example Malaysia and the Republic of Korea, high-profile cases of corruption, bribery and the magnitude of IFFs have led to public outrage. In the former, for example, a scandal involving a $6.5 billion bond offering for 1Malaysia Development Berhad, the country's State-owned fund, has led to investigations of corruption and money-laundering across six countries.[10]

With regard to gender, despite some progress, gender-based discrimination is still prevalent in both developed and developing countries (World Economic Forum, 2020).

[10]   See   https://www.reuters.com/article/us-malaysia-politics-1mdb-goldman/malaysia-files-criminal-charges-against-17-goldman-sachs-executives-idUSKCN1UZ0DI.

In this regard, the report is aligned with the centrality given to gender equality in the achievement of the Sustainable Development Goals (United Nations Entity for Gender Equality and the Empowerment of Women (UN-Women), 2018). The report also subscribes to Sen's (1999) contention that "nothing, arguably, is as important today, in the political economy of development as an adequate recognition of political, economic and social participation and leadership of women. This is indeed a crucial aspect of 'development as freedom'". The report addresses IFFs and gender issues in two ways. First, it considers women as agents of development and change. Many studies have underlined the low level of representation of women in senior corporate management across countries and industries (Elborgh-Woytek et al., 2013; International Labour Organization, 2019; Crédit Suisse, 2019). As a consequence, there is substantial and growing evidence concerning the business case for gender diversity in senior leadership positions across the public and private sectors (McKinsey Global Institute, 2015). This report subscribes to target 16.7 of "responsive, inclusive, participatory and representative decision-making at all levels" in institutions to turn them into critical enablers of equity. In this regard, chapter 4 investigates the status of gender diversity and inclusion in the management and leadership of key institutions from whose ranks facilitators and regulators of IFFs operate. And second, in chapter 5, the report reviews existing findings on the impact of IFFs on women and considers the implications of injecting finance from curbing or reclaiming IFFs on labour force allocation.

The capabilities framework provided the foundations for the United Nations Human Development Index, leading it to become one the most authoritative international sources of welfare comparisons between countries (Fukuda-Parr, 2003; Fukuda-Parr and Kumar, 2006). More recently, greater consideration for the role of human capital in poverty alleviation has led to the adoption of a multidimensional measure of poverty in the World Bank report *Poverty and Shared Prosperity 2018* (World Bank, 2018). When considering this measure, which includes consumption, education and access to basic infrastructure, poverty levels are 50 per cent higher than when relying solely on monetary poverty. In sub-Saharan Africa, 28.2 per cent out of a total of 64.3 per cent multidimensionally poor experience shortfalls in consumption levels. Studies have also shown that education is a game changer in the economic history of developed countries (Piketty, 2019).

For the planet: Environmental sustainability and climate change
Climate change intensifies the occurrence and the manifestation of natural disasters (see, for example, Eckstein et al., 2019) and the climate crisis negatively affects the path towards achieving the Sustainable Development Goals. From Mozambique to countries

in the Caribbean, cyclones and tropical storms have resulted in the loss of life and have crippled economies. Floods destroy agricultural produce. Droughts in the Sahel and Horn of Africa contribute to the rise of the number of hungry on the continent and are a threat to peace and instability in the two regions (World Food Programme, United States of America, 2017). Some sources of IFFs, such as illegal logging, fishing and mineral extraction are closely connected with substantial environmental costs, as well as the impoverishment of individuals and communities that rely on those resources to sustain their existence. In addition, it is estimated that globally, countries forego an estimated $7 billion to $12 billion in potential fiscal revenue each year as well as reduced tourism activity (World Bank, 2019). This report attempts to capture some of the implications of IFFs for environmental sustainability and with regard to climate change in Africa (chapter 5). The analysis also confronts the magnitude of IFFs with that of climate finance related to the Paris Agreement under the United Nations Framework Convention on Climate Change (Paris Agreement). The Paris Agreement, signed by 195 countries in December 2015, was a landmark achievement as it set out a framework to combat climate change and set the target of holding temperature increases to "well below 2°C" with efforts to hold the increase to 1.5°C (United Nations Framework Convention on Climate Change (UNFCCC), 2015). In 2009, at the fifteenth Conference of the Parties to the UNFCCC in Copenhagen, developed countries committed to a goal of mobilizing jointly $100 billion per year by 2020 to support climate change mitigation actions in developing countries. Six years later, this goal remained unfulfilled, and the twenty-first Conference of the Parties extended the goal of mobilizing jointly $100 billion per year through 2025 (UNFCCC, 2019). The present report investigates the state of climate change-related factors across countries with different exposures to IFFs (chapter 5). It considers institutional and government revenue channels, both key elements in building climate-related resilience. The findings are then used to argue that considering the slow pace of progress in efforts to curb and reclaim IFFs, a bridge should be made between negotiations on IFFs and negotiations on climate finance.

For peace: Illicit trade and the financing of conflict

Challenges to peace and security in Africa are "increasingly complex" (United Nations, Security Council, 2019:4). In this regard, it is difficult to capture the extent to which the flows estimated in chapter 2 originate in illicit activities aimed at conflict or terrorism financing. Similarly, the integration of peace and development perspectives in the analysis of the relationship between IFFs and sustainable development is limited by data constraints. Rather, this report begins with the premise that peace and security are prerequisites for sustainable development, as emphasized in the African Union theme for 2020, "Silencing the guns". A 2018 policy brief by the Oslo Peace Centre on conflicts in Africa during 1946–2018 showed that the number of conflict-affected countries on the continent increased from 14 in 2017 to 17 in 2018, the second highest number since 1946. Altogether, the number of battle-related deaths were estimated to be about 15,000 in 2018. Concerns for peace and security and the need to address components of IFFs as part of such efforts are frequently expressed in multilateral gatherings. In September 2019, for example, in its statement following the adoption of General Assembly resolution 71/315 on the implementation of the recommendations contained in the report of the Secretary-General on the causes of conflict in Africa and the promotion of durable peace and sustainable development in Africa, the Group of 77 and China called for taking concrete steps to address the root causes of conflict in Africa. The statement listed among such causes "illicit trade in and proliferation of arms, especially small arms and light weapons, as well as the illicit exploitation, trafficking and trade of high-value natural resources".[11]

IFFs contribute to the financing of terrorism in Africa. International Criminal Police Organization et al. (2018) states that terrorists and armed insurgents' activities in Africa are highly suspected to be funded by financial proceeds originating from transnational organized crime activities. These include, but are not limited to, trafficking of humans, drugs, cultural artefacts, stolen motor vehicles and various illicit goods, and illegal poaching. Taken together, the illicit exploitation of natural and environmental resources, including gold, diamonds, oil, charcoal, other minerals, timber and wildlife, and illegal taxation, confiscation and looting, account for 64 per cent of finance linked to security threats and conflicts (International Criminal Police Organization et al., 2018). It is further estimated that of the $31.5 billion in IFFs generated annually in conflict areas, 96 per cent is used by organized criminal groups, including to fuel violent conflict. *The World Atlas of Illicit Flows* further identifies more than 1,000 routes used for smuggling and illicit flows, including in Africa.

This report's examination of the specific case of mining (chapter 3) is motivated both by the sector's prominence as a source of IFFs and by its continued association with conflict situations. As of September 2019, for example, the Security Council report of the United Nations Secretary-General – Strengthening the partnership between the United Nations and the African Union on issues of peace and security in Africa, including on the work of the United Nations Office to the African Union – highlights situations in the Central African Republic, the Democratic Republic of the Congo, Libya, South Sudan and the Sudan, and the Sahel and Horn of Africa (United Nations, Security Council, 2019). Most of these countries or regions are rich in natural resources. In Middle Africa, protracted armed conflict, including activities by non-State armed groups, is associated with significant transborder

[11] See https://www.g77.org/statement/getstatement.php?id=190910.

dimensions and terrorism. Transborder dimensions are also critical in the Sahel. In South Sudan, the United Nations Panel of Experts on South Sudan identified lack of oversight in defence spending and the practice of bypassing accountability mechanisms to procure arms before the war through mismanagement of the country's oil resources as playing key roles in enabling the illicit financing of weapons. The experts underlined violation of international human rights law and of international humanitarian law by all parties (United Nations Security Council, 2016). However, although oil, gold and other minerals have a stronger association with conflict financing, other natural resources, such as timber from illegal logging, also play a role in fuelling instability (UNECA, 2015).

For prosperity: Implications of illicit financial flows on inequality, economic growth and structural transformation

The primary motivation to tackle IFFs also comes from human rights considerations. IFFs are considered violations of human rights (United Nations, General Assembly, 2017). The second motivation comes from the association of IFFs with inequality and the impact this has on growth and poverty reduction. Although not the main determinant of inequality, IFFs add fuel to wealth concentration at the global level. The World Bank, for example, states that IFFs "are a symptom of problems that institutionalize inequality and constrain prosperity… Addressing the causes of illicit financial flows and restricting the illicit movement of capital out of developing countries undoubtedly support economic development and growth" (World Bank, 2016:3).

Tax evasion and aggressive tax avoidance are likely to be among the main channels of the impact of IFFs on inequality. However, available evidence points to a complex web of association between tax and inequality. On one hand, aggressive tax optimization strategies are disproportionately more prevalent among the richest groups and large corporations. In Denmark, Norway and Sweden, for example, tax avoidance represented about 25 per cent of the tax of the top 0.01 per cent of households, whereas it was estimated to affect an average of 2.8 per cent of the taxes of the remainder of the population (Alstadsæter et al., 2018). Additional analysis based on the Crédit Suisse Global Wealth Databook and the annual Forbes billionaires list also shows that there is increasing wealth concentration. The number of billionaires owning as much wealth as half the world's population fell from 43 in 2017 to 26 in 2018 (Oxfam, 2018). In contrast to these trends, there was a new billionaire every two days over the years 2017 and 2018, yet the wealth of the poorest half of the world's population dropped by 11 per cent during the same period. On the other hand, taxpayers at the top of the wealth or income scale are also those who make the most significant contributions to total income tax in many countries. In the United Kingdom of Great Britain and Northern Ireland, for instance, policy reforms contributed to making the tax system more progressive. As a result, the top 1 per cent earners now contribute a third of the country's income tax, a reflection of an increase of their share of total income tax payments from 25 to 30 per cent since 2010 (Adam, 2019).

Recently, concerns about high levels of inequality and their effects on poverty reduction have returned to the fore. Research shows that it takes two to three generations in Nordic countries and nine generations in emerging economies for a child born into a poor family to reach the average income (OECD, 2018a). The share of global wealth owned by the world's richest 1 per cent rose from 42.5 per cent in 2008, at the time of the financial crisis, to 50.1 per cent in 2017, a value of $140 trillion (Crédit Suisse, 2017). The Crédit Suisse report also estimates that the number of millionaires fell after the 2008 crisis but recovered fast and increased to 36 million, three times the 2000 level. Most of these millionaires were in the United States, followed by Europe, and 22 per cent were in emerging economies such as China. In contrast, 70 per cent of the world's working-age population, 3.5 billion adults, accounted for just 2.7 per cent of global wealth. Most of this population are in African countries and India.

In Africa, at the aggregate continental level, inequality indicators have followed a downward decline. However, 10 out of the 19 most unequal countries in the world are in Africa (United Nations Development Programme (UNDP), 2017). Reasons for such high levels of inequality include the highly dualistic economic structure of some countries, such as higher income levels in multinational companies, especially in the extractive sector, a main conduit for IFFs, and where linkages with other sectors of the economy are limited (UNCTAD, 2017). The latest available data show that poverty reduction and distributional issues remain critical in Africa. The causal factors include insufficient levels of economic growth, weak institutions and limited success in channelling growth into poverty reduction due to heavy reliance on extractive industries (World Bank, 2018). Findings from Nkurunziza (2014) also reveal that in the absence of capital flight, income per capita would have been 1.5 per cent higher and the poverty rate nearly 2 percentage points lower than they were at the time of the analysis.

More generally, the worse the distribution of income is, the lower the share of current and additional income that goes to the poor, and therefore the smaller the poverty-reducing effect of growth. High levels of initial income inequality reduce future growth even after controlling for initial levels of GDP and human capital (Birdsall et al., 1995; Knowles, 2001). Analysis of data over the period 1987–1998 also shows that developing countries with rising incomes and improving distributions reduced poverty seven times as fast as growing economies with increasing inequality (Ravallion, 2001). There is also evidence that a highly unequal distribution of human capital, that is, unequal access to health and education, is a major constraint to poverty reduction in Latin America and sub-Saharan Africa (Birdsall et al., 1995; Birdsall and Londono, 1997). This concern is of great relevance to Africa as the average continental poverty rate stands at 40 per cent and is on the rise in several countries in sub-Saharan Africa, including in fragile and conflict-affected situations (World Bank, 2018). The number of people living in extreme poverty in sub-Saharan Africa, for instance, increased from an estimated 278 million in 1990 to 413 million in 2015. With regard to distributional aspects, in 12 African countries the living standard of the poorest 40 per cent is worsening rather than improving (World Bank, 2018). At this pace, the World Bank 2018 report estimates that extreme poverty in sub-Saharan Africa will still be at double-digit levels in 2030. To reverse this trend, African countries need to realize historically unprecedented and sustained economic growth rates while making sure that such growth is highly inclusive.

In addition to the inequality, growth and poverty reduction channel, IFFs might also impact negatively on many economies subject to rising debt. Indeed, there is empirical evidence of the close connection between IFFs and a rising public debt ratio (Ndikumana, 2003; Beja, 2006; Ndikumana and Boyce, 2011). On one hand, IFFs can lead to flight-driven external borrowing. On the other hand, foreign loans can trigger debt-fuelled capital flight, thereby compounding government indebtedness. These concerns are motivated by the previous occurrence of a debt crisis in the history of many African countries. High levels of poverty and unsustainable debt burdens made these countries eligible for special assistance from IMF and the World Bank and led them to be part of the group of "heavily indebted poor countries" established in 1996.

The present report examines the relationship between IFFs and structural transformation (chapter 5). Structural transformation is broadly defined as the reallocation of economic activity across agriculture, manufacturing and services. More specifically, the drivers of the reallocation of resources towards the non-agricultural sector are increases in agricultural productivity that relax a subsistence food consumption constraint, a reduction in constraints to labour mobility between sectors and increases in capital formation. Structural transformation is generally analysed through the following measures of economic activity at the sectoral level: employment shares and value-added shares on the production side, and final consumption expenditure shares on the consumption side. Stylized facts on structural transformation based on long-term historical series from developed countries show that increases in GDP per capita have been associated with decreases in both the employment share and the nominal value-added share in agriculture and increases in both the employment share and the nominal value-added share in services. Technological factors, policies, regulations and institutional as well as cultural factors that influence labour retention in traditional sectors such as agriculture can act as barriers to labour mobility and slow down the expected shift of labour towards services (Messina, 2006; Hayashi and Prescott, 2008).

However, it should be born in mind that this report's quantitative analysis of IFFs and structural transformation should be considered for illustrative purposes only, rather than definitive. Indeed, IFFs affect the integrity of many key economic indicators. At a recent expert meeting on measurement of IFFs in the context of the UNCTAD–UNODC Task Force, for instance, participants raised concerns about whether GDP and associated economic statistics could still constitute valid indicators of the economic dynamism of the domestic economy if such indicators reflected the international arrangements of MNEs rather than a country's real economy. Furthermore, in a context of high dependency on MNE activities, national accounts are vulnerable to "even minor organizational change by large multinational enterprises".[12] Similarly, the report discusses the opacity of data across many global value chains due to the dominance of MNEs in global trade in goods and services (chapter 4). This limits any attempt to better collect data to understand productivity shifts across sectors.

This report does not set out to analyse the impact of IFFs on capital accumulation and investment, yet it must be emphasized that IFFs also negatively impact the economy through the domestic investment channel. Past research on the impact of capital flight on domestic investment has found that as of 1990, Africa had incurred an estimated 16 per cent loss in output due to the resulting financial leakages (Collier et al., 2001) and that it lowered the annual rate of productive capital accumulation in sub-Saharan Africa by about 1 per cent (Nkurunziza, 2014).

Estimating the extent of asset recovery and what it could mean for the Sustainable Development Goals at the local level
This report considers the magnitude of African wealth stored in offshore accounts and the missed opportunities that this generates (chapter 6). However, the report distances itself from perceptions of Africa being a special case in this regard. Indeed, studies on the distribution of the source of offshore wealth find that "offshore wealth is not easily explained by tax, financial or institutional factors" (Alstadsæter et al., 2018). In this regard, official data from the Switzerland National Bank, for example, shows that African countries do not feature in the top 10 of countries that own a greater share of wealth stored in banks in Switzerland than their share of world GDP. The list of countries is heterogeneous and includes countries with highly developed domestic financial industries, as well as countries with poorly developed financial institutions. The most prominent are Saudi Arabia, the United Arab Emirates, Spain, France, Belgium, Argentina, the Bolivarian Republic of Venezuela, Egypt and Jordan (Alstadsæter et al., 2018).

---

[12] See https://unctad.org/en/pages/newsdetails.aspx?OriginalVersionID=2206.

The experience of both developed and developing countries shows that reclaiming IFFs is a worthwhile exercise. France, for example, recovered €372 million of taxes and penalties between 2013 and 2019 due to the revelations in the papers leaked from a law firm in Panama. If earmarked, it is estimated that these funds could make it possible to build 24 primary schools of 20 pupils per class, or two large public hospitals, based on rates for a large metropolis in France (France, Assemblée Nationale, 2019). Despite slow progress overall, some African countries have been successful in establishing the ground for capital repatriation. By 2018, the OECD-supported Africa Initiative helped African members to identify more than €90 million in additional tax revenues.[13] Nigeria successfully recovered $0.5 billion from Swiss banks in 2005 (UNODC and World Bank, 2007).

This report uses data from the UNODC–World Bank StAR and the International Centre for Tax and Development (ICTD) and United Nations University World Institute for Development Economics Research (UNU-WIDER) government revenue database to chart the state of play of government revenue across Africa and how IFFs feature in domestic resource mobilization efforts (chapter 6). The analysis is situated in the context of a growing number of cases of fund repatriation being allocated to development projects. There is increasing interest in showcasing the extent to which the repatriation of funds to Africa could result in major investments on the continent's journey to economic and social transformation. AfDB, for example, estimates that the annual value of corruption in Africa far exceeds the investment needed to achieve universal electricity access for the continent by 2025, which will range between $60 billion and $90 billion per year (AfDB, 2017). With regard to IFFs, corruption is only accounted for if it implies a cross-border transfer of funds. Some cases of fund repatriation underline specific efforts to earmark funds for specific projects. In 2004 and 2012, for example, following criminal investigations into allegations of corruption and money-laundering from Angola, Angola and Switzerland allocated the recovered funds to the establishment of a hospital, infrastructure, water supply and local capacity-building for reintegration of displaced persons. In a similar initiative, the United Kingdom and the United Republic of Tanzania used recovered funds for primary schools in the country, including the financing of teaching materials and school desks in remote rural areas. The present report builds on these insights as well as on earlier studies on the dynamics of socioeconomic indicators and oil policies and regulations in a case study from Nigeria (UNCTAD, 2017; Chérel-Robson, 2017).

---

[13]   See https://www.oecd.org/tax/transparency/international-community-has-achieved-unprecedented-success-fighting-offshore-tax-evasion.htm.

Chapter 1 annex
Estimates of the cost of illicit financial flows from Africa and worldwide (various years)

Africa	Cost, billions of dollars
Trade misinvoicing[a]	
High-level Panel on Illicit Financial Flows from Africa (UNECA, 2015)	40.2 (2010)
Ndikumana and Boyce (2018)	30 (2015)
Global Financial Integrity (2019)	.45[b] or 131[c] (2015)
Kar and Cartwright-Smith (2009)	52.9 (2008)
Transfer pricing manipulation	
Lower-end estimates, median: OECD (2015), Janský and Palanský (2018), Tørsløv et al. (2018)	4.8 (2015)
Higher-end estimates, median: Crivelli et al. (2015), Cobham and Janský (2018)	55.4 (2015)
Treaty shopping: Beer and Loeprick (2018), all countries	3.4 (2015)
Personal tax evasion by high net worth individuals: Zucman (2014)	9.6 (2014)
IFFs related to corruption: AfDB (2015)	148 (per annum)
IFFs related to corruption: Yikona et al. (2011), estimates for Malawi	0.44 (over 10 years)
Domestic tax losses (defined as domestic tax gap)	
Yikona et al. (2011), estimates for Malawi	0.42 (2009)
Yikona et al. (2011), estimates for Namibia	0.84 (2009)
Worldwide	
Estimated global annual IFFs	
Cobham and Janský (2018), globally per year	500 (per annum)
Tørsløv et al. (2018), globally per year	200 (per annum)
International tax avoidance: UNCTAD (2014), global estimate	70–120 (per annum)
Transnational organized crime	
May (2017), global estimate of value 11 criminal activities	1 600–2 200 (per annum)
UNODC (2011), global estimate of transnational organized crime activities	650 (per annum)
UNODC (2018), global estimate of migrant trafficking	5.5 - 7.0 (2016)
Estimates of global money-laundering	
Schneider and Buehn (2013)	603 (2006 per annum)
UNODC[d]	800–2 000 (per annum)

Source: UNCTAD compilation of estimates from various publicly available reports and publications.
[a] The main difference between the Global Financial Integrity and Ndikumana and Boyce (2018) methodologies is that the latter authors' methodology allows for the possibility of reverse flows of capital flight and that net import misinvoicing (and net trade misinvoicing overall) can result in a downward adjustment of capital flight estimates (Boyce and Ndikumana, 2012).
[b] Global Financial Integrity (2019) based on United Nations International Trade Statistics Database (United Nations Comtrade) data, reflecting estimates for 2015.
[c] Global Financial Integrity (2019) based on the IMF Direction of Trade Statistics (DOTS), reflecting estimates for 2015. IMF DOTS includes a larger sample of African countries than United Nations Comtrade.
[d] See https://www.unodc.org/unodc/en/money-laundering/globalization.html.

Chapter 2

Estimating the magnitude of illicit financial flows related to extractive commodity exports from Africa

The measurement of trade-related IFFs in Africa is critical to combating them. While refining the methods of estimating and classifying trade-related IFFs to help policymakers establish their priorities and devise appropriate policy responses, this report considers but does not delve deeply into recent debates about methodology. Rather, it starts from the presumption that even under the most conservative estimates, extractive export-related IFFs from African countries are of an order of magnitude that gives rise to serious concerns. Reliable estimates are key to curbing IFFs and to creating sensible policies to tackle them. As highlighted in the conceptual framework of this report (see chapter 1), trade misinvoicing is a key channel for moving illicit value across borders.

**IFFs OF AT LEAST
$40 billion**

linked to
extractive commodities

HIGH-VALUE,
LOW-WEIGHT COMMODITIES

drive illicit trade outflows

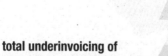

**total underinvoicing of
extractive commodity
exports from Africa**

gold
77%

diamonds
12%

platinum
6%

other
commodities
5%

This chapter adopts the partner-country trade gap method applied to official trade statistics for African countries and specific commodity groups to estimate the magnitude of trade misinvoicing. The chapter identifies and explores country-specific issues linked to statistical anomalies with regard to trade recording and extractive sectors that are at a high risk of illicit outflows. The estimates presented in this chapter show that export underinvoicing as a channel for illicit outflows is of critical importance for the continent. This chapter also reviews logistical and statistical reasons for the identified partner-country trade gaps and links them to current trade recording practices. It also presents case studies discussing the complex interrelationships between various illicit activities that contribute to trade-related illicit outflows. The chapter concludes that the partner-country trade gap method can be a potentially powerful tool to identify commodities that are at risk of trade-related illicit outflows and also alert countries to serious anomalies in the recording of trade statistics.

2.1 Counting the losses: Methodological issues in estimating illicit financial flows

The three main methods in the empirical literature focusing on the quantification of IFFs are: (a) the partner-country trade gap method;[14] (b) the balance of payment residual method; and (c) the price filter analysis method. The partner-country trade gap method, which is used in this chapter, compares the export value reported by country A to country B with the import value reported by country B from country A and after some adjustments tries to infer the magnitude of trade misinvoicing from the extent of the calculated trade gap. This method relies on mirror statistics, based on the principle of double accounting in international trade statistics and with a focus on discrepancies in the same trade flow recorded in two different countries at the commodity group level.

The balance of payments residual model, which is used to measure capital flight,[15] quantifies IFFs as unrecorded capital outflows and is measured as the missing residual in the balance of payments, after corrections for underreported external borrowing and the partner-country trade gap. The terms "capital flight" and "illicit financial flows" are sometimes used interchangeably, but they are distinctly different concepts. Capital flight can be illicit, depending on the definition, but not all IFFs are capital flight (for example,

---

[14]   In this report the partner-country trade gap method, which is the same as the IMF DOTS method for trade misinvoicing, uses United Nations Comtrade data.

[15]   Capital flight represents outflows of financial resources from a country in each period that are not recorded in official government statistics (Ndikumana and Boyce, 2018). The definition of capital flight used in this chapter is linked to the balance of payments residual method and is conceptually different than capital leaving a country due to a political or economic event.

smuggling). Capital flight may be illicit through illegal acquisition, transfer, holding abroad, or some combination of the three. Illicitly acquired capital is money obtained through embezzlement, bribes, extortion, tax evasion or criminal activities. Wealth acquired by these means is often transferred abroad clandestinely to evade legal scrutiny as to its origins. Conceptually, IFFs include not only capital flight but also payments for smuggled imports, transactions connected with illicit trade in drugs and other contraband and outflows of illicitly acquired funds that were domestically laundered before flowing abroad through recorded channels. These are illicit, but they are not capital flight, since these illicit funds are recorded in the balance of payments (Ndikumana et al., 2014).

The price-filter analysis, in comparison with the other two approaches, relies on transaction-level microdata and estimates the price range of a specific commodity over time to distinguish between normal and abnormal pricing (Carbonnier and Mehrotra, 2018; Ahene-Codjoe and Alu, 2019). The analysis either relies on the distribution of prices over time and its outliers (interquartile range price filter) or the comparison of transaction-level prices to free market prices ("arm's length price filter").

This chapter represents a systematic effort to apply the partner-country trade gap method to intra- and extracontinental African trade utilizing United Nations Comtrade data for eight extractive commodity groups.[16] Trade misinvoicing, the fraudulent issuing of an invoice to shift funds abroad, is estimated by exploring discrepancies in mirror trade statistics, which has a long-standing history in the detection of customs fraud (Morgenstern, 1963; Bhagwati, 1964, 1967). Mirror trade statistics compare the bilateral export flows of one country to the respective reported import flows of the partner country. Ideally, the value of the two trade statistics should only differ by the cost, insurance, freight (c.i.f.), but large discrepancies can arise due to valid logistical or statistical reasons as well as deliberate misinvoicing. A study by WCO (2018) highlights that mirror trade gaps[17] identified by the partner-country method do not distinguish between trade misinvoicing and random reporting errors. Although the statistical properties of trade misinvoicing and random errors can be assumed to be different, this is not the case for systematic errors generated by how international trade statistics are recorded. There are challenges in using the partner-country trade gap for the purpose of inferring illicitly motivated customs fraud ranging from differences in valuation, time lags in shipping, destination and product misclassification (section 2.3).

Table 1 provides an overview of four different trade gaps that can arise when comparing mirror trade statistics and their underlying motivation. Since this chapter focuses on

---

[16] Gold, platinum, diamonds, copper, iron, aluminium, manganese, petroleum oil and gas.
[17] The mirror trade gap is the discrepancy between mirror trade statistics, which is the same trade flow reported as export by country A and import by country B.

primary extractive commodities which account for over half of African exports (figure 3), only the export side is analysed. A positive partner-country trade gap arises when the value of exports is lower than the value of imports recorded by the partner country. This practice of export underinvoicing whereby the exporting firm understates the value of exports is used to conceal trade profits abroad (WCO, 2018). Thus, commodities leave the country, but the corresponding financial flows partly stay in foreign accounts. This deprives developing countries of much needed foreign exchange and erodes the tax base of economies already under pressure to mobilize domestic resources for the financing of the Sustainable Development Goals.

Table 1
Classification of the outcome of the partner-country trade gap

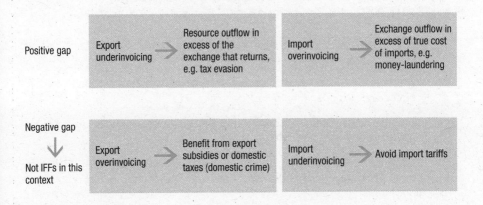

Source: UNCTAD secretariat.
Note: A positive gap in the partner-country trade gap can be used to infer illicit outflows and a negative gap can be used to infer illicit inflows depending on the country and commodity context in question.

On the import side, a positive gap can be associated with a practice called import overinvoicing, which is another way to disguise capital flight as a form of trade payment (WCO, 2018). Typically, an importer overstates the value of imports to allow the outflow of excess funds to foreign accounts instead of only paying for imports. Trade-related IFFs are generated by both practices and will lead to excessive funds or merchandise, greater than indicated in official records, leaving the country. This practice is also referred to as technical smuggling in contrast to "pure" smuggling,[18] which will only be captured by the mirror trade gap if the merchandise is imported to the partner country legally. Additionally, if both trading partners collude in falsifying the value of an invoice, it will not be captured by the mirror trade gap since both trading partners will report the same value in their trade statistics. Reviewing a variety of motives for trade misinvoicing, Bhagwati (1967) concludes that underinvoicing of exports, rather than overinvoicing of imports, is used as a vehicle for capital flight, given that export controls are often less restrictive. There are also other reasons for trade misinvoicing such as export overinvoicing to benefit from subsidies or import underinvoicing to avoid tariffs (Nitsch, 2011). Although both are fraudulent and linked to illicit activities, they do not fit in the context analysed here, focusing on exports of primary extractive resources from the continent (Nitsch, 2011; UNECA, 2015; WCO, 2018). Thus, in the context of this analysis, export overinvoicing and import underinvoicing are not considered illicit financial inflows, which represents a major methodological difference between this report and approaches used by Global Financial Integrity (Global Financial Integrity, 2017, 2019) or capital flight measures (Ndikumana and Boyce, 2018).

This chapter contributes to the measurement of trade-related IFFs via the partner-country trade gap method by:

(a)   Identifying the partner-country trade gap model of best fit for primary extractive commodities exports from Africa;

(b)   Reflecting the first systematic mirror trade analysis for the continent with a focus on both intra-African and extracontinental African trade;

(c)   Placing particular emphasis on primary commodities in Africa and their value chains (including increasingly centralized aspects of trading in Europe) and transit trade;

(d)   Discussing country- and commodity-specific case studies in Madagascar and Zambia, and the gold trade in East Africa, South Africa and Switzerland;

(e)   Providing an in-depth analysis of trade-recording practices and data quality uncertainties in African countries (that is, informal economy, porous borders, selection bias, non-reporting of data, and the like, which in turn impacts IFFs as both are linked to institutional quality).[19]

---

[18]   Pure smuggling is when goods are exported clandestinely and then imported clandestinely to the next country. This practice is associated with trade in illicit goods such as drugs, in contrast to technical smuggling, which is a fraudulent statement about the value of merchandise trade through official channels and thus being partially recorded in trade statistics.

[19]   A country's institutional capacity impacts its ability to enforce customs and border controls, which in turn impacts both the accuracy of its trade statistics and the probability of IFFs.

Trade-related illicit financial flows in the literature

The literature on trade-related IFFs has graduated from estimates based on total exports and imports to more country- and product-specific analyses, as the limitations of international merchandise trade statistics to accurately trace international trade have become clear.

The report of the High-level Panel on Illicit Financial Flows from Africa (UNECA, 2015) considers the whole continent and specific country–commodity pairs. It concludes that the largest shares of illicit outflows from Africa in precious metals, iron and steel, and ores are generated by the Southern African Customs Union; Zambia alone accounted for 65 per cent of trade misinvoicing in copper. The difficulties in using international trade statistics from Southern Africa are the subject of a more detailed discussion in section 2.3.

It has been estimated that as much as 50 per cent of illicit outflows from Africa are generated via trade mispricing and more than half of trade-related IFFs stem from the extractive sector (UNECA and African Minerals Development Centre, 2017). This and other studies have highlighted the importance of the extractive sector in generating IFFs and the role that the international community could play in combating them (UNCTAD, 2016). In the case of mining, MNEs increasingly centralize their trading operations, which raises the risk of trade mispricing. Singapore and Switzerland are among the most attractive places for centralizing trade operations due to tax incentives for multinational trading companies (UNECA and African Minerals Development Centre, 2017). Switzerland accounts for around a third of the global transit trade in key commodities such as oil, metals and agricultural goods (Lannen et al., 2016).

Table 2 provides a summary of country-level estimates of IFFs in Africa. For example, Ahene-Codjoe and Alu (2019) find evidence of a significant and abnormal undervaluation of commodity exports from Ghana. Using contemporaneous market reference prices and interquartile-range price filter methods, the authors find that abnormally undervalued export of gold (gold bullion and unwrought gold) equalled $3.8 billion or 11 per cent of the total export value ($35.6 billion) of gold between 2011 and 2017. Their estimates for cocoa beans and cocoa paste show that 2.7 per cent of the $12.6 billion worth of cocoa beans exported was undervalued and that 7.5 per cent of the total export of cocoa paste ($1.8 billion) was also undervalued. The authors argue that this corresponds to significant IFF risks due to the presence of many MNEs in the industry and corroborates existing literature that IFFs via commodity trading are a concern for Ghana. In another study, Nicolaou-Manias and Wu (2016) estimate the extent of trade mispricing for five African countries using the IMF DOTS methodology. These authors find declining trade mispricing in South Africa and Zambia for the period 2013–2015 and in Nigeria for the period 2013–2014. However, Egypt and Morocco exhibited significant and increasing trade mispricing from 2013–2014.

Table 2

Summary of country estimates of illicit financial flows

	Study	Method and/or results
Angola	Ndikumana and Boyce (2018)	Capital flight of $60 billion during 1986–2015
Cote d'Ivoire	UNCTAD (2016)	Net cocoa export misinvoicing of $3.7 billion during 1995–2014
	Ndikumana and Boyce (2018)	Capital flight of $32 billion during 1970–2015
Democratic Republic of the Congo	Cathey et al. (2018)	Eurostat data and price filter analysis to detect undervalued European Union imports. Undervalued amount of European Union imports from the Democratic Republic of the Congo: €9.95 billion during 2000–2010
Egypt	Nicolaou-Manias and Wu (2016)	Gross excluding reversal (GER) method; $32.6 billion during 2013–2014
Ghana	Ahene-Codjoe and Alu (2019)	Micro-level data provided by the Ghana Revenue Authority (2011–2017): Abnormally undervalued export of gold was $3.8 billion and of cocoa, $12.6 billion
	Marur (2019)	Mirror trade data between Ghana, Switzerland and the United Kingdom during 2000–2017: Gold $6 billion; cocoa $4.3 billion
Kenya	Letete and Sarr (2017)	Uses Ndikumana estimate from the Political Economy Research Institute database and links it to institutions
Madagascar	Chalendard et al. (2016)	Import underinvoicing and mirror trade data to detect customs fraud. Customs fraud reduced non-oil customs revenue (duties and import value-added tax) by at least 30 per cent in 2014
Morocco	Nicolaou-Manias and Wu (2016)	GER method; $16.6 billion during 2013–2014
Nigeria	UNCTAD (2016)	Oil export misinvoicing at $44 billion and import misinvoicing at $45 billion during 1996–2014
	Nicolaou-Manias and Wu (2016)	GER method; $48 billion during 2013–2014
South Africa	UNCTAD (2016)	Net export misinvoicing during 2000–2014: Silver and platinum, $24 billion; iron, $57 billion
	Ndikumana and Boyce (2018)	Capital flight: $198 billion during 1970–2015
	Nicolaou-Manias and Wu (2016)	GER method; $67 billion during 2013–2015
Zambia	UNCTAD (2016)	Net export misinvoicing of copper: $14.5 billion during 1995–2014
	Nicolaou-Manias and Wu (2016)	GER method; $12.5 billion during 2013–2015

Source: UNCTAD secretariat.
Note: The GER method only considers positive gaps and sets negative trade gaps, resulting from the partner-country method, to zero.

The studies summarized in table 2 reflect a wide range of estimates of IFFs and capital flight, data and empirical approaches to measurement. This makes a comparison of estimators across studies impossible. At the time of writing, there are insufficient studies exploring the statistical reasons for bilateral trade asymmetries, especially in Africa (United Nations Statistics Division (UNSD), 2019). This chapter aims to address some of the criticisms raised in the literature by better controlling for c.i.f. and by providing an in-depth analysis of the recording of international trade statistics, while highlighting the idiosyncrasies of individual countries. The chapter also aims to provide an Africa-centred partner-country trade gap analysis by focusing on key commodities and their value chains that are of particular importance to the continent (in terms of total exports) and that have been highlighted as being prone to illicit outflows (UNECA, 2015; UNCTAD, 2016).

In this chapter, the analysis focuses on intra- and extracontinental African mirror trade gaps and considers the drivers of illicit outflows in this context. The lack of information on how intra-African trade statistics are recorded is a major obstacle to accurately assessing the status quo of regional and continental trade integration. The role of industry-specific features, such as the high degree of concentration in commodity trading, bonded warehouses for metals and petroleum exports via pipelines and how these features are reflected in international trade statistics is also highlighted.

2.2 Africa: Empirical analysis of the commodity-based partner-country trade gap

Rationale and sample selection

The importance of the mining and minerals sector led to the creation of the African Mining Vision (AMV), adopted by the first African Union Conference of African Ministers Responsible for Mineral Resources Development, held in Addis Ababa in 2008. The aim of AMV is to use the mineral wealth of Africa to eradicate poverty and achieve structural transformation and socioeconomic development. It is the most comprehensive continental framework governing mining and aims to integrate mining into national development policies, by ensuring that communities see real benefits, countries negotiate contracts that generate fair resource rents and that the mining industry becomes a strategic element of continental industrialization (UNECA, 2011).

The primary commodities included in the sample are those identified in previous studies as drivers of illicit outflows and extractive commodities that matter for the continent.

Most African economies are heavily dependent on the export of primary commodities (46 out of 54 are commodity dependent).[20] Eighteen countries are dependent on minerals, ores and metals exports, 17 on the export of agricultural products and 11 on fuel exports. There is also empirical evidence that the degree of trade misinvoicing varies over commodity groups and is linked to commodity-specific characteristics (UNCTAD, 2016). For example, high-value, low-weight commodities such as diamonds, gold and other precious metals appear to be more prone to smuggling and have been linked to IFFs, corruption and illicit arms trafficking (IMF, 2014; Berman et al., 2017). A feature of trade in primary extractive commodities that makes them vulnerable to trade misinvoicing is market concentration. As the large-scale extraction of natural resources is highly capital intensive, MNE market concentration is significant given their substantial financial and market power, enabling them to exert significant influence over government regulations together with the technical expertise to circumvent domestic laws (UNCTAD, 2016). Similarly, major agglomerates in extractive industries, which both mine and trade commodities, can exert considerable influence over prices and key elements of the value chain.

The distinction between intra- and extracontinental African trade for the calculation of the partner-country trade gap matters since trade patterns in terms of size and products are different. In addition, key players and motives for fraudulent customs invoicing differ. Furthermore, the quality of intra-African trade data is generally lower as trade recording at porous land borders is often more challenging than at ports. Therefore, the partner-country trade gap patterns are expected to differ for intra- and extracontinental African exports of extractive resources.

Countries need to
improve the recording
of intra-African trade statistics, especially over land borders

Figure 3 shows commodity exports by group as a share of total African exports. Primary extractive commodities constituted more than 50 per cent of total exports during 2000–2018, with oil and gas exports contributing around 40 per cent of total

[20] A country is export commodity-dependent when more than 60 per cent of its total merchandise exports are composed of commodities. African countries that are not export commodity dependent include Cabo Verde, Egypt, Eswatini, Lesotho, Mauritius, Morocco, South Africa and Tunisia.

exports. Since many of the identified commodities only make up a small percentage of total African exports not all are included in the final analysis. Manganese is the last commodity included in the analysis because the share of total exports of the other listed commodities was too small at the time of writing.

Figure 3
Commodity exports by group, 2000–2018
(Percentage of total African exports, by value)

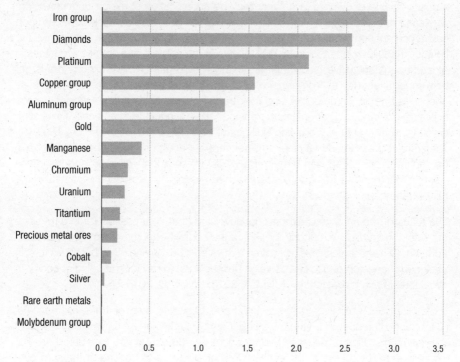

Source: UNCTAD calculations based on UN Comtrade.

The method
This section outlines the method used to estimate the extent of partner-country (mirror) trade gaps (*DX*) focusing on commodity exports from Africa and its mirror, that is, imports from Africa reported by the rest of the world. Building on Ndikumana and Boyce

(2018), the following equation denotes the difference between import (*M*) and export values (*X*) correcting for the c.i.f. (*β*):

$$DX_{i,t} = \sum_{j=1,k=1}^{JK} (M_{ji,t}^k - \beta X_{ij,t}^k)$$

In this equation, *DX* captures statistical and logistical errors in mirror trade data, as well as intentional export misinvoicing. Given the limitations of international trade reporting, a positive value of *DX* in a given year may be an indication of export underinvoicing, whereas a negative value is more difficult to explain as to some extent this depends upon how a primary commodity is traded. A negative value of *DX* cannot be readily linked to IFFs for the following reasons: (a) illicit inflows in the context of extractive industries in Africa is counterintuitive; and (b) large negative trade gaps (where exports are larger than imports reported by the partner country) are likely to be linked to the characteristics of specific primary commodities and their trade patterns (for example, copper storage in bonded warehouses, or upstream transformation in industrial free zones). (*β*) is c.i.f., which is usually set at 1.1 following Ndikumana and Boyce (2018) and UNCTAD (2016). Therefore, it is assumed that c.i.f. is 10 per cent of the export value. In section 2.3, this procedure is compared with data in the OECD International Transport and Insurance Cost for Merchandise Trade database, which allows for a more accurate estimate of the mirror trade gap.

The focus of the analysis is export underinvoicing (that is, a positive trade gap) since this is the most relevant conduit for IFFs in the context of primary commodity exports from Africa. Trade underinvoicing is often motivated by exporting MNE incentives to shift foreign exchange abroad to settle foreign transactions, to pay for smuggled goods or to avoid foreign exchange controls (UNECA, 2015; UNCTAD, 2016).

Table 3 shows various partner-country trade gap estimates of trade-related IFFs. Significant differences in methodology exist and are reflected in the variation in size of the estimators. First, a negative partner-country trade gap is not considered an illicit inflow (as in Global Financial Integrity, 2019) or set to zero. Second, if the sum over all partner-country trade gaps is negative it will not be attributed to illicit inflows (as in Ndikumana and Boyce, 2018) but is explained by particularities in commodity-specific trade recording. Third, the level of data aggregation used in all the studies with the exception of UNECA (2015) and Global Financial Integrity (2019) is total trade, which does not allow for a commodity-driven analysis. Fourth, this chapter focuses on illicit outflows related to extractive industry exports, thus does not take the import side, agricultural or manufactured products, into account.

Table 3

Africa: Different estimates of trade-related illicit financial flows

(Billons of dollars)

	UNECA (2015): annual average 2000–2010	Global Financial Integrity (2019): 2015 estimate (DOTS)	Global Financial Integrity (2019): 2015 estimate (United Nations Comtrade)	Ndikuman and Boyce (2018): 2015	UNCTAD (2020): 2015 Estimate[a]
Positive export gap[b]		39	11		40
Positive import and export gap[c]		65	23	38	
Total	16[d]–29				

Note: The group of countries included and the time period are not consistent across studies.

[a] The present report. Focuses on extracontinental African exports and eight commodity groups; 80 per cent of the results are driven by South Africa and largely by gold. Other countries include Angola, Benin, Burundi, the Central African Republic, Egypt, Eswatini, the Gambia, Guinea, Lesotho, Madagascar, Malawi, Mauritius, Morocco, Mozambique, the Niger, Rwanda, Senegal, Togo, Uganda, the United Republic of Tanzania and Zimbabwe.

[b] A positive export gap signifies that a country's reported exports of a specific commodity are lower than imports reported by the partner country. This may be an indicator of systematic export underinvoicing, intended to conceal trade profits abroad, such as in tax havens. A firm interested in moving capital out of a country would underinvoice its exports, thus bringing reduced foreign exchange into the country.

[c] A positive import gap is an indicator of systematic import overinvoicing, intended to disguise capital flight as a form of trade payment. Both positive export and import gaps can be indicative of trade-related illicit outflows.

[d] The total from UNECA (2015) reflects the five top commodities.

Global Financial Integrity (2019) notes that globally, sub-Saharan Africa has the highest propensity for trade misinvoicing and is the only region in which outflows exceed inflows. In 2015, IFFs (as reported in United Nations Comtrade) are estimated at $45 billion and illicit outflows are equal to $23 billion (table 3). The present report's estimate of $40 billion in export underinvoicing is based on the net export gap and is the sum of all positive individual country estimates in 2015 (covering 21 African countries and the eight selected commodity groups). Despite significant differences in methodologies for trade-related illicit outflows from the continent, some convergence on findings exist; IFFs are large, have increased over time and trade in primary extractive commodities is a major contributor (UNECA, 2015; Östensson, 2018). Estimates based on total trade should only be considered as indicative, since calculating the mirror trade gap over the sum of all commodity groups can conceal large commodity-specific heterogeneities. Furthermore, due to significant differences in the data used (for example, level of aggregation, total, Harmonized System four- or six-digit level or Standard International Trade Classification) and how IFFs are defined, estimates are not comparable across studies.

An additional premise underlying mirror trade gap-based estimates of IFFs is that trade statistics reported by developed countries are generally more accurate and thus discrepancies in partner-country trade statistics are mainly driven by trade-related IFFs from developing countries. Therefore, the mirror trade gap is usually calculated vis-à-vis developed countries only and then scaled up by their share in total trade (see, for example, Ndikumana and Boyce, 2018; Global Financial Integrity, 2019). This does not allow for the analysis of intra-African discrepancies nor account for the fact that although primary commodities are still traded in Europe, the latter is no longer the largest consumer. Another concern is attributing partner-country trade gaps as being directly linked to illicit flows, which has been widely criticized in the literature for being too simplistic (De Wulf, 1981; Nitsch, 2011). Other sources of error being of a purely logistical nature have gained insufficient weight in recent discussions. For example, the analysis by Hong and Pak (2017) of the partner-country trade gap between Japan and the United States shows that even between developed countries, these gaps persist. Similarly, Bundhoo-Jouglah et al. (2005) analyse asymmetries in bilateral trade between Germany and the United Kingdom and ascribe the differences to accounting standards. Other statistical challenges are discussed in section 2.3.

Table 4 summarizes the descriptive statistics for global, extracontinental and intra-African trade derived from the partner-country trade gap model. There are no significance levels presented, as a regression model is not estimated, but rather an indicator for potential illicit outflows, which is used in the regression analyses presented in chapter 5. The global, intra- and extracontinental African trade for the period 2000–2018 summarized in table 4 covers eight commodities (as specified in table A.2) and highlights some interesting findings. For example, only one third of recorded trade is intra-African, which reflects the extracontinental export orientation in Africa for primary commodities. The average trade value, meaning the sum of all trade values divided by the number of observations, of extracontinental African trade is seven times as large as intra-African trade, $63 million versus $8.5 million. The maximum trade value for extracontinental African trade is seven times as large as for intra-African trade. Imports recorded by the rest of the world stemming from the continent are on average larger than exports recorded by African countries.

Table 4

Descriptive statistics: Global, extracontinental and intra-African trade and trade gaps, 2000–2018

		Number of observations	Average trade value (millions of dollars)	Standard deviation	Minimum	Maximum
Global trade	Import	80 571	44	501	0	36 990
	Export	74 302	43	476	0	34 384
	M-1.1*export	113 390	1	155	-10 416	14 881
Extracontinental	Import	50 814	64	626	0	36 990
	Export	46 361	62	596	0	34 384
	M-1.1*export	72 217	2	189	-10 416	14 881
Intra-Africa	Import	29 757	7	88	0	5 112
	Export	27 941	10	109	0	4 700
	M-1.1*export	39 501	-2	60	-4 751	1 006

Source: UNCTAD calculations based on United Nations Comtrade.
Note: M-1.1*export denotes imports minus exports (including 10 per cent of export value proxy for c.i.f.).

Figure 4 shows the results of the partner-country trade gap clustered by the eight commodity groups. Some general trends emerge. First, the trade gap for gold from South Africa (since 2011) has a significant impact on the overall African trade gap. South Africa has a distinctive trade recording system, as illustrated by the observed gold trade reporting. Gold from South Africa, for historic reasons, had no trading partner country assigned before 2011. Since then, gold has been reported in United Nations Comtrade, and therefore included in this report, even though the reporting of this commodity remains special (Ndikumana and Boyce, 2019). Second, all high-value commodities, gold, platinum and diamonds (for example, from Eswatini, Lesotho, South Africa and the United Republic of Tanzania) tend to have a positive trade gap, whereas petroleum and copper exports tend to exhibit a negative one. In fact, all major petroleum exporting countries (Algeria, Angola, Nigeria and Tunisia) to some extent have large negative export trade gaps, with the exception of Egypt, which has a large positive gap. On average, iron, aluminium and manganese also have positive export gaps.

Figure 4
Sum of partner-country trade gaps by commodity group

(Millions of dollars)

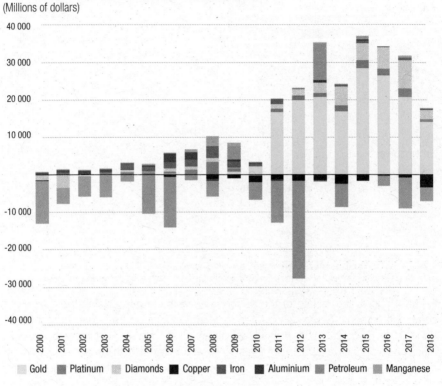

Gold   Platinum   Diamonds   Copper   Iron   Aluminium   Petroleum   Manganese

Source: UNCTAD calculations based on United Nations Comtrade.

The estimated partner-country trade gap consists of 109,451 observations; 40,803 are matched along the country commodity axis; 37,330 are orphan imports, meaning there are no commodity exports reported by the African State for the same year; and 31,318 are lost exports, meaning for the same year and commodity, the partner country did not report any imports. Figure 5 shows the amount of total exports covered in the sample. For many countries that primarily export mining commodities or petroleum, a large share of exports is included. For other countries, such as agricultural exporters or those with greater export diversification, a smaller share is covered.

Figure 5

Exports covered by the sample, 2000-2018

(Percentage of total exports)

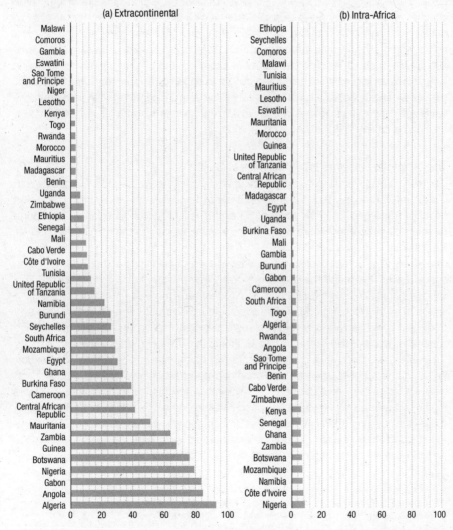

Source: UNCTAD calculations based on United Nations Comtrade.

The findings show that during the period 2010–2014, there were eight countries[21] in which the partner-country trade gap was positive and increasing and that during the period 2015–2018, there were five countries[22]. This suggests that these countries are at increasing risk of trade-related illicit outflows via export underinvoicing. Three different countries during the periods 2010–2014[23] and 2015–2018[24] had a positive but decreasing trend in the size of the partner-country trade gap, implying that the risk of illicit outflows via export underinvoicing was decreasing over these periods for a subsample of countries. For the remaining countries, the partner-country trade gap is either stable over time or no time trend can be assigned due to too few observations for the years considered, or too much volatility to discern a clear trend. Although countries have up to two years to report data in United Nations Comtrade, not all countries provided data for 2018.

Intra-African asymmetries in bilateral trade data

Generally, a positive net export gap can be an indicator of export underinvoicing, which is a channel through which value leaves the country illicitly. It is more difficult to link a negative trade gap to IFFs as this could simply reflect the underreporting of imports by the partner country. Figure 6 shows the annual average of the mirror trade gap for intra-African trade from 2000 to 2018. With regard to intra-African trade, the largest outliers are Ghana and Nigeria, with a negative average trade gap of more than $1 billion annually, which explains the negative average intra-African trade gap in table 4. This suggests that exports from Ghana and Nigeria are more rigorously recorded than imports by neighbouring countries. The largest positive outliers are Mozambique and South Africa, with an annual average of more than $250 million per year. Benin and Togo are the largest positive outliers when weighting the mirror trade gap by total exports (figure 7). According to the statistics of trading partners, both Benin and Togo export large amounts of gold, whereas both countries report exporting only small amounts and have limited gold reserves. A possible explanation for this is that gold from the Sahel region is exported via Togo and is inaccurately recorded as originating from Togo in the partner country (Extractive Industries Transparency Initiative (EITI) Togo, 2013). The recording of trade statistics at porous land borders is a challenge for many countries and the lack of customs enforcement can be a threat to national security, because organized crime will use the same trade routes for illicit trade, potentially in arms.

---

[21] Burundi, Eswatini, Gambia, Lesotho, Mali, South Africa, Togo, United Republic of Tanzania.
[22] Benin, Burundi, Lesotho, Togo, United Republic of Tanzania.
[23] Benin, Egypt, Madagascar.
[24] Egypt, Gambia, South Africa.

Figure 6
Intra-African partner-country trade gap, annual average 2000–2018
(Millions of dollars)

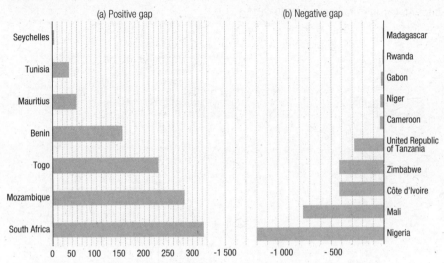

* Countries with an inconclusive gap are Algeria, Angola, Botswana, Burkina Faso, Burundi, Cabo Verde, the Central African Republic, the Comoros, Egypt, Eswatini, Ethiopia, the Gambia, Ghana, Guinea, Kenya, Lesotho, Malawi, Mauritania, Morocco, Namibia, Sao Tome and Principe, Senegal, Uganda and Zambia.

Source: UNCTAD calculations based on United Nations Comtrade.

For the intra-African partner-country trade gap, results are mainly inconclusive meaning that there is no consistent trend over time, that is, a large positive gap in one year followed by a negative gap in the next. These patterns cannot easily be attributed to errors in trade recording and systemic illicit behaviour. Where volatile fluctuations in a country's export trade gap are difficult to logically explain, they are placed in the inconclusive gap category (figure 6).

Figure 7 shows the same results as figure 6 but with country estimates weighted by total exports, which produces a different ranking of estimates.[25] When weighted by trade the

[25] The weighting of the partner-country trade gap is a delicate question. Generally, countries that trade more will have larger partner-country trade gaps, and this should be considered via weighting by GDP or total exports. Here the trade gap is weighted by total exports, which allows for a comparison between the intra- and extracontinental African trade gap, weighted by intra- and extracontinental African export value. At the same time, weighting by total exports introduces distortions when the trade gap is driven by systemic non-reporting on either side of the trading partners. Therefore, in chapter 5, which uses only the extracontinental African trade gap estimates, GDP is used for weighting purposes and Benin and Togo remain the largest outliers (for further information, see Schuster and Davis, 2020).

largest positive outliers are Benin and Togo, which may be attributed to gold trade rules of origin issues, as outlined above.

Figure 7

Intra-African mirror trade gap, 2000–2018

(Percentage of total exports, by value)

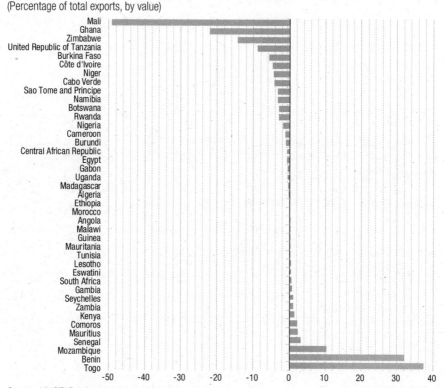

Source: UNCTAD calculations based on United Nations Comtrade.

According to Mayaki in "Colonialism was a system of illicit financial flows", most pre-independence infrastructure primarily linked mines to ports and was geared towards the extraction of minerals and agricultural products. Much of that infrastructure still stands in most of Africa (*Africa Renewal*, 2020). The lack of recorded intra-African trade is partly a function of such embedded historical and economic factors. For example, until 2008, the export statistics of Uganda were calculated at the port of Mombasa in Kenya, a legacy of colonial practices (Jerven, 2013), thus neglecting any intra-African trade in official statistics. When the Uganda Bureau of Statistics surveyed trade, it concluded that informal cross-border trade was significant and contributed immensely to household welfare and growth (Kuteesa et al., 2010). Similarly, a United Nations Comtrade metadata survey showed that Sierra Leone did not include land border trade in the statistics reported to United Nations Comtrade.[26] As some countries do not report, or only sporadically report, the suitability of United Nations Comtrade data for the analysis of intra-African trade is questionable. Improving intra-African trade statistics is an important pillar for understanding opportunities for regional trade integration.

Another hurdle for the analysis is that informal cross-border trade is sizeable and important for many African economies. For some borders and specific products, informal trade might be as high as formal trade. For example, a recent survey concluded that the number of products being exported from Benin to Nigeria were five times greater than official records showed (Bensassi et al., 2016). Informal cross-border trade and porous borders mean that data at land borders is not collected rigorously, which in turn may limit the usefulness of the partner-country trade gap analysis for the inference of IFFs linked to intra-African trade. A systematic approach to assessing informal cross-border trade and its formalization will be necessary to identify growth potential and risks associated with intra-African trade. Informal cross-border trade should not be equated with IFFs, but illicit cross-border trade may use the same routes as other informal cross-border trade. However, the partner-country trade gap method can also be used to identify issues with trade recording and customs inefficiencies. For example, if all trade partners report importing a specific commodity at a higher value than a country's own export statistics, this might be an indication of significant informal (possibly illicit) cross-border activities or smuggling.

Extracontinental African asymmetries in bilateral trade data

Figure 8 shows the sum of mirror trade gaps, covering the eight commodity groups included in the sample. The largest outlier is South Africa, with a positive trade gap of $10 billion annually. If trade in gold is excluded, the annual average is $4 billion. The largest negative outlier is Algeria, with an annual average of almost $6 billion.

Based on the selected commodity sample, 23 out of 45 African countries covered in the analysis experience a positive and time-persistent partner-country trade gap, which can be used to infer illicit outflows via extracontinental trade in extractive resources (for data coverage, see table A.1). The extent of the trade gap is linked to the volume of total trade and data quality. This is in comparison with intra-African trade (figure 6), in which only seven countries fall into the time-persistent positive group, which allows for the inference of illicit outflows; these seven countries lost, on average, around $1 billion per year between 2000 and 2018. The results for intra-African trade are expected to be

---

[26]   See https://comtrade.un.org/survey/.

more mixed as it is generally easier to record trade at ports than at land borders, and may also be due to some countries not reporting on intra-customs-union trade.

When weighting the trade gap by total exports (figure 9), the largest positive outliers are Togo and Benin even though total trade covered in the sample is less than 10 per cent. This is mainly driven by countries reporting gold imports from these countries while at the same time they are not major gold producers. It may be that gold exported via Togo and Benin from the Sahel region is inaccurately recorded in partner countries. When weighting the trade gap by total exports the gap is large, since these orphan imports are not recorded in the total exports of either Benin or Togo.

Figure 8
Extracontinental partner-country trade gap, annual average 2000–2018
(Millions of dollars)

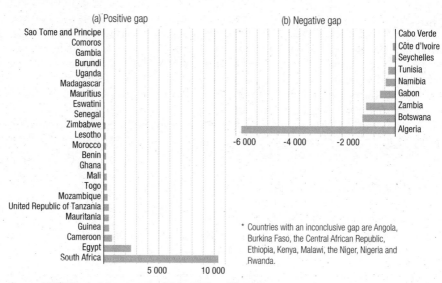

* Countries with an inconclusive gap are Angola, Burkina Faso, the Central African Republic, Ethiopia, Kenya, Malawi, the Niger, Nigeria and Rwanda.

Source: UNCTAD calculations based on United Nations Comtrade.

Generally, countries can be divided into three groups. For countries that have a consistently positive mirror trade gap, a case can be made for linking the positive export gap to export underinvoicing and thus illicit outflows. Given that many primary resources are stored in bonded warehouses, a persistent negative trade gap is expected in the data. For countries in the negative or inconclusive groups no inference can be made about trade misinvoicing. This does not mean that these countries do not have trade-related illicit outflows, but rather that trade statistics are recorded in a way that makes it impossible to detect trade gaps that are associated with export underinvoicing. For countries with a persistent negative gap, any correlation with commodity prices must be carefully analysed (box 2). A negative correlation between the commodity-specific trade gap and commodity price, as for example in Zambia, is linked to the amount of commodity kept in stock, as any profit-maximizing firm has an incentive to sell more copper when prices are high, reducing the stock in bonded warehouses and decreasing the mirror trade gap. The third group consists of countries with large mirror trade gaps, but they vary significantly over time. This group is much harder to explain because if there was systematic trade misinvoicing that could be clearly detected in macro-level trade data, drivers should be consistent over time, or only change with significant political or economic events. For the 23 countries where there is a positive indication of systemic export underinvoicing, commodity and trade-related illicit outflows were an estimated average of almost $18 billion per year during 2000–2018 (figure 8).

Figure 9
Extracontinental African mirror trade gap, 2000–2018

(Percentage of total exports, by value)

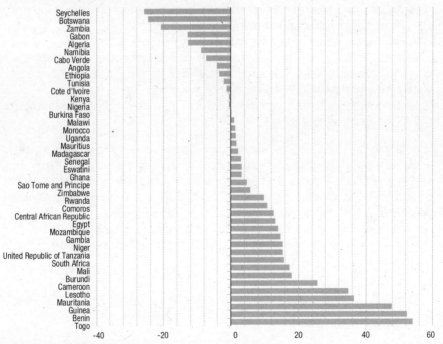

Source: UNCTAD calculations based on United Nations Comtrade.

When comparing the pattern of intra- and extracontinental African trade gaps by country for the period 2000–2018 (figures 6 and 8) three interesting points emerge. First, the number of countries where the results of the partner-country trade gap method leads to inconclusive results is much larger for intra-African trade. This might be related to greater uncertainty concerning the recording of intra-African trade statistics. Second, some interesting cases emerge where the extracontinental African trade gap does not allow for the inference of illicit flows, but where the intra-African situation is different (see Seychelles and Tunisia). Third, when the trade gap is weighted by total trade, Benin and Togo are the largest positive outliers and both their intra- and extra-African trade gaps are largely driven by gold trade.

Box 2
Zambia: Exploring the copper trade gap

Based on United Nations Comtrade data, Zambia reports more than 50 per cent of its copper exports to Switzerland. In contrast, Switzerland does not report any copper imports from Zambia. This is termed merchanting and is often observed in trade data for commodity trading hubs such as Switzerland and the United Kingdom. The trading company Glencore, which has its headquarters in Switzerland and has a subsidiary in Zambia called Mopani Copper Mine, may be taken as an example; the company initially purchases copper that will be reported as an export to Switzerland. Typically, the copper does not physically enter Switzerland but is stored, for example, in one of the bonded warehouses of the London Metal Exchange, before entering other final destination markets, or is resold during shipping.

Such practices can lead to large mirror trade gaps. There will be a large negative gap between Switzerland and Zambia, which could prompt the assumption of massive export overinvoicing and a large positive trade gap between Zambia and the final destination country, which could be interpreted as export underinvoicing. Although UNCTAD (2016) has highlighted this problem, the suggested remedy, that is, the exclusion of exports from Zambia to Switzerland, would lead to a substantial positive bias in the mirror trade gap. Box 2 figure 1 shows the extent of the mirror trade data mismatch as reported by UNCTAD (2016), excluding copper exports from Zambia to Switzerland.

Box 2 figure 1

Partner-country trade gap: Zambia copper exports, excluding Switzerland as destination market

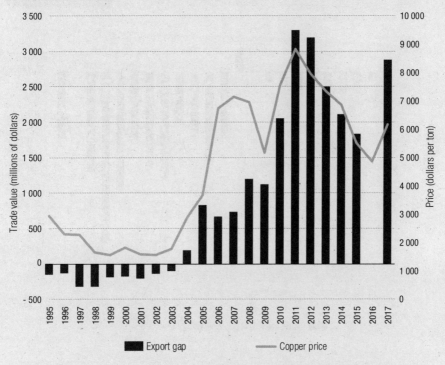

Source: UNCTAD calculations based on United Nations Comtrade and copper price data from the London Metal Exchange.

The results change significantly when including Switzerland in the difference between reported copper exports by Zambia and imports from Zambia reported by the rest of the world. Exports reported by Zambia to the rest of the world are larger than Zambian imports reported by the rest of the world, leading to an extensive negative trade gap. Furthermore, box 2 figure 2 shows the link between the size of the trade gap, total export value and price of copper. The trade gap is strongly negatively correlated with both the total export value and the copper price (that is, when copper prices and total exports increase, the trade gap decreases).

Box 2 figure 2

Partner-country trade gap: Zambia copper exports, all destination markets

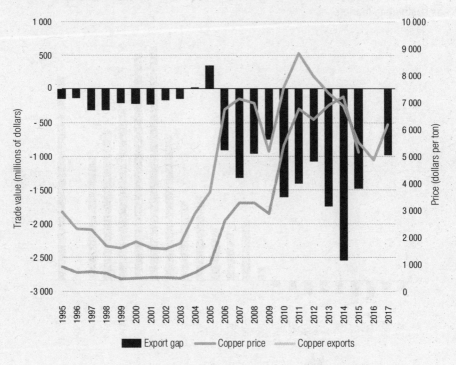

Source: UNCTAD calculations based on United Nations Comtrade and copper price data from the London Metal Exchange.

Box 2 figure 3 shows total copper exports from Zambia to the world and total copper imports reported by the rest of world. The import value is consistently below the export value, which is surprising since imports are generally recorded more rigorously, and the import value also includes c.i.f. There are two potential explanations for the lost copper exports, namely, storage in bonded warehouses and downstream transformation in industrial free zones. Countries that follow the special trade recording system do not report trade related to bonded warehouses and all types of industrial free zones, which means that if copper from Zambia was imported to an industrial free zone and then sufficiently transformed it would not appear as imports in international trade statistics. The bonded warehouses of the London Metal Exchange hold large volumes of metals such as copper, aluminium, lead, nickel, zinc and precious metals. The Exchange houses as much as 250,750 metric tons of copper at any given time.[a] The evident negative correlation between the mirror trade gap and the copper price (-0.81) supports the hypothesis of copper being stored in bonded warehouses. The higher the demand and ultimately, the price, the more copper stocks will be sold from the warehouse, entering countries import statistics and closing the mirror trade gap.

Box 2 figure 3

Partner-country trade gap: Zambia copper exports and imports as reported by the rest of the world

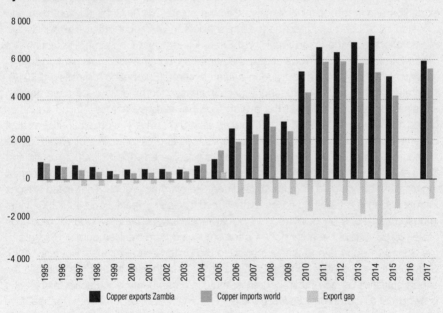

Source: UNCTAD calculations based on United Nations Comtrade.

Although there is no evidence of export underinvoicing using the partner-country trade gap approach, Zambia is still experiencing significant losses related to the minerals industry, but via different channels that are largely undetectable in trade statistics.

Source: UNCTAD secretariat.
[a] See https://www.lme.com/en-GB/Metals/Non-ferrous/Copper#tabIndex=0.

The special role of gold as a conduit for illicit financial flows
Gold, due to its physical properties, high value, low weight and tradability on international markets, is at high risk of money-laundering by organized crime networks (Financial Action Task Force, 2015) and smuggling. Switzerland refines between 40 and 70 per cent of the world's gold production. During the refining process, the gold loses all traces of its origin and is traded as Swiss gold on international markets (Switzerland, Interdepartmental Coordinating Group on Combating Money-Laundering and the Financing of Terrorism, 2015; Mbiyavanga, 2019).

Collier (2007) has highlighted the considerable economic and development costs associated with conflict, which in the African context is closely linked to the illicit extraction and trade of minerals (also Berman et al., 2017). Gold, tin, tantalum and tungsten have been identified as fuelling conflicts in many countries. Recognition of this is reflected in the Dodd-Frank Wall Street Reform and Consumer Protection Act (Dodd-Frank Act) section 1552 and by the European Commission implementing special regulatory regimes related to trade in these elements (European Commission, 2017). Estimates also show that exogenous price increases (commodity price super cycles) explained up to one fourth of the average level of violence across African countries during the period 1997–2010 (Berman et al., 2017). The United Nations Panel of Experts on Illegal Exploitation of Natural Resources and Other Forms of Wealth of the Democratic Republic of the Congo (United Nations, Security Council, 2002) found that Kampala's largest gold trading companies, Machanga Ltd and Uganda Commercial Impex, were buying gold from Ituri-based non-State armed groups. The United Nations Security Council established a Committee (Security Council resolution 1533 (2004)) that imposed sanctions on gold trade with that region under Security Council resolution 1596 (2005). This is because gold is often smuggled from the Democratic Republic of the Congo to Uganda and then exported to the United Arab Emirates (Reuters, 2019; United Nations, Security Council, 2002), and much of this trade is not reflected in the export statistics of the African countries; thus, large amounts of potential tax revenue is being lost to the country in which the gold is mined. Gold exports from Uganda have risen significantly over recent years, even though the country has only modest reserves (figure 10). Furthermore, recorded imports by the United Arab Emirates from Uganda are much larger than recorded exports from Uganda to the United Arab Emirates, which implies potential export underinvoicing and/or smuggling.

Figure 10
Uganda and the United Arab Emirates: Gold imports and exports
(Trade value in millions of dollars)

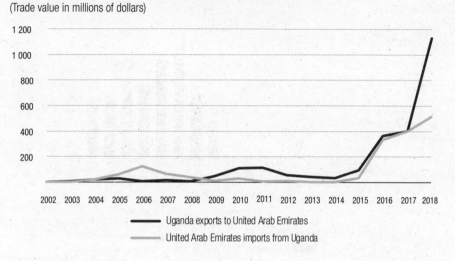

Source: UNCTAD calculations based on United Nations Comtrade.

This is also reflected in the results of the partner-country trade gap, whereby countries generally tend to have large positive trade gaps related to gold exports (in order of trade gap, South Africa, Togo, Benin, the United Republic of Tanzania, Mali, Burundi, Madagascar, Senegal and Kenya). The trade gap is correlated with the gold price on international markets. Figure 11 highlights the relationship between commodity prices and the size of the partner-country trade gap over time. For gold there is a strong positive correlation (0.85), whereas for petroleum there is a strong negative correlation (-0.68). The correlation of prices and the export gap is partially driven by the fact that both are linked to total export value (that is, if prices rise, the total export value increases and the export gap also rises). This shows the importance of different trading patterns and risks associated with diverse commodities and that gold has a high risk of related illicit outflows.

Figure 11
Madagascar: Partner-country trade gap and commodity prices
(Millions of dollars)

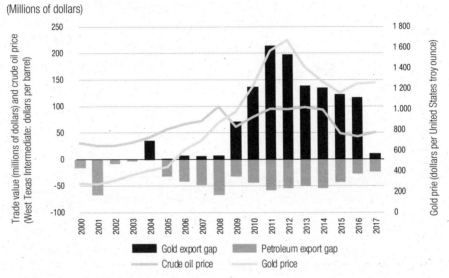

Source: UNCTAD calculations based on United Nations Comtrade and the IMF primary commodity price system for crude oil and gold price data.

2.3 Challenges in matching bilateral merchandise trade statistics

There are a multitude of challenges in matching bilateral trade data. Ideally, exports of country A to country B should be equivalent to imports of country B from country A, minus c.i.f., based on the principal of double accounting in trade statistics. Valid logistical and statistical reasons for asymmetries in bilateral trade statistics include: exchange rate volatility both between trade partners and vis-à-vis the value in which data is reported in United Nations Comtrade (which uses quarterly averages to convert figures into dollars); uncertainty surrounding the quality; destination mismatches; different classifications for the same good; timing and currency valuation (long sea cargoes, delayed customs processing or storing in warehouses can lead to trade being recorded in different years and goods being valued at different prices due to exchange rate volatility); and trade recording in customs unions and at land borders (Nitsch, 2011; Marur, 2019; UNSD, 2019).

Cost, freight, insurance

This encompasses the costs that occur when transporting goods from one country to another. The standard in international trade statistics is to report the export value, exclusive of these costs (that is, free-on-board) and the import value inclusive of c.i.f. (UNDS, 2011). Under the World Trade Organization (WTO) General Agreement on Tariffs and Trade of 1994, members may opt to include the value of freight, insurance and handling costs in the transaction value at the point of entry to a customs territory. For the partner-country trade gap analyses, it is important to account for these differences in valuation. In two survey rounds covering 34 African countries, all except South Africa reported the value of imported goods as inclusive of c.i.f. The South African Revenue Service reports both exports and imports as free-on-board. Other countries that report imports exclusive of c.i.f. are Australia, Brazil, Canada, the Dominican Republic, Mexico and Palau. This matters for the analysis because for these countries there is no need to control for c.i.f. when analysing the partner-country trade gap.

The standard practice in the partner-country trade gap method is to add 10 per cent to the export value of all countries in a sample to account for differences in valuation (Bhagwati, 1967; Nicolaou-Manias and Wu, 2016; UNCTAD, 2016; Ndikumana and Boyce, 2019). This approach has been widely criticized in the literature for being too simplistic (Nitsch, 2011; Marur, 2019). Nicolaou-Manias and Wu (2016) compare the results of the partner-country trade method using 10 per cent and 5 per cent to account for c.i.f. (as suggested by the South African Revenue Service) for a group of African countries; the impact on the estimated trade gap was significant. The 2018 release of IMF DOTS suggests a uniform 6 per cent markup on the export value for the calculation of trade gaps (Marini et al., 2018). In reality, c.i.f. differs significantly along the axes of distance between countries, mode of transport, value of merchandise and other commodity-specific characteristics such as weight. Furthermore, the cost is expressed as a percentage of the total value and will therefore vary over time, often countercyclical to commodity prices.

As the partner-country trade gap method has evolved from using total exports to being commodity specific, it is important to account for commodity-specific valuation differences. The OECD International Transport and Insurance Cost for Merchandise Trade database, which is classified by partner and commodity group over time, is analysed to explore the actual costs (Miao and Fortanier, 2017). For the 71,792 export observations in the OECD database, 50,556 can be matched along the exporter partner–commodity axis with the OECD c.i.f. estimates, covering around 70 per cent of export observations. The subsample covers 65 per cent of extracontinental African bilateral country–commodity matches and 80 per cent of intra-African matches of the whole sample. On further analysis, the missing matches seem random and correlate with total export observations by country. Table 5 shows the matched subsample focusing on intra- versus extracontinental African trade costs, classified by commodity group and with an emphasis on landlocked countries.

Table 5
Cost of freight and insurance, by commodity group, 2000–2018

Commodity group	Extracontinental			Intra-African			Landlocked countries		
	Number of observations	Average (percentage)	Standard deviation	Number of observations	Average (percentage)	Standard deviation	Number of observations	Average (percentage)	Standard deviation
Gold	1 846	2.1	0.019	54	2.7	0.021	330	2.1	0.019
Platinum	453	2.2	0.017	111	2.1	0.021	43	2.4	0.022
Diamonds	1 823	1.9	0.021	335	1.3	0.021	349	1.8	0.023
Copper	10 878	4.8	0.023	6 544	4.5	0.031	1 114	2.7	0.028
Iron group	13 226	7.9	0.035	10 452	7.8	0.040	2 242	3.3	0.028
Aluminium	11 508	5.6	0.030	8 242	5.9	0.034	2 515	5.2	0.039
Petroleum	8.701	5.9	0.032	6 581	7.3	0.036	1 536	3.4	0.031
Manganese	2 281	9.5	0.054	607	8.4	0.053	1 339	4.9	0.063
	50 716	6.0		32 925	6.5		8 481	4.1	

Source: UNCTAD calculations based on the OECD International Transport and Insurance Cost for Merchandise Trade database.
Note: Landlocked countries in the sample: Botswana, Burkina Faso, Burundi, Central African Republic, Eswatini, Ethiopia, Lesotho, Malawi, Mali, Niger, Rwanda, Uganda, Zambia, Zimbabwe.

A variety of factors will impact c.i.f. such as geography (distance, landlocked or island status) and infrastructure (quality of transport facilities, as well as information and communication technologies) for transport costs (Limão and Venables, 2001). From the OECD database, the following trends are observable:

(a)   For high value commodities (gold, platinum and diamonds), c.i.f. is around 2 per cent of export value (table 5);

(b)   Copper, aluminium and petroleum are close to the 6 per cent of c.i.f. recommended by IMF;

(c)   Manganese and iron are closer to the 10 per cent adjustment widely used in the literature;

(d)   For intra- and extra-African trade, c.i.f. follow a similar pattern. However, the trade costs for landlocked countries seem to be lower than for all intra-African trade. In this case, the following needs to be determined: whether the cost for the final destination is included or only until the next border or transit point.

The gradual shift from estimating the partner-country trade gap based on total trade vis-à-vis partner countries towards the more detailed commodity-based approach needs more precise estimates of c.i.f. Adding 10 per cent of export value to account for the difference in valuation might be a good proxy when using total exports but hides significant heterogeneity across commodity groups.

Trade reporting within an African customs union

This chapter has presented an in-depth partner-country commodity-based analysis of trade misinvoicing, while also taking account of statistical errors stemming from the international merchandise trade statistics. The quality of available data varies across countries. For example, 55 per cent of developed countries use customs declarations as the main source of international trade statistics, and supplement these with other administrative records associated with taxation and enterprise surveys. In contrast, 98 per cent of developing countries rely purely on customs declarations (UNSD, 2008).

Other statistical challenges in matching bilateral trade data are linked to differences in trade reporting. The results of the 2006 and 2016 national compilation and dissemination practices survey conducted each decade by UNSD is used to highlight trade reporting differences in the African context. The survey covers up-to-date information on national compilation and dissemination practices, as well as the degree of compliance with United Nations guidelines (for more information, see Schuster and Davis, 2020). The survey results for 2006 and 2016 are not robust. For example, in 2016, Madagascar and Seychelles reported not being members of a customs union. Yet both countries are members of the Common Market for Eastern and Southern Africa, which has operated as a customs union since 2009, and are also part of the Southern African Development Community, which has operated as a customs union since 2010. Furthermore, some countries such as Botswana, Cameroon and the Gambia do not report intraunion trade, whereas others do, including Ethiopia, Lesotho, Malawi, Namibia, Rwanda and Sierra Leone. South Africa indicated that it did not report intraunion trade in 2006 but did so in 2016. This creates an additional layer of potential statistical error as not all countries are covered in the survey, some answers do not identify one or the other case precisely and trade reporting changes over time. This makes it necessary to undertake a careful descriptive data analysis to identify changes in intra-Africa trade patterns that can be attributed to changes in reporting.

Trade reporting systems

The trade reporting system governs how individual transactions are recorded at the national level and is the foundation of aggregates reported in United Nations Comtrade. There are two different types of trade reporting systems, general and special. In the case of the general trade system, the economic territory and the statistical system are consistent, meaning that all merchandise entering and leaving the country will be recorded. The special trade system allows for some exceptions, such as special economic zones, bonded customs warehouses or industrial free zones. Countries that apply the special trade system account for a smaller proportion of trade than countries that use the general trade system. If countries use different trade reporting systems, it introduces another statistical reason for discrepancies in mirror trade data.

The survey does not clarify why South Africa switched from the general to the special system between 2006 and 2016. The South African Revenue Service reports that it follows a hybrid special strict trade reporting system, which includes warehoused goods for local consumption, but goods imported and exported for processing are excluded from trade statistics. Efforts are being made to move towards the general trading system to allow for a better international comparison of trade statistics. The importance of the different application of trade systems is directly linked to the relative size of special economic zones in Africa. If a country uses the special reporting system but its special economic zones are relatively small compared with total international trade, such discrepancies might be ignored. Generally, the value of the metadata survey would be significantly increased if the results could be checked for inconsistencies with the countries when queries arise. In addition, the presentation of the results does not allow for a comparative analysis without manually summarizing them and would benefit end users if they could be downloaded in a spreadsheet. The change in numbering of survey questions, especially without a correspondence table, is another non-standard anomaly, which makes a comparative analysis by end users more difficult. Other relevant questions related to the timing of regime switches, such as "When did you switch from the special to the general trade system reporting?" would make the survey results more meaningful and allow for a better comparison across time.

2.4 Concluding remarks

The magnitude of trade mispricing in Africa based on a range of estimates varies from $30 billion to $52 billion per annum. The scarcity of available geological information in Africa and the resulting information asymmetry between mining companies that have the means to acquire private information about reserves and Governments makes the extractive sector particularly prone to illicit outflows (UNECA and African Minerals Development Centre, 2017). There are only rough estimates of potential reserves available on the continent, as significant information gaps impede robust data collection on mineral and metal resources in Africa (World Bank, 2017b). As noted for gold, high-value low-weight commodities are especially prone to smuggling (UNCTAD, 2016). With rapidly rising demand, the risk of smuggling of rare earth minerals is increasing and their improved governance should be a policy priority for well-endowed countries and requires comprehensive geological surveys.

There is uncertainty with regard to the quality of African trade statistics, especially for intra-African trade. The United Nations Comtrade metadata survey, which could shed light on what is covered in international trade statistics, lacks a comprehensive and consistent database. The frequency of reporting and quality of trade data is linked to institutional capacity and so is the probability of trade-related illicit financial outflows; thus, there is a downward bias in the estimates in this chapter, since countries that have the highest probability of incurring trade misinvoicing also have the highest probability of low-quality trade reporting, of being excluded from the sample due to non-reporting or of missing too many years of data (only countries with at least 10 observations between 2000 and 2018 are included).

Only **45 out of 54** African countries report trade data in a continuous manner

Informal cross-border trade is estimated to be as large as officially recorded trade for some country borders and specific products in Africa (Morrissey et al., 2015). This renders the partner-country trade gap method less significant for the detection of systemic trade misinvoicing for intra-African trade as errors and variation in the data is more prevalent, which hinders the scope for inference about trade-related IFFs with a reasonable confidence interval. Nonetheless, the method adds value to the analysis of intra-African trade patterns because it helps identify gaps in trade recording and, together with production or resource endowments information, could be used to identify potential rules of origin violations.

The partner-country trade gap method cannot capture the origin of IFFs but reflects a channel through which funds leave a country. Even when trade misinvoicing can be clearly recognized, it does not facilitate the identification of the underlying crime (for a critique of the method, see Forstarter, 2017). This may be due to the circumvention of capital controls, the evasion of taxes, the laundering of proceeds of crime, bribery or the financing of terrorism. However, the method can identify industries with a high risk of IFFs or at least alert government officials to areas in which trade is not being properly recorded as a good first line of defence, as it is based on publicly available data.

These limitations bring to light the necessity of a triangulated approach to identify IFFs, including information on other criminal activities that generate cross-border financial flows and evasive intrafirm trading that can drain countries' financial resources without the necessity of fraudulent invoices, to generate a comprehensive picture of the scale of IFFs. Even if trade misinvoicing can be clearly identified, customs fraud will only be captured by the mirror trade gap if smuggling or misinvoicing is only one sided. However, if trade partners at both ends of the transaction collude, the trade value reported in both countries will be equal. Other non-commercial pathways of IFFs are more opaque and it is thus more difficult to quantify their magnitude.

Chapter 2 annex

Table A.1

Data availability in United Nations Comtrade, 2000–2018

	Years
Algeria	2000–2017 (no gold exports)
Angola	2007, 2009–2018
Benin	2000–2018
Botswana	2000–2018
Burkina Faso	2000–2005, 2007–2017
Burundi	2000–2017
Côte d'Ivoire	2000–2017
Comoros	2000–2013
Cabo Verde	2000–2007, 2009–2018
Cameroon	2000–2017
Central African Republic	2000–2017
Egypt	2000–2018
Eswatini	2000–2007, 2013–2017
Ethiopia	2000–2016
Gabon	2000–2009
Gambia	2000–2017
Ghana	2000–2001, 2003–2013, 2016–2018
Guinea	2000–2002, 2004–2008, 2013–2015
Kenya	2000–2010, 2013, 2017–2018
Lesotho	2000–2004, 2008–2015, 2017
Madagascar	2000–2018
Malawi	2000–2017
Mali	2000–2008, 2010–2012, 2016, 2017
Mauritania	2000–2014, 2016, 2017
Morocco	2000–2017
Mozambique	2000–2018
Namibia	2000–2018
Niger	2000–2016
Nigeria	2000–2003, 2006–2014, 2016–2018
Rwanda	2001–2016
Sao Tome and Principe	2000–2018
Senegal	2000–2018
Seychelles	2000–2008, 2010–2018
South Africa	2000–2018 (no gold or platinum: 2000, 2002)
Togo	2000–2005, 2007–2017
Tunisia	2000–2017
Uganda	2000–2018
United Republic of Tanzania	2000–2018
Zambia	2000–2015, 2017–2018
Zimbabwe	2000–2002, 2004–2018

Table A.1

Data availability in United Nations Comtrade, 2000–2018 *(continuation)*

	Years
Countries excluded due to missing years:	
Congo	2007–2014, 2017
Djibouti	2009
Eritrea	2003
Guinea-Bissau	2003–2005
Libya	2007–2010
Sierra Leone	2000, 2002, 2014–2017
Sudan*	2000–2011
Sudan	2012, 2015, 2017
No data available	
Chad	
Democratic Republic of the Congo	
Equatorial Guinea	
Liberia	
Somalia	
South Sudan	

Source: UNCTAD calculations based on United Nations Comtrade as at November 2019.
* Reference corresponds to the name in use historically during the period covered by the data.

Table A.2

Commodities of interest and their derivative products

(Harmonized System four-digit level, 1992)

	Gold	Platinum	Diamonds	Copper	Iron	Bauxite	Petroleum	Manganese
Raw material (commodity)	-	-	-	2603, 7401	2601	2606	2709	2602
				Copper ores	Iron ores	Aluminium ores	Petroleum oils, crude	Manganese ores
Refined products (first derivative)	7108	7110	7102	7402, 7403	7201–7212	7601	2710	8111
	Gold	Platinum	Diamonds	7405–7412	Iron	7603–7609	Petroleum oils, not crude	Manganese and articles thereof
				Copper		Aluminium and articles thereof		
				7404		7602		
				Non-ferrous base metal: waste and scrap		Aluminium, waste and scrap		
By-products (second derivative)					2821	2818	2711	2820
					Iron oxides	Aluminium oxide	Petroleum gases	Manganese oxide

Source: UNCTAD secretariat.

Chapter 3
Global enablers of illicit financial flows

IFFs have multiple origins and ways of crossing borders. Chapter 2 focuses on trade mispricing as one of the core mechanisms supporting IFFs. It shows the complex layers that lie behind the tracking of related practices, from data architecture, to historical legacy, to the current capacity of customs across the continent. Moving into the realm of the international legal system, this chapter highlights key foundations of the international taxation system (section 3.1), surveys selected mechanisms for tax evasion and tax avoidance (section 3.2) and sheds light on some of the system's global actors (section 3.3). The exposé does not cover ongoing reforms of international corporate taxation as these are addressed in chapter 7. Rather, taking stock of the shortcomings in the international taxation system, section 3.4 discusses the global movement for tax justice and the engagement of African stakeholders in reform processes, followed by some concluding remarks.

LOOPHOLES IN MANY TAX TREATIES

in Africa

leave countries vulnerable to tax avoidance

WITHOUT MINIMUM STANDARDS FOR INVESTMENT TREATIES

African countries risk

a race to the bottom to attract FDI

FDI

3.1 Key foundations of the international taxation system

From the Westphalian system to the international corporate taxation system

The foundations of the principles that underline the international taxation system are anchored in what has become known as the Westphalian system. Based on a scholarly body of work that dates back to sixteenth- and seventeenth-century Europe, the Westphalian system core characteristics of territoriality, sovereignty, equality and non-intervention have come to prevail in the international legal system despite debate on and criticism of their adequacy (Osiander, 2001; Picciotto, 2013). As argued in this chapter and in chapter 4, these principles have come to prevail and explain both the dominance of unilateral taxation systems and the complexity of multilateral reforms.

In 1923, at a time when African countries were still under colonial rule, four economists, professors Bruins, Einaudi, Seligman and Sir Josiah Stamp worked under the auspices of the League of Nations to lay the ground for the first model tax conventions. In what has become known as the "report by the four economists", their proposal was that income from business activities should be taxed by the country of source while in return the country of residence should have the primary right to tax income from investments such as dividends, royalties or interests.

The Financial and Fiscal Commission of the United Nations carried forward the work until 1954, when the Commission was dissolved. Two years later, the predecessor of OECD, the Organization for European Economic Cooperation (OEEC), established a Fiscal Committee with the aim of inheriting the role of the dissolved United Nations Commission.[27] Archives from OECD also show that the creation of the Fiscal Committee initially encountered opposition from some members due to their wish to focus on the use of a bilateral treaty strategy and avoid an international treaty binding OEEC member States. By 1959, the OEEC Council recommended for adoption the proposals made by member States in their bilateral conventions, namely on: (a) avoidance of double taxation on income, capital and estates of deceased persons; and (b) avoidance of double taxation on indirect taxes such as turnover taxes. The OECD Model Tax Convention, first published in 1963 as the *Draft Double Taxation Convention on Income and Capital*, subsequently became the industry standard (Picciotto, 2013). OECD estimates that by 2017, it had been used as the basis of more than 3,000 tax treaties around the world (OECD, 2017)[28].

[27] See https://archives.eui.eu/en/fonds/173529?item=OEEC.FC.
[28] See https://www.oecd.org/tax/treaties/tax-treaties-2017-update-to-oecd-model-tax-convention-released.htm.

Permanent establishment and the arm's length principle
The OECD Model Tax Convention on Income and on Capital (OECD Model Tax Convention) includes the same compromise between country of source and country of residence as the United Nations Model Double Taxation Convention between Developed and Developing Countries (United Nations Model Tax Convention). In effect, it means that the country of source has the right to tax active income while the country of residence has the right to tax passive investment.[29] In other words, both the United Nations and OECD tax conventions imply that the country of source is not entitled to tax income from foreign corporations even when such income originates from business activities in its territory (OECD, 2017).[30] Both models grant countries flexibility in defining corporations' country of residence using formal registration, place of management or any similar criterion. It is this flexibility that allows multinational corporations to move their residence to countries with preferential tax regimes even when they do not have any significant business activities in those countries. It is also this flexibility that sets the basis for BEPS.

Both the United Nations and OECD conventions stipulate that corporations not only pay taxes to the country in which they have legal residence but also to the countries in which they have a permanent establishment, a key legal concept in the determination of the source of income, whose definition was originally laid out in article 5 of the OECD Model Tax Convention. The list of the types of establishment that qualify for permanent establishment is broad and is based on an actual physical presence in the territory. Exceptions include facilities that only serve the purpose of storage, display or delivery. Permanent establishment is of critical relevance in the services economy as the taxation of services provided by foreign companies is growing in importance as a tax treaty issue.

The United Nations Model Tax Convention, in its most recent version, provides two options that allow developing countries to tax service providers. The first is the service permanent establishment provision, which expands the definition of permanent establishment to include foreign companies if they have a physical presence providing services in the country for more than a certain length of time. The second is a new article permitting developing countries to impose withholding taxes on management, consultancy and technical service fees, regardless of whether the provider of those services is physically

---

[29] The exact definitions of active income, passive income and portfolio income depend on a country's regulations. For taxation purposes, income received from business activities or wages, commissions and payment for services rendered are generally considered as active. Passive income includes regular earnings from a source other than an employer or contractor, that is, rental real estate and stock dividends and other activities as defined in a country's regulations and the tax treaties it is party to

[30] See https://martinhearson.net/2012/10/17/would-a-new-article-in-the-un-model-tax-treaty-be-a-fundmaental-change-to-international-tax/.

present at all in the country. Both provisions are popular in Africa. However, in a study covering 149 tax treaties in force in sub-Saharan countries, only 33 per cent were found to include the service permanent establishment provision and 36 per cent, the service withholding tax (Hearson, forthcoming). The prevalence of tax treaties that omit both provisions is considered by taxation specialists to be a major constraint on the ability to increase integration by Africa into the global service economy (Hearson, forthcoming).

Both the OECD Committee on Taxation and Fiscal Policy and the United Nations Committee of Experts on International Cooperation in Tax Matters have endorsed the arm's length principle, another core pillar of international taxation. It stipulates that transactions between entities of the same MNE are priced as if they happened between independent enterprises. In practice, the application of the principle should require the ability to identify a comparable product and price. While for standardized products this is relatively easy, it is difficult if not impossible for highly complex products or intangibles such as intellectual property or trademarks. As markets are thinner in developing countries, there is consensus that even with the best intentions, the arm's length principle is difficult to implement (Waris, 2017).

3.2 Selected mechanisms for tax evasion, tax avoidance and money-laundering

This section offers a brief overview of key features of the operationalization of tax avoidance and evasion in commercial activities. The main mechanisms for tax avoidance and evasion include trade mispricing, abusive transfer pricing, profit shifting and tax arbitraging. The discussion focuses on the latter three and also the use of tax havens and secrecy jurisdictions (for trade mispricing, see chapter 2).

Abusive transfer pricing and profit shifting
In a globalized economy, MNEs operate their cross-border investments through the most tax efficient corporate structures (UNCTAD, 2015a), spreading their functions, assets and risks across multiple related entities located in different jurisdictions. In the case of many African countries, this practice has resulted in value-adding activities being transferred away from where the initial economic activity took place (World Bank, 2017a). These cross-border movements of goods and services require transfer pricing, a standard practice within MNEs that was not originally meant to be illegal. As such, transfer pricing operations have both an accounting dimension and an economic

efficiency objective. Notwithstanding these motivations, part of the theoretical economic literature has shown that a multinational company can manipulate transfer prices between subsidiaries located in different countries with a view to reducing their overall tax burden (Horst, 1971; Kant, 1990). Similarly, some studies on MNEs have established that the risk that multinational companies manipulate transfer pricing between their subsidiaries to make more profits appear in low-tax countries is mitigated when the foreign subsidiary is located in a competitive market (Schjelderup and Sorgard, 1997). This argument would imply that African countries where markets are less competitive would be more vulnerable to transfer pricing.

From an operational perspective, abusive transfer pricing, a form of trade mispricing, is enabled through the application of the arm's length principle. The practice is based on the excessive manipulation by MNEs of prices of cross-border transactions between related parties. The end result of abusive transfer pricing is to artificially shift profits from high-tax jurisdictions to low- or no-tax jurisdictions through the following three key channels:[31]

(a) Trade mispricing through the manipulation of intragroup import and export prices whereby affiliates in high-tax countries import goods and services at high prices from firms in low-tax countries;

(b) Debt shifting through intragroup financing, whereby an affiliate in a high-tax jurisdiction borrows from an affiliate in a low-tax jurisdiction and pays an artificially high interest rate to reduce its profits and tax burden;

(c) Location of intangibles and intellectual property (for example, brands, research and development and algorithms) whereby an entity holds its intangible assets and intellectual property in a tax haven and charges its affiliates service fees for using these assets.

The BEPS reform package intends to curtail abusive transfer pricing (OECD, 2018b; chapter 7). The ambition is that the new set of measures will lead to greater alignment between profit outcomes and economic substance, by considering the true economic contribution by entities in a given tax jurisdiction.

Tax arbitraging and tax treaty shopping

There are more than 500 bilateral tax treaties in force in Africa (Hearson, forthcoming). Tax treaties play an important role in where and how profits, income and wealth are

---

[31] For real case examples of profit shifting, see Hearson (forthcoming).

taxed. These treaties were originally set up to harmonize tax treatment of cross-border investment and prevent investors incurring double taxation, that is, income is taxed in the source country where the activity takes place and also in the country where the investor or shareholder is located. Tax treaties have three main characteristics. First, they limit the rate at which the source State can impose withholding taxes. Second, they limit what can be subject to tax, for example through the definition of "permanent establishment", which sets a minimum threshold of activity that must take place in a country before its Government can levy tax on the profits generated there by the taxpayer concerned. Third, tax treaties exempt some types of income earned in the source country from taxation in that country altogether, for example taxes on capital gains in particular circumstances.

Interestingly, caution in the inclusion of tax avoidance in definitions of IFFs, as discussed in the introductory chapter, is in contrast to its mention in the OECD Model Tax Convention, whose preamble states the Convention's intention to avoid double taxation "without creating opportunities for non-taxation or reduced taxation through tax evasion or avoidance (including through treaty-shopping arrangements aimed at obtaining reliefs provided in this Convention for the indirect benefit of residents of third States)" (OECD, 2017). The evidence of substantial losses due to tax evasion and tax avoidance in both developed and developing countries shows that these objectives have not been fully met. Rather, tax treaties provide unintended opportunities for tax avoidance through differences in clauses and concessions contained therein. Consequently, businesses can take advantage of more favourable tax treaties available in some jurisdictions by structuring their activities through these jurisdictions, reduce their tax liabilities and thus make use of tax arbitrage (OECD, 2017).[32] The practice of structuring a multinational business in such a way as to take advantage of differences in tax treaties is called tax treaty shopping.

Some of the root causes of the validation of international tax avoidance and tax evasion lie in established theoretical arguments in some of the economic literature. In the tradition of rational choice explanations, an individual will choose to take the risk of tax evasion if deducting the costs of the consequent punishment of being caught from the individual's (income-defined) expected utility of the benefits of not paying taxes yields positive gains (Allingham and Sandmo, 1972; Yitzhaki, 1974). Furthermore, proponents of a narrow

---

[32] A famous example of exploiting legal loopholes and tax treaties is the exploitation of differences between definitions of tax residency in the law in Ireland and the United States. According to the law in Ireland, a company's residence is determined on the basis of the location from which the company is run, whereas United States law focuses on where the company is registered. If a company puts its intellectual property into a company registered in Ireland but controlled from a tax haven such as Bermuda with which Ireland has a tax treaty, in Ireland, the company is considered to be a tax resident in Bermuda, while in the United States, it is considered to be a tax resident of Ireland. As a result, royalty payments between them are untaxed or only minimally taxed.

utilitarian perspective argue that private sector spending is more efficient, and it should therefore keep the power to make decisions on how the money should be spent (Benk et al., 2015; Preobragenskaya and McGee, 2016). More generally, empirical studies show that financial rewards alone insufficiently explain tax evasion (for an overview of evidence from experiments, see Torgler, 2002, 2003; Feld and Frey 2006). Rather, "tax morale", a moral obligation to pay taxes and "a belief in contributing to society by paying taxes" (Torgler and Schneider, 2009:230) are the main motivations for individuals and firms to comply (Luttmer and Singhal, 2014).

Conscious of international competition in international corporate taxation, many countries commit to double taxation treaties with a view to attracting higher levels of FDI (Barthel et al., 2009). Such decisions are based on assumptions of how taxation affects the operational mode of MNEs. On one hand, firms' locational decisions on large fixed-cost investment projects in a given jurisdiction depend on the effective average tax rate on the returns from the investment, taking into account depreciation allowances and other provisions that affect the tax base (Devereux and Griffith, 1998, 2003). On the other hand, the amount of real investment to undertake in a given location depends on the effective marginal tax rate, that is, the tax rate on an extra dollar of income generated by investment. Inefficiency arises from a divergence between the social and private returns. As the decision maker, the firm maximizes its private rather than social returns. With regard to the objective of attracting higher levels of investment, econometric studies on the relationship between FDI and double taxation treaties show variance in results and underline the estimation and data challenges involved in such exercises (Neumayer, 2006; Barthel et al., 2010). These inconclusive empirical findings on the importance of tax treaties for FDI location decisions are also due to the complexity of the drivers of FDI decision-making in MNEs (Carr et al., 2001; Bergstrand and Egger, 2007). Highlighting the secondary role of taxation among these drivers in sub-Saharan Africa, recent findings suggest that treaties are not associated with increases in FDI in low-income economies (Beer and Loeprick, 2018).

In addition to their limited impact on FDI attraction, tax treaties have other flaws. First, many of the tax treaties signed by African countries are high risk as they omit many of the clauses, available through international and regional model tax conventions, that might limit the risk of tax avoidance (Wijnen and de Goede, 2013; Hearson, 2016). For example, both the United Nations and the OECD Model Tax Conventions include a provision that protects developing countries against tax avoidance through indirect transfers of real property. However, a large number of tax treaties signed by developing countries still omit this provision, leaving them vulnerable to the avoidance of capital gains tax arising from the profit realized on the sale of non-inventory assets such as the sale of stocks, bonds, real estate and precious metals (see Hearson, forthcoming).

Second, many treaties, especially older ones, lack anti-abuse clauses and provisions for mutual assistance between tax authorities (Hearson, forthcoming). The revenue costs to African countries from tax treaty shopping are estimated to have amounted to $3.4 billion in 2015 (Beer and Loeprick, 2018). Researchers from IMF and the World Bank further estimate the cost of treaty shopping in Africa to be about 20 to 26 per cent of corporate income tax revenue from each treaty with an investment hub (Beer and Loeprick, 2018). Their findings show that treaty shopping reduced revenue by 5 per cent in all African countries (equivalent to $3.4 billion across the continent in 2015) and 14 per cent in those countries that have at least one treaty with an investment hub. This is the only estimate of the comprehensive costs of tax treaties in African countries to date. The revenue foregone has been specifically attributed to reductions in dividend and interest withholding tax. Janský and Palanský (2018), for example, provide illustrative country-level estimates of profit shifting and compare estimated corporate tax revenue losses, relative to their GDP and tax revenues, including for 14 African countries (Benin, Botswana, Burkina Faso, Cabo Verde, Côte d'Ivoire, Guinea-Bissau, Morocco, Mozambique, the Niger, Nigeria, South Africa, Togo, Uganda and Zambia).

Secrecy-based tax havens and non-cooperative jurisdictions

Tax havens provide critical services that enable abusive tax avoidance and tax evasion. They offer low or zero taxation, moderate or light financial regulation, banking secrecy and anonymity. Tax havens are particularly attractive to high-net-worth individuals. Estimates show that the resulting loss amounts to 2.5 per cent of total tax revenue in Africa (Zucman, 2014). Definitions and criteria applied in identifying tax havens and similar concepts vary across institutions. For OECD, for example, tax havens are countries or jurisdictions with financial centres that contain financial institutions that deal primarily with non-residents and/or in foreign currency on a scale out of proportion to the size of the host economy; and in which non-resident-owned or -controlled institutions play a significant role.[33] For IMF (2000), offshore financial centres (OFCs) have relatively large numbers of financial institutions engaged primarily in business with non-residents).[34] Garcia-Bernardo et al. (2017) identify two types of OFCs, sink OFCs and conduit OFCs. A sink OFC is a jurisdiction in which a disproportional amount of value disappears from the economic system. In this classification, the top five sink OFCs are the British Virgin Islands, China, Jersey, Bermuda and Cayman Islands. A conduit OFC is a jurisdiction through which a disproportional

---

[33] See https://stats.oecd.org/glossary/detail.asp?ID=5988.
[34] See https://www.imf.org/external/np/mae/oshore/2000/eng/back.htm.

amount of value moves towards sink OFCs, and the top five are the Netherlands, the United Kingdom, Switzerland, Singapore and Ireland. OECD and European Union lists of tax havens and non-cooperative tax jurisdictions are discussed in box 3.

Although the terms tax haven and OFC are often used interchangeably, UNCTAD (2015a) specifies that the former refers to a political jurisdiction. In addition, tax havens not only offer the possibility of escaping from taxes but also from many other rules and regulations (UNCTAD, 2015a). In such cases, prosecution of economic and financial crimes and judicial cooperation with other countries are often limited, hence the associated term of "secrecy jurisdictions". In contrast, OFCs comprise accountants, lawyers and bankers, and their associated trust companies and financial intermediaries, who sell services to the residents of other territories or jurisdictions wishing to exploit the mechanisms created by legislation in the tax havens and secrecy jurisdictions.[35]

The prevalence of offshore investment hubs underlines the link between investment and taxation. These links are further discussed in chapter 4. An offshore investment hub is defined according to four criteria initially developed by OECD: (a) no or low taxes; (b) lack of effective exchange of information; (c) lack of transparency; and (d) no requirement of substantial activity. UNCTAD (2015a) found 42 hubs that complied with these criteria and classified them into two groups, as follows:

- Jurisdictions identified as tax havens: These include small jurisdictions whose economy is entirely, or almost entirely, dedicated to the provision of offshore financial services.

- Jurisdictions (not identified as tax havens) offering special purpose entities or other entities that facilitate transit investment: These are larger jurisdictions with substantial real economic activity that act as major global investment hubs for MNEs due to their favourable tax and investment conditions.

It is estimated that between 30 and 50 per cent of global FDI is channelled through networks of offshore shell companies (UNCTAD, 2015a; Haberly and Wójcik, 2015; Bolwijn et al., 2018). Henry (2012) estimates that as at 2010, at least $21 trillion to $32 trillion had been invested through offshore secrecy jurisdictions. Secrecy is typically provided in relation to ownership registration and transparency, which obscures the

---

[35] The Corporate Tax Haven Index of the Tax Justice Network ranks jurisdictions according to how aggressively and extensively they contribute to helping MNEs avoid paying tax and erode the tax revenues of other countries (see https://www.taxjustice.net/). The ranking also indicates how much each place contributes to a global "race to the bottom" in corporate taxes. In 2019, the ranking was led by British Virgin Islands, Bermuda and Cayman Islands, followed by the Netherlands, Switzerland, Luxembourg, Jersey, Singapore, Bahamas and Hong Kong (China).

ultimate account holders and obstructs investigations on tax matters. Secrecy is of concern in much broader terms as it facilitates not only tax evasion, but also the laundering of proceeds of crime and corruption.[36]

An estimated
30-50%
of global FDI is channelled
through offshore shell companies

Box 3
The measurement of illicit financial flows for Sustainable Development Goal indicator 16.4.1

Several institutions have established lists of tax havens. The OECD Committee on Fiscal Affairs' 2002 list of uncooperative tax havens based on tax transparency and exchange of information included seven jurisdictions (Andorra, Liberia, Liechtenstein, the Marshall Islands, Monaco, Nauru and Vanuatu), but all subsequently made commitments and were removed from the list.[a]

The European Union list of non-cooperative jurisdictions for tax purposes is updated periodically. Listed countries are identified based on recognized international tax standards, namely, transparency, fair taxation and implementation of the OECD BEPS minimum standards. As of October 2019, the list comprised the following jurisdictions: American Samoa, Belize, Fiji, Guam, Marshall Islands, Oman, Samoa, Trinidad and Tobago, United States Virgin Islands, Vanuatu.[b]

Oxfam (2019) notes that the European Union list does not include Bermuda, British Virgin Islands, Cayman Islands, Hong Kong (China), Panama, nor countries that are "too big to be listed", such as Switzerland and the United States. Moreover, European Union member States are exempted from the list, including Ireland, Luxembourg and the Netherlands.

Source: UNCTAD secretariat.
[a] See https://www.oecd.org/countries/monaco/list-of-unco-operative-tax-havens.htm.
[b] See https://www.consilium.europa.eu/en/policies/eu-list-of-non-cooperative-jurisdictions/.

[36] The Financial Secrecy Index of the Tax Justice Network measures not only the level of secrecy of jurisdictions, but also their role globally in enabling practices that enable money-laundering, tax evasion and the concentration of untaxed wealth. The ranking shows that the world's most important providers of financial secrecy include some of the wealthiest economies. The top 10 out of the 112 jurisdictions ranked in 2019 were as follows: Cayman Islands, United States, Switzerland, Hong Kong (China), Singapore, Luxembourg, Japan, Netherlands, British Virgin Islands, United Arab Emirates. The top ranking African countries in 2020 were Kenya (ranked 24), Nigeria (34), Angola (35), Egypt (46), Mauritius (51), Cameroon (53) and South Africa (58).

Corruption and money-laundering

It is generally established that IFFs in Africa and corruption are closely interrelated (Reed and Fontana, 2011; Ayogu and Gbadebo-Smith, 2014). Corruption is variously defined as concerning "the use or misuse of public office for private gain", "State capture", "patronage and nepotism" and "administrative corruption" (Campos and Pradhan, 2007). More specifically, articles 15 through 25 of the United Nations Convention against Corruption (2003) list a series of acts associated with corruption as follows: the active or passive bribery of domestic or foreign public officials, including staff of international organizations; the embezzlement and misappropriation or other diversion of property by a public official; the obstruction of justice; the active and passive trading in influence; and the abuse of functions and illicit enrichment. Reed and Fontana (2011) identify three main mechanisms through which corruption contributes to IFFs. First, corruption is a source of proceeds, often in the form of bribes. Second, it is a means to facilitate the creation of illicit funds, such as corrupt tax administrators who ignore tax evasion or interpret tax regulation to reduce the tax burden of a taxpayer in return for a bribe. Third, corruption can be an enabler of IFFs by compromising the institutions tasked with anti-money-laundering obligations. For example, entities with anti-money-laundering obligations may collude with clients to not fulfil their obligations or financial intelligence units may be prevented from performing their function by not being provided with sufficient independence, legal powers and resources.

With regard to the first mechanism, there is ample evidence of the two-way relationship between corruption proceeds and origins of IFFs. Studies on the illicit trade of wildlife, for example, have underlined the correlation between ivory trade and State corruption (Lemieux and Clarke, 2009; Douglas and Alie, 2014). Corruption within institutions mandated to enforce wildlife legislation makes it difficult to curb illegal wildlife trade (Abotsi et al., 2016). In addition, there is evidence that this illegal trade, estimated to be a multibillion-dollar business, also provides funding to finance the bribing of public officials (Anderson and Jooste, 2014). With regard to transfer mechanisms, the symbiotic relationship between corruption and money-laundering, in particular, has been subject to scrutiny (Chaikin and Sharman, 2009). On one hand, corruption facilitates money-laundering and, on the other hand, money-laundering makes grand corruption possible and profitable (Reed and Fontana, 2011; Chaikin and Sharman, 2009; UNODC and World Bank, 2007).

In the context of money-laundering, corruption proceeds often result from the payment of commissions, payments from a protective "umbrella" or stakes of corrupt politicians in established businesses. In the legal jargon, corrupt acts are labelled as "predicate offence", "underlying offence", "criminal conduct", "unlawful activity" or "infraction sous-jacente", depending on the country's legal tradition (World Bank, 2004). In legal terms, "property" is defined broadly to include assets of every kind, including corporeal or incorporeal, moveable or immoveable, tangible or intangible and legal documents or instruments, showing evidence not only of title but also interest in related assets (World Bank, 2004). Money-laundering operations generally require criminals to use intermediaries, either individuals or legal persons, through schemes that add opacity and establish distance between them and the identity of the account owners. As part of these schemes, corporate vehicles and trusts are among the most often used mechanisms in cases of money-laundering (World Bank, 2004).

With regard to the magnitude of the revenue and other losses due to corruption in Africa, AfDB (2015) estimates that around $148 million per annum is lost to corruption. In addition, Bates (2006) and Ayogu and Gbadebo-Smith (2014) argue that by destroying "institutions as investment" the net losses from corruption are likely to be far greater than the first-level account of bribery.

3.3 Global actors of the network of tax evasion, tax avoidance and money-laundering

Perpetrators of tax-related IFFs are to be found among MNEs and high-net-worth individuals. For these actors, IFFs are facilitated by a large network of entities comprising non-financial institutions such as tax advisors, lawyers, accountants, notaries, trust and company service providers, real estate agents and providers of gambling services, as well as banks, wealth management firms and other financial institutions.

Tax advisory firms and other non-financial institutions
Facilitators of tax-related IFFs operate mostly from tax advisory firms. *The Global Tax Advisory Market in 2019* report estimates that the market was worth $34.4 billion in 2018. The global tax market grew by 6.5 per cent between 2018 and 2019, a higher rate than the 5.3 per cent growth rate registered between 2017 and 2018 (Source Global Research, 2019). The market is expected to continue on this upward trend in 2020 and beyond, with the world's largest consulting firms, the so-called big four, controlling 87 per cent of market share. The report further reveals that the financial services sector is the largest sector for global tax work, with almost a third of the world's tax advisory market in 2017, valued at $6.64 billion. Amid the different areas of work, transfer pricing is a major source of business, with a market value of $5.18 billion in 2018. *The Global Tax Market in 2019* report singles out three major drivers of tax advisory work: a complex global

tax landscape; a growing convergence between tax and risk management, including reputational risk; and foresight on automation. The appetite for risk is a critical element of tax optimization schemes and partly explains why large tax advisory firms are often cited in ongoing investigations of tax evasion and aggressive tax optimization schemes.[37]

The evidence of poor tax compliance of European offshore account holders shows the extent of the central role played by financial institutions in making tax evasion possible. Although not all offshore private wealth evades taxes, the rate of non-compliance to tax obligations is generally high, with estimates ranging between 75 and 90 per cent across countries for which compliance data is available (Alstadsæter et al., 2018). Furthermore, Zucman (2017) argues that the apparent increase in compliance rates among European account holders is a mechanical consequence of the fact that the volume of assets held in Switzerland by European individuals in their own name has gone down, whereas the volume of funds channelled through screening entities has not. As part of compliance requirements in the financial sector, the role of these screening entities is to verify each onboarding customer against a number of sanction lists and criminal databases that are issued by global law enforcement agencies.

Money-laundering relies on the services of non-financial businesses and professions that include lawyers, accountants, notaries, trust and company service providers, real estate agents, providers of gambling services and online gaming services and dealers in precious stones and metals, among others. Among the traditional actors, money launderers count on the confidential and privileged nature of the lawyer–client relationship, although anti-money-laundering compliance requirements have now been extended to them. Among other key actors, the increasing role of the luxury industry and of real estate as vehicles for money-laundering has been a cause for concern (European Parliament, 2017).

Banks and other financial institutions

Funds from IFFs are ultimately deposited in financial institutions such as banks; securities, mortgage and insurance brokers; and currency exchange agencies (World Bank, 2004). Financial institutions can be unknowingly vulnerable to money-laundering given the variety of services they provide and the global dimension of their operations. However, they can also be complicit in money-laundering schemes. Famous cases of indictment of banks for anti-money-laundering lapses or sanctions violations by the United States Department of Justice provide evidence of the central role that financial institutions play in the facilitation of IFFs. For example, in 2012, after many years of legal

[37] See, for example, https://www.icij.org/investigations/luanda-leaks/read-the-luanda-leaks-documents/.

proceedings, HSBC Holdings agreed to forfeit $1.256 billion for anti-money-laundering violations and illegally conducting transactions on behalf of customers in a group of countries subject to sanctions enforced by the United States Office of Foreign Assets Control at the time of the transactions.[38] Financial institutions in the informal sector also house facilitators of IFFs. Taxing those in the informal sector is difficult owing to the absence of data, mobility of individuals and inability of individuals to pay tax (Ezenagu, 2019). A telling example of unrecorded inflows and outflows is the transfer of remittances through informal channels, such as the hawala system (UNODC, 2018).

Under Sustainable Development Goal 16, the objective of curbing IFFs is noted alongside that of ensuring responsive, inclusive, participatory and representative decision-making at all levels. The lack of gender diversity in the decision-making bodies of banks and other institutions was put in the spotlight in the aftermath of the 2008 global financial crisis. Poor gender diversity in senior leadership positions in financial institutions and the role of groupthink and reckless decision-making in provoking the crisis was underlined.[39] In a series of papers that followed the crisis, IMF research showed that the presence of women and a higher share of women on the boards of banks was associated with greater bank stability and a lower share of non-performing loans (Sahay et al., 2017). However, there has been little change in gender diversity performance among the leadership of financial institutions and there is limited evidence from studies based on econometric methods in ascertaining innate behavioural differences between men and women. Instead, research results pinpoint the role of acquired behaviours in determining group attitudes and decision-making. Studies on gender parity show poor performance in the global financial services sector. Across all positions, women represent 32 per cent of new recruits in financial services globally and 17 per cent in asset management (Boston Consulting Group, the Sutton Trust, 2014).

3.4 The movement for tax justice

Key actors in the global fight for tax justice
The present report argues that the fundamental flaws of the international corporate taxation system are sustained by the dominant principles of the Westphalian system (Palan, 2002). However, until the early 2000s, the international corporate taxation system proved to be resilient to calls for change due to the growing complexity of

---

[38] See https://www.justice.gov/opa/pr/hsbc-holdings-plc-and-hsbc-bank-usa-na-admit-anti-money-laundering-and-sanctions-violations.

[39] See https://www.theguardian.com/business/2018/sep/05/if-it-was-lehman-sisters-it-would-be-a-different-world-christine-lagarde.

international trade, the growth in international flows of capital, the growth of the service industry and the disruptive effect of the digital economy. The seeds of change were planted in the aftermath of the 2008 global financial crisis. As most countries faced soaring government debt, media reports about MNE profit-shifting activities were met with increased attention by some Group of 20 countries.

At the multilateral level, a few initiatives were established as early as the 1980s to improve tax-related standards. The Multilateral Convention on Mutual Administrative Assistance in Tax Matters was developed by OECD and the Council of Europe in 1988, updated in 2010 and signed by 130 jurisdictions (OECD, 2019b). In the same vein, the Global Forum on Transparency and Exchange of Information for Tax Purposes was set to be the multilateral framework through which the international standards on tax transparency and exchange of information would be monitored and reviewed. Finally, the Financial Action Task Force was established as an intergovernmental body that develops and promotes policies to protect the global financial system against money-laundering, terrorist financing and the financing of the proliferation of weapons of mass destruction. As such, the Financial Action Task Force recommendations are recognized as the global anti-money-laundering and counter-terrorist financing standard.

There has also been increasing awareness among African countries on having given away more taxing rights than other regions during their bilateral treaty negotiations (Daurer, 2014; Hearson, 2016). A press release by a group of finance ministers from developing countries, for example, stated: "The global tax system is stacked in favour of paying taxes in the headquarters countries of transnational companies, rather than in the countries where raw materials are produced. International tax and investment treaties need to be revised to give preference to paying tax in 'source' countries" (Francophone [Low-Income Countries] Finance Ministers Network, 2014). Strikingly, tax justice has become a rallying point for a coalition of civil society organizations, supported by academic research and revelations by investigative journalists and whistle-blowers.

Civil society organizations have uncovered many cases of IFFs, raised public awareness and put pressure on revising harmful practices. They play a vital role in closing the gap between IFFs being considered as a technical issue and as a political and social concern. Investigative journalists have also played a key role in uncovering the mechanics, spread and magnitude of IFFs. Following the release of a group of papers in 2017, for example, and the public attention that followed, in a number of countries, legislative bodies conducted enquiries into transfer pricing and tax avoidance (see, for example, France, Assemblée Nationale, 2019; chapter 7).

The movement for tax justice has been active on many fronts in Africa. African countries created the African Tax Administration Forum (ATAF) in 2009, initially to stimulate the exchange of information and collaboration between national tax authorities. In addition to information exchange, ATAF aims to improve the capacity of African tax administrations, improve revenue collection, provide a voice for African countries on regional and global platforms to influence the international tax debate, and develop and support partnerships between African countries and development partners.

With regard to tax treaties, many developing countries have begun to reconsider their content. Malawi, Rwanda, Senegal, South Africa and Zambia are among those countries that have cancelled or renegotiated tax treaties in recent years, while others, such as Uganda, have undertaken reviews (Hearson, 2015). Perhaps in response to the international debate and the threat of further cancellations, Ireland and the Netherlands, for example, have reviewed the impact of their treaty networks on developing countries and offered partial renegotiations (Netherlands, Ministry of Finance, 2013; Ireland, Ministry of Finance, 2015). The net effects of these negotiations have yet to be fully assessed. In addition, civil society groups have begun to mount campaigns against particular tax treaties, for example, a lawsuit challenging a treaty between Kenya and Mauritius.[40]

With regard to abusive transfer pricing and tax avoidance, the consideration of affiliates of MNEs as separate independent entities has been increasingly contested. The intensification of global value chains and the resulting increase in trade in intermediates have led affiliates to become ever more integrated. However, as noted by the Independent Commission for Reform of International Corporate Taxation (2018), "revisions to transfer pricing rules continue to cling to the underlying fiction that an MNE consists of separate independent entities transacting with each other at arm's length." Yet the corresponding accounting treatment of MNEs as consisting of separate entities is also reflected in tax treaties negotiated with African countries and in the national tax law of African countries.

---

[40] The Tax Justice Network Africa challenged the Kenya–Mauritius tax treaty signed in 2012. It highlighted that the treaty never came into force because the Government of Kenya did not follow the ratification procedures required by law. In addition to the procedural issue, Tax Justice Network Africa claimed that the tax treaty led to revenue loss and encouraged tax avoidance. In 2019, the High Court in Kenya agreed with the position of Tax Justice Network Africa on the procedural issue but held that it had not successfully proven the claim of revenue loss and tax avoidance and did not bring expert witnesses to substantiate the claim. Thus, the court could not rule on that claim, but ruled that the tax treaty was invalid. At the time of writing, the case is on appeal. At the same time, a new treaty to avoid double taxation was signed between the two countries in 2019 (Lewis et al., 2013; ActionAid, 2016; www.theeastafrican.co.ke/business/Court-nullifies-Kenya-tax-deal-with-Mauritius/2560-5052628-948m33/index.html).

Towards a reshuffling of taxing rights? The state of African engagement in international taxation reform

The limited institutional capacity in most African countries on international taxation issues is an illustration of the inadequacy of the international taxation system of the past 100 years. It is widely agreed, for example, that the separate entity approach and the tools to implement it are likely too complex and expensive for many African countries to manage (Waris, 2017). Similarly, dynamics of engagement in international taxation reform are shaped by substantial differences in institutional capacity and emerging imbalances in the likely impact of new regulations. Reed and Fontana (2011), for example, observe that regimes on anti-money-laundering imposed on developing countries have been much stricter than those forced on secrecy jurisdictions in advanced countries.

In 2012, further to decisions made in the aftermath of the financial crisis, in the context of fostering more transparency on international taxation and better alignment of taxation with economic activity, the Group of 20 called on OECD to reform the international corporate tax system. In 2013, OECD published a report titled "Addressing base erosion and profit shifting". The report documents the impact of profit shifting by multinational corporations. Furthermore, acknowledging the changing landscape of globalization, it states that the current conventions may not have kept pace with changes in global business practices. The report further states that some multinational corporations have engaged in aggressive tax optimization practices which raise "serious compliance and fairness issues" (OECD, 2013).

As part of the BEPS Framework, from 2012 to 2015, OECD and the Group of 20 undertook a review of the OECD international corporate tax instruments. Efforts were directed at closing the gap in international rules, in particular those that "allow corporate profits to disappear or be artificially shifted to low/no tax environments, where little or no economic activity takes place" (OECD, 2016). The initiative also meant to reform the permanent establishment definition and curb the tendency of multinational corporations to avoid permanent establishment status in countries in which they have significant business activities.

A major outcome of the review was the creation of a multilateral instrument to introduce changes to existing tax treaties. The instrument includes options for anti-abuse rules and rules to prevent avoidance in specific areas, including permanent establishment and capital gains. Other important outcomes were the introduction of a framework for country-by-country reporting of financial data by MNEs and, in 2016, the creation of an innovative "inclusive monitoring framework" which now counts 136 countries, including 25 from Africa.[41] In the years that have followed, OECD has embarked on an ambitious project to reform the international corporation system. However, as shown in the discussion of the state of progress in the reforms of the international taxation regime in chapter 7, this is proving challenging. In practice, the challenge lies in the definition of new rules that would satisfy all parties, developed and developing countries and corporations active across different global industries, combined with the embeddedness of digitalization across value chains.

There have also been more calls for collaboration on international taxation in the context of the Sustainable Development Goals. In this context, in 2016, the United Nations, the World Bank, IMF and OECD launched the Platform for Collaboration on Tax. The Platform aims to better frame technical advice to developing countries as they seek both more capacity support and greater influence in designing international rules in light of the growing importance of taxation in the debate on how to achieve the Goals. While the initiative illustrates broad interest in the topic, there has only been one global conference of the Platform to date.[42]

Notwithstanding capacity constraints, a number of African countries are present in international tax bodies (table 6). African countries that have not joined the BEPS Framework have not done so for a number of reasons. First, many cannot comply with the four "minimum standards" set by the Group of 20 and OECD, namely, country-by-country reporting of corporate financial information; preventing tax treaty abuse; curbing harmful tax competition; and resolving disputes between States that create double taxation. Second, countries are sceptical about their ability to participate meaningfully in the Framework's intense Paris-based work programme. Third, the availability of adequate human resources is limited, which is a major hindrance to fully engaging with, presenting and defending an African position (ATAF, 2019). The outcome statement of the ATAF meeting highlights the disconnect between the policy and administrative levels of a country, emphasizing challenges of information-sharing between the two. On one hand, commitments at the policy level to join the BEPS Framework have been made without consideration of the compliance burden entailed. On the other hand, revenue officials participating in negotiations often struggle to g.ain the political support to follow through on their negotiating positions.

---

[41] See https://www.oecd.org/tax/beps/g20-finance-ministers-endorse-reforms-to-the-international-tax-system-for-curbing-avoidance-by-multinational-enterprises.htm.
[42] See https://www.oecd.org/ctp/platform-for-collaboration-on-tax.htm.

Table 6
African representation in international tax bodies, as at September 2019

Organization or agreement	Number of African members	Countries (steering groups only)
Global Forum on Transparency and Exchange of Information for Tax Purposes	31	
Steering group	2	*Ghana, Kenya*
Multilateral Convention on Mutual Administrative Assistance in Tax Matters	10	
Multilateral Competent Authority Agreement on the Exchange of Country-by-Country Reports	7	
Common Reporting Standard [on automatic exchange of information] Multilateral Competent Authority Agreement	6	
Inclusive Framework on BEPS	25	
Steering group	4	*Côte d'Ivoire, Nigeria, Senegal, South Africa*
Multilateral Instrument on BEPS	12	
United Nations Committee of Experts on International Cooperation in Tax Matters	6	Djibouti, Ghana, Kenya, Liberia, Nigeria, Zambia

Source: Hearson (forthcoming) based on OECD and United Nations membership lists.

3.5 Concluding remarks

This chapter has focused on a selected set of avenues for enabling IFFs. All of them are likely to have a detrimental effect on financing for development. Tax treaty shopping, in particular, exemplifies the complexity of international taxation and stiff tax competition among countries. Considering the dominant features of the current international corporate system, race to the bottom as a strategy for attracting FDI is likely to continue. While the fiscal costs of a treaty might be a price worth paying for its investment promotion benefits, the evidence that tax treaties attract investment into developing countries is contested and unclear (Sauvant and Sachs, 2009; Hearson, 2018). Moreover, this debate should account for the effect of tax treaty shopping on the competitiveness of local firms. As only international firms can shift profits and reduce prices through lower taxes, local firms are subject to higher local tax rates. As shown in chapter 4, potential development gains or losses can be further exacerbated by the interaction between taxation issues, international investment agreements and the regulatory framework of mining value chains.

In light of the 2030 Agenda for Sustainable Development, the fundamental features of the international taxation system underline the need for further research on the distributional impact of profit shifting. Although not addressed in this report, there is evidence that globally, profit shifting results in reduced corporate income taxes (Zucman, 2019). Considering the financing needs of African countries, some of the losses might be compensated by a broadening of the tax base, as investigated in chapter 6.

Chapter 4

The regulatory environment of illicit financial flows with a special focus on selected sectors

This chapter provides an overview of the regulatory environment within which IFFs are conducted. It focuses on selected sectors while also addressing the wider regulatory environment. IFFs stem from some parts of the productive economy (chapters 1–3). In Africa, extractive industries have been singled out (UNECA, 2016). In what follows, cross-cutting data constraints across value chains are highlighted (section 4.1) with a brief rationale behind the focus on extractives. The regulatory framework within which IFFs in extractive industries operate is discussed in section 4.2. Section 4.3 sheds light on other sectors that are also prone to high risks of illicit practices. Section 4.4 offers an introduction to the broader regulatory environment on taxation, corruption and money-laundering. In addition to the regulations in home States, FDI projects are subject to binding bilateral agreements between home and host States, and these are examined in section 4.5. Finally, much like the international legal system discussed in chapter 3, the broader imbalance in terms of engagement between investors and the host country in the sectors most prone to IFFs is partly rooted in the structural inequalities of the international economic system, and these are examined in section 4.6, followed by some concluding remarks.

IN AFRICA, TAXATION CLAUSES IN MINING CONTRACTS VARY WIDELY.

For example, royalty rates range from:

5%
on gold in Ghana

2-2.5%
on copper in the
Democratic Republic of the Congo

0.075%
on bauxite and
3%
on iron ore in Guinea

AFRICAN COUNTRIES MUST COORDINATE MORE

on tax in the mining sector

4.1 Data opacity across value chains and the special case of extractives

Difficulties in the analysis of IFF risks across value chains are compounded by the opacity that characterize some of its segments. Indeed, a company's supply chain can involve multiple tiers of suppliers, potentially delaying the company's request for compliance information about upstream suppliers. Companies could submit inquiries to their first-tier suppliers, that in turn could either provide the required information or initiate the inquiry process up the supply chain to the next tier. The process could continue until inquiries reach the level of the production facility. These difficulties were apparent in the application of the 2012 Dodd-Frank Act on industries involved in consumer products. The application of the disclosure requirement of the Act revealed that a majority of companies with final products that relied on minerals as intermediates were unable to determine the country of origin of the conflict minerals in their products and whether such minerals benefited or financed armed groups in the countries covered (United States, Government Accountability Office, 2015).

With regard to sectoral characteristics, research on the sources of risks of IFFs shows that a mineral such as gold is more prone to IFFs than an agricultural product such as cocoa (Brugger and Engebretsen, 2019). For the latter, the risks are mostly related to smuggling, and in the gold sector, the risks are present from exploration to the awarding of contracts, through production, processing, assaying, selling, customs and final export (Brugger and Engebretsen, 2019). At the exploration stage for example, illicit practices include inflating expenditure, bribery and illicit transfers of trade samples collected. During the production stage, there is also evidence that the tax deductibility of internal loans that surpasses a permissible threshold as a result of reinvestment or expansion may result in a particular risk (Miyandazi, 2019).

The sources of IFFs in the extractive sector can be classified in three categories (Le Billion, 2011): proceeds of corruption derived from the abuse of public authority for personal gain; revenues from illegal resource exploitation that prevent the State from receiving its legal share; and tax evasion initiated by the investor. These three causes are not mutually exclusive and often occur together. The first cause, corruption and its associated dysfunctional institutions, is often cited as a key enabler of the negative association between natural resource abundance and development, leading to what has been coined the "resource curse" and the so-called "paradox of plenty" (Auty, 1993; Sachs and Warner, 1995; Karl, 1997).

The magnitude of the second cause, illegal exploitation and trading of minerals, is such that transparency initiatives such as the Kimberley Process Certification Scheme help uncover the extent of discrepancies between actual and reported production in the minerals sector. It has been shown, for example, that due to smuggling and underreporting, the global production of diamonds was nearly twice as large as previously estimated, although the lack of more recent data limits further investigation of the issue (World Bank, 2008).

With regard to the third cause, tax evasion, countries need to weigh the costs and benefits associated with building specialist capacity for assessing tax in the extractive sector. If the tax office believes there is a consistent and wide gap between the market and the values reported by exporters, it may warrant investing in the specialized information and expertise, as well as laboratory services, needed to verify and potentially challenge exporters' declared values. Building these sector-specific auditing capabilities can be expensive and challenging, as it requires deep knowledge about how prices are set and deals are struck for each product. Tax assessors also need a detailed understanding about how tax filings are impacted by other aspects specific to extractive industries, such as the importation of specialized machinery, the procurement of technical services and hedging and financing arrangements – especially the use of debt – which can be more challenging to assess (United Nations, 2017). Finally, more general tax avoidance challenges associated with, for example, capital gains tax and indirect transfers, are also significant across mining value chains.

4.2 Illicit financial flows and the regulatory framework of the extractive sector in Africa

As stated in chapter 2, mining policies and activities in Africa should be guided by the African Union AMV. Mining operations should also be subject to several international guiding principles such as the United Nations Guiding Principles on Business and Human Rights. These frameworks are soft law instruments and as such are not legally binding. This section focuses on the dominant features of domestic legislation of relevance to extractive industries and on mining contracts.

The legal and regulatory framework at the domestic level
The extractive sector is subject to the hierarchy of the legal norms of the host country. Although practices of domestication of international laws vary, domestic laws are

the default rules when no other special normative regime referring to the primacy of international law over domestic law applies (Chibundu, 2010). As shown in figure 12, the hierarchy of legal norms includes the constitution, followed by a body of national laws that comprise the mining code, and laws on investment, trade, taxation, labour protection, infrastructure and environmental protection and other country-specific legislation.[43] The constitution sets out the most fundamental principles for the governance of economic activities, such as State sovereignty over natural resources, ownership and protection of property, the protection of local communities and protection of the environment and human rights. It enacts the permanent State sovereignty over natural resources, citizens' right to a healthy environment and the need to protect the environment for both present and future generations (LEX Africa, 2019).[44] Constitutional law also governs the distribution of power among different government entities and agencies. For example, the constitutional law of Ghana requires parliamentary ratification of all mining contracts involved in the granting of rights or concessions on behalf of the Government. Finally, FDI projects in extractive industries are also governed by the enabling framework for investment, including the tax code, and environmental and foreign exchange regulations. Despite the wide array of legislation, as shown in figure 12, most countries lack implementation and enforcement capacity, especially in assessing IFFs (Musselli and Bürgi Bonanomi, 2020).

A comprehensive analysis of transfer pricing legislation in Africa by the World Bank found that most African countries do not have an appropriate transfer pricing framework (Guj et al., 2017). Transfer pricing is addressed either in the general tax law or a financial act. Examples of countries in which some of these acts address anti-avoidance include Côte d'Ivoire, Madagascar, Mali and Sierra Leone (Guj et al., 2017:94). Although most countries have a mining code, despite the adoption of AMV, aimed at making the African mining sector an engine for the transformation of the continent, several analyses show that even during commodity booms, many mineral-rich countries have not improved their socioeconomic performance (UNCTAD, 2017). Growing concerns for the sector's poor development record, evidence of the magnitude of IFFs and the emergence of civil society organizations working on transparency issues, contributed to a trend leading to the review of mining codes in Africa (Bridge, 2004).

---

[43] For a summary of the mining law regime in about 15 African countries, including on the relevant authorities and legislation, acquisition of rights, rules on indigenous peoples' rights, disposal of rights, the environment, health and safety, royalties and taxes, see DLA Piper (2012) and LEX Africa (2019).

[44] Constitutional law of Mozambique, Namibia and Nigeria (LEX Africa, 2019).

Figure 12

Legal and regulatory framework in the mining sector in Africa

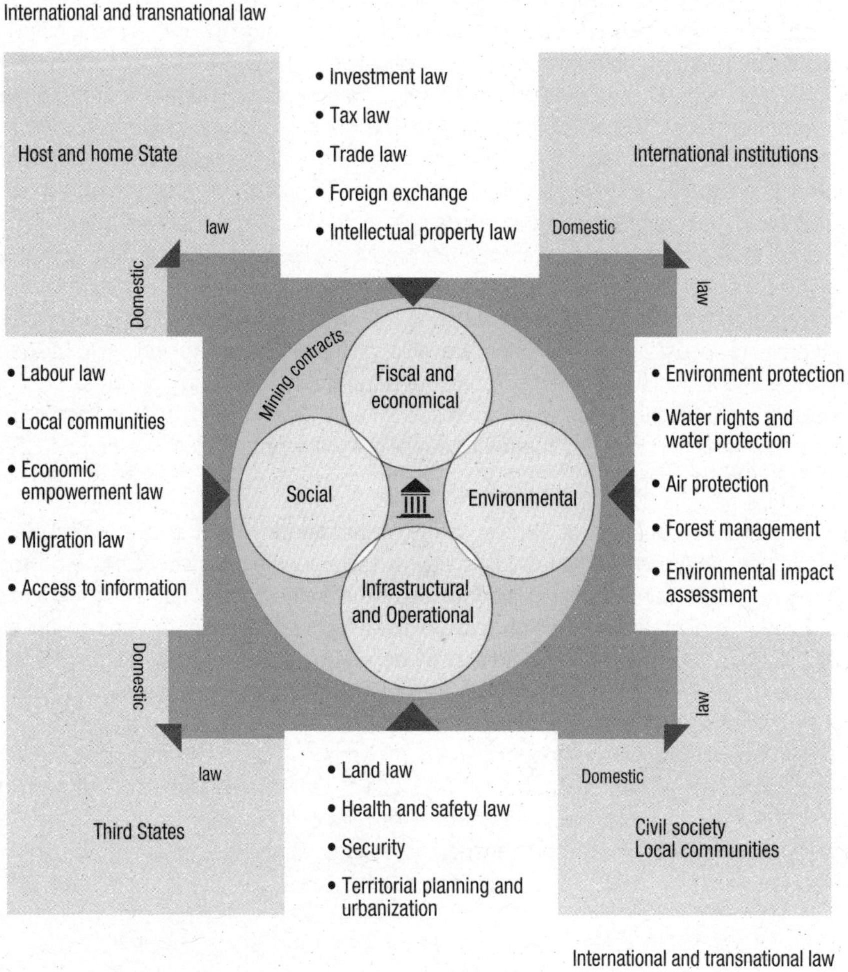

International and transnational law

Host and home State

- Investment law
- Tax law
- Trade law
- Foreign exchange law
- Intellectual property law

International institutions

Domestic

law

Domestic

Mining contracts

Fiscal and economical

Social

Environmental

Infrastructural and Operational

- Labour law
- Local communities
- Economic empowerment law
- Migration law
- Access to information

- Environment protection
- Water rights and water protection
- Air protection
- Forest management
- Environmental impact assessment

Domestic

law

Domestic

law

Third States

- Land law
- Health and safety law
- Security
- Territorial planning and urbanization

Civil society
Local communities

International and transnational law

Source: UNCTAD secretariat.

Mining contracts

Mining contracts are widely used across the mining sector as a complement to domestic legislation.[45] An examination of contracts covering gold, copper and cobalt, aluminium and bauxite across a sample of three countries (the Democratic Republic of the Congo, Ghana and Guinea) reveals a high level of variance in their fiscal clauses (table 7). Royalties, for example, can range from, in Ghana, 5 per cent of the revenue on gold, as prescribed in the mining code to, in Guinea, 0.075 per cent on bauxite and 3 per cent on iron ore. Mining contracts also vary in terms of the treatment of affiliated company transactions. For example, in Guinea, different companies have different contractual provisions on the obligation to comply with the best transfer pricing practices and that of the pre-emptive right of the State to purchase the mineral products when it considers the transfer price too low. In contrast, in the Democratic Republic of the Congo, contracts do not make any mention of such transactions. Rather, the 2018 Mining Code stipulates that transactions between affiliates be conducted on an arm's length basis.

The examination of publicly available contracts in a sample of African countries shows that mining contracts play a significant role in mining investments on the continent.[46] State participation varies and includes either shares to be held by State-owned companies or shares held by the Government. Mining contracts also increasingly include provisions on their development contribution. In the contracts examined in table 7, these range from 20 per cent of royalties as required by domestic legislation in Ghana to 0.5–1 per cent of the revenue and subject to the Community Development Agreement between the company and the local community in Guinea.

It is also common for such mining contracts to include a stabilization clause, which freezes the applicable domestic law during the period of the project. While contracts are normally concluded under and subject to domestic law, mining contracts are often internationalized and apply international law or provide recourse to international dispute settlement mechanisms, a provision that is also readily available in the bilateral investment treaties between the home country of most investors and the African host country in which the project is located.

---

[45] Confidential interviews by a member of the present report's team with partners from two law firms with offices in mineral-rich countries in Africa.
[46] Ibid. See https://resourcecontracts.org/.

Table 7
Selection of fiscal clauses in mining contracts in the Democratic Republic of the Congo, Ghana and Guinea

	Democratic Republic of the Congo	Ghana	Guinea
Resource	Copper and cobalt	Gold	Aluminium and bauxite
Year of signature	2005–2010	2008–2015	2010–2018
Payment recipient	Government and State-owned enterprise	Government	Government and State-owned enterprise
Royalties	2–2.5 per cent of the revenue, less certain costs under most contracts	5 per cent of the revenue, as prescribed by the Mining Code	0.075 per cent on bauxite, 3 per cent on iron ore and other non-ferrous minerals, as prescribed by the Mining Code
Bonus	Either a one-off payment or a combination of a fixed fee and a monthly fee or extra fees determined by the production capacity of the mine. The amount of the payment ranges from $100,000 to $100 million, depending on the size of the project and the terms of the contract	$30,000–$50,000 as consideration of the granting of the mining lease	Applicable law
State participation	17.5–30 per cent shares to be held by the State-owned enterprise, 10 per cent shares to be held by the Government, subject to further increase	10 per cent free carried interest for the Government as prescribed by the Mining Code, subject to further participation in the mining operation	5–15 per cent non-contributive shares held by the Government or State-owned enterprise, either with or without the right to purchase additional shares
Rental fees	Most contracts do not have such a clause; therefore, the Mining Code 2018 shall apply: $0.2–$0.4 per hectare per year during exploration; $0.4–$0.8 per hectare per year during exploitation	From 8.5 to 260 Ghanaian cedi per half year	$10–$20 per square kilometre during exploration, $75–$300 per square kilometre during exploitation, depending on the type of licence and times of renewal
Corporate income tax	30 per cent, the same rate provided in certain contracts and the Mining Code 2018, which shall apply when contracts do not include such a clause. Mining companies are also subject to windfall profit tax, as provided in the Mining Code 2018	35 per cent, as prescribed by the Income Tax Act 2015	35 per cent, but most contracts provide certain tax incentives, such as tax holidays (normally 5–6 years) or a lower tax rate at the beginning of exploitation

Table 7
Selection of fiscal clauses in mining contracts in the Democratic Republic of the Congo, Ghana and Guinea *(continuation)*

	Democratic Republic of the Congo	Ghana	Guinea
Development contribution	0.3 per cent of the revenue or other amount agreed in the contract	20 per cent of the royalty contributed to a development fund, as prescribed by the legislation	0.5–1 per cent of the revenue, subject to the Community Development Agreement concluded between the company and the local community
Affiliated company transactions	No relevant terms in contracts, but according to the Mining Code 2018, any business transaction between affiliates shall be conducted on an arm's length basis	Standard term in most contracts: (a) A fair and reasonable price for services and provide justifications when required; (b) All transactions on the basis of competitive international prices and upon fair and reasonable terms and conditions; (c) Notify the minister of all transactions and supply details when required	Great variance among mining contracts, which may include some of the following elements: (a) Arm's length principle and best transfer pricing practices should be complied with; (b) Obligation to declare and report affiliated transactions included in most contracts; (c) Prior approval for either the transfer pricing method or the affiliated transaction is required under certain circumstances; (d) Pre-emption right of the State to purchase the mineral products when it considers the transfer price too low
Stabilization	From the date of signature to the entire duration of the agreement, covering both fiscal and non-fiscal issues	No stabilization clause in most contracts	During the period of the mining concession, most stabilization clauses only cover taxation and custom duties

Source: UNCTAD secretariat and https://resourcecontracts.org/.
Note: In 2019, only 15 out of 27 countries in sub-Saharan Africa disclosed contracts on investment projects in the extractive sector and only six of these disclosed sufficient details for analysis.

4.3 Other selected sectors with high risks of illicit financial flows

Telecommunications and private equity

The other two sectors in which tax avoidance issues have received attention due to their high-profile nature are telecommunications and private equity. Sub-Saharan Africa is the world's fastest growing market for mobile telecommunications. The total number of subscribers is expected to increase from 456 million in 2018 to over 600 million by 2025, half of the continent's population (GSMA, 2019). A common tax evasion practice known as "SIM[subscriber identification module] box fraud", for example, involves operators making false declarations of incoming international call minutes to reduce the tax payable to the Government (UNECA, 2015).

The telecommunications sector is also prone to market concentration as it is dominated by a small number of multinational corporations and contributes to an estimated 8.5 per cent of GDP at the continental level and raises about $15.6 billion in taxes. This relatively limited competition has allowed companies to generate significant rents (Matheson and Petit, 2017). As shown in box 4, the telecommunications sector has also been subjected to several tax disputes. These disputes have uncovered the complex interactions between the establishment status of affiliates, tax treaty shopping and the implications of the application of the domestic tax code.

Sectors most vulnerable to IFFs
and tax disputes
include extractives, financial services and telecommunications

With regard to private equity, in addition to publicly owned direct investors, there are also high-profile cases in the area of social impact investors. Private equity investment structures typically involve a pooling vehicle located in an intermediate jurisdiction. Mauritius is often the chosen location in Africa (Hearson, forthcoming). This provides a number of tax and non-tax benefits that investors argue are crucial to the business model (Carter, 2017). However, the tax treaty networks of Mauritius and other pooling jurisdictions can reduce the ability of the country in which the investment takes place to tax dividends and interest payments and capital gains. Investors argue that eliminating such taxes allows them to invest more widely in Africa, that the economic burden of withholding taxes would ultimately fall on the recipient of the investment and that the alternative to pooling offshore would be to use an onshore jurisdiction in an OECD country that had an advantageous treaty with the recipient country (Carter, 2017).

Box 4

Tax dispute on capital gains: The case of mobile telecommunications from Kuwait in Uganda

An ongoing dispute exists between the Uganda Revenue Authority and the mobile telecommunications company Zain, from Kuwait. The dispute concerns the sale of the latter's subsidiary in Uganda. At the time, Zain International owned Zain Africa BV, which had equity in 26 companies, all registered in the Netherlands. As a result, the sale took place through the transfer of shares in a holding company based in the Netherlands. At stake is a tax assessment of $85 million. The Uganda Revenue Authority states that Zain is liable to pay capital gains tax on the transaction, although it took the form of an offshore indirect transfer in the Netherlands. Indirect transfers of companies whose value derives primarily from immovable property (in this case, telecommunications infrastructure) are taxable under the domestic tax code of Uganda, but not under the tax treaty between the Netherlands and Uganda.

Zain declined to pay, stating that the Uganda Revenue Authority had no jurisdiction to levy tax on Zain Africa BV because it was resident in the Netherlands and did not source the income from Uganda. The Uganda High Court in Kampala initially ruled in favour of Zain in December 2011. The case attracted attention across the 26 countries in which Zain operates in Africa. However, the tax law of Uganda includes an anti-abuse rule designed to prevent treaty shopping. In its ruling in favour of the Uganda Revenue Authority in 2014, the Court of Appeal only covered a procedural matter. It is therefore unclear whether the Revenue Authority or Zain would be successful with regard to the content, as Zain has not appealed further. The Revenue Authority cannot enforce its tax assessment without assistance from the Netherlands, which the treaty provides for, since Zain no longer has any assets in Uganda.

The indirect transfer can be illustrated as follows.

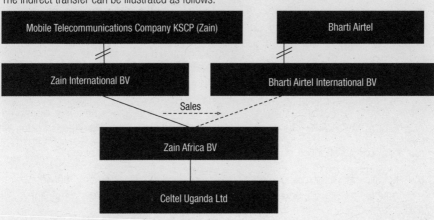

Source: Hearson and Kangave, 2016.

New technologies and the digital economy

The emergence of new business models stemming from the digital economy has given rise to a number of challenges related to IFFs in both developed and developing countries. With regard to taxation, an OECD paper points to three ways in which digitalized businesses are harder to tax under existing rules: the ability to generate value in a country without a physical presence; the importance of data, a new and different type of commodity; and the importance of intangible assets (OECD, 2018c; UNCTAD, 2019b). Nonetheless, digital business models also allow firms to avoid tax liabilities that Governments intend them to pay. For example, intangible assets are hard to value and easy to move, which makes them an important tool in profit-shifting strategies; the minimal physical presence needed for digital business models allows firms to design business structures that circumvent existing permanent establishment rules.

African Governments are seeking to address this problem through a variety of routes beyond simply corporate income tax. To address the main problem of low corporate income taxes, some African countries have adopted a range of innovative measures (Hearson, 2018). Kenya, for example, recently designed a proposal to expand its definition of permanent establishment, to include digital advertising platforms. Some African countries have been seeking to use other taxes to respond to the situation. This includes value-added tax, which, for example, South Africa has now imposed on sales of applications through mobile platforms. Uganda has attempted to levy value-added tax on foreign providers of digital services. Several countries, including Uganda and Zimbabwe, have also introduced taxes on digital financial transactions.

Furthermore, digital technologies have expanded opportunities for cybercrime and offered platforms to trade illegal goods and services by offering a wide range of features that facilitate the illegal transfer and use of money (Tropina, 2016), including the following the following:

(a) Automation, speed and cross-border nature, which allow money to be quickly transferred across different jurisdictions;

(b) Anonymity, which reduces the ability to perform customer checks;

(c) Complexity of online transactions, which allows for multiple activities;

(d) Insufficient or no regulation of most intermediaries operating online, which enables transactions to take place without anti-money-laundering measures.

Malhotra (2010) notes that the above features allow for the division of transactions into small amounts, below the reporting threshold, and for them to be performed rapidly through different institutions and jurisdictions. As a result, it becomes nearly impossible to detect IFFs and trace them back to their origins. They thus provide a means to distance money from illegal sources and the means to illegally transfer money from legal sources.

There are several tools associated with money-laundering and digital technologies, such as mobile banking or online non-bank payment services. Online non-bank payment services, in particular, are prone to IFFs, owing to their largely unregulated nature. These services provide a fast, cheap and anonymous means to make payments and international transfers, which makes them vulnerable to illicit transfers.

4.4 Cross-cutting regulations of relevance to illicit financial flows

Taxation standards and legislations

Transparency and cooperation between tax administrations globally is key in the fight against tax evasion and tax avoidance. In this regard, the Multilateral Convention on Mutual Administrative Assistance in Tax Matters, established in 1988 and originally limited to OECD and Council of Europe members, has, since 2008, been open to all interested countries. By joining this agreement, countries can obtain the right to request information on their taxpayers' affairs from all other signatories. The Convention also offers the legal framework through which to cooperate when investigating multinational taxpayers, without the need to negotiate dozens of bilateral deals. To date, 10 African countries have joined the convention (Hearson, forthcoming). However, the need for compliance with this Convention has been underlined as not adequate to African countries due to capacity constraints (UNECA, 2015). Similarly, the Global Forum on Transparency and Exchange of Information for Tax Purposes conducts peer reviews of countries' compliance with OECD information-exchange standards and is backed by the threat of "defensive measures" from the Group of 20 (Hearson, forthcoming).[47] After ATAF, it is the tax body with the most African members, namely, 31.[48]

By joining, countries agree to be peer reviewed, but they also have more leverage if they seek access to tax information from another Global Forum member.

Most sub-Saharan African countries established a domestic transfer pricing regime only during the last decade; there are a few exceptions, such as South Africa in 1995 and

[47] See https://www.oecd.org/tax/transparency/.
[48] For the list of members, see www.oecd.org/tax/transparency/about-the-global-forum/members/.

Kenya in 2006. As at March 2019, about half of the countries in sub-Saharan Africa still did not have any form of domestic transfer pricing rules and therefore could not challenge MNEs through local judicial authorities (AndersenTax, 2019). Indeed, when domestic transfer pricing rules are available, they are the superior legal source and international instruments such as the OECD Transfer Pricing Guidelines for Multinational Enterprises and Tax Administrations can only be used as secondary sources; if no transfer pricing rules are available under the domestic regime and no guidance has been provided by the authority, the tax administrators cannot choose the rules ex post to the detriment of taxpayers. In effect, the few transfer pricing cases published in Africa suggest that most of the countries concerned did not have their first transfer pricing judgment until recently, for example, Zimbabwe in 2017, and Ghana, Malawi and South Africa in 2018. As a result, the transfer pricing methods and the applicability of the OECD Transfer Pricing Guidelines were at the centre of the debate in several of the cases.[49]

In Malawi, domestic transfer pricing regulations were already available at the time of a landmark dispute in 2016.[50] However, the audit report produced by the Malawi Revenue Authority did not refer to domestic regulations, but instead relied on the OECD Guidelines and directly quoted article 9 of the OECD Model Tax Convention to define the arm's length principle. In response to this, the judges stated that "where local legislation provides for the law, it is always imperative to apply that law" and international instruments can be used "in interpreting that local law". The tax administrator should "strictly follow the dictates of the law as enacted by the legislature" and "any slight departure from the law is not allowed". Therefore, the court of Malawi ruled the application of the OECD Guidelines and not the domestic transfer pricing regulations to be illegal.

In the other two cases, respectively in Kenya and Zambia, the courts ruled that the OECD Guidelines can be used by taxpayers for transfer price calculation, although these rules are not part of the domestic legal system. The court in Zambia, for example, acknowledged the use of the OECD Guidelines and the United Nations *Practical Manual on Transfer Pricing for Developing Countries* when there is a lacuna in domestic legislations at the time of the case. However, the court pointed out that the domestic transfer pricing regulation was issued in 2018 and should now become the first reference point for transfer pricing practices.[51] Interestingly, the court in Kenya expressed its concern about the lack of relevant transfer pricing rules in the judgment and said that while "unfortunately our Act is silent on such methods to be employed or

---

[49]   For the first transfer pricing case in South Africa, see Brink (2018).
[50]   See https://www.africataxjournal.com/wp-content/uploads/2018/08/TP-MALAWI-JUDICIAL-REVIEW-Eastern-Produce-MW-Ltd-vs-MRA-Transfer-Pricing-Applicability-of-OEC...-2.pdf.
[51]   Nestle Zambia Trading Ltd v Zambia Revenue Authority, Tax Appeals Tribunal, 2018/TAT/03/DT, available at https://www.africataxjournal.com/wp-content/uploads/2019/04/Nestle-vs-ZRA-TP-Case-2019.pdf.

used", the court hoped that the Kenya Revenue Authority would "lead in the initiative to make rules in this regard".[52]

Corruption and money-laundering

Several international instruments have established legal obligations of relevance to the regulation of IFFs. The following conventions criminalize either the origin of IFFs, corruption, money-laundering or the use of flows, such as in the financing of terrorism: United Nations Convention against Illicit Traffic in Narcotic Drugs and Psychotropic Substances, 1988; International Convention for the Suppression of the Financing of Terrorism, 1999; United Nations Convention against Transnational Organized Crime, 2000; United Nations Convention against Corruption, 2003; and a number of United Nations Security Council resolutions establishing targeted financial sanction regimes applied to terrorist groups.

With regard to corruption, the United Nations Convention against Corruption covers five main areas, namely, preventive measures, criminalization and law enforcement, international cooperation, asset recovery and technical assistance and information exchange. In addition, as part of their anti-corruption initiatives at the domestic level, a majority of countries globally have enacted laws that require officials to disclose their financial information (assets, income and liabilities) through financial disclosure frameworks. According to Guj et al. (2017), 176 countries have enacted respective laws, including all high-income OECD countries, 89 per cent of countries in sub-Saharan Africa and 61 per cent in the Middle East and North Africa.

Anti-money-laundering laws and regulations are critical in the fight against corruption as they criminalize a type of conduct that is related to the corrupt act itself (World Bank, 2004). In terms of money-laundering, the set of global standards on the fight against the laundering of the proceeds of crime that has become the main reference is the 40 recommendations of the Financial Action Task Force (2003). While not binding, these recommendations set out several requirements for combating money-laundering. Critically, they recommend that countries should criminalize money-laundering so that these actions can be prosecuted. Financial institutions should be obliged to keep records of all transactions and perform customer due diligence. This entails knowing company ownership, or the beneficial owner of a customer that is a legal entity. Additional due diligence is required for politically exposed persons as, typically, these are particularly at risk of large-scale corruption. However, definitions of politically exposed persons differ across countries.

[52] Unilever Kenya Ltd v Commissioner of Income Tax [2005], Income Tax Appeal No. 753 of 2003 at 15, available at https://www.africataxjournal.com/wp-content/uploads/2018/08/Unilever-Kenya-Ltd-v-Commissioner-KRA-Income-Tax-Appeal-753-of-2003.pdf.

In countries with anti-money-laundering legislation, both financial institutions (banks, insurance companies and currency exchange services) and designated non-financial businesses and professions (for example, lawyers, accountants and casinos) are required by law to notify a public agency when they find a suspicious transaction report. These agencies are mostly financial intelligence units. While almost all countries have a financial intelligence unit, their institutional set-ups and capacities in terms of mandate and resources differ widely. As in all other countries, it is critical that financial intelligence units in African countries be shielded from political pressure so that they can perform their functions independently (IMF, 2004).

4.5 The prevalence of bilateralism

Investment treaties, taxation and dispute settlement mechanisms
IFFs from commercial activities are operated within an environment framed by international investment agreements, notably bilateral investment treaties, regional treaties and others. In addition to bilateral investment treaties, international investment agreements also comprise treaties with investment provisions. These typically consist of three types of treaties: broad economic treaties that include obligations commonly found in bilateral investment treaties (for example, a free trade agreement with an investment chapter); treaties with limited investment-related provisions (for example, only those concerning the establishment of investments or the free transfer of investment-related funds); and treaties that only contain framework clauses such as the ones on cooperation in the area of investment and/or for a mandate for future negotiations on investment issues (UNCTAD, 2018).

Bilateral investment treaties constitute the main form of investment agreements used by African countries to attract FDI. There are now over 3,000 international agreements concluded by around 180 countries.[53] Their attractiveness is such that in 2018, countries signed some 40 new international investment agreements, including 30 bilateral investment treaties and 10 treaties with investment provisions, bringing the treaty universe to 3,317 agreements (UNCTAD, 2019c). Out of these, by January 2019, African countries alone had signed close to 1,000 international investment agreements, of which around 200 were intra-African, including numerous regional agreements. Regional agreements comprise the Investment Agreement for the Common Market for Eastern and Southern Africa Common Investment Area, the Economic Community

[53] See https://investmentpolicy.unctad.org/international-investment-agreements.

of West African States Supplementary Act on Investments and the Southern African Development Community Protocol on Finance and Investment, among others. In addition, many countries are increasingly bound by extraregional agreements such as the East African Community–United States Trade and Investment Framework Agreement, the European Union–Southern African Development Community Economic Partnership Agreement and the Economic Community of West African States–United States Trade and Investment Framework Agreement.[54]

These treaties confer a series of rights and obligations on contracting parties. In bilateral investment treaties, in particular, the obligations of States include the commitment to not discriminate against foreign investors by offering them national or most-favoured nation treatment, to offer fair and equitable treatment and to not expropriate investment without compensation. In addition, bilateral investment treaties mainly include a dispute settlement clause that allows investors to sue host States, typically bypassing domestic courts and allowing investors to directly bring international arbitration proceedings, most often at the International Centre for Settlement of Investment Disputes or under the United Nations Commission on International Trade Law arbitration rules. However, originally based on a system of ad hoc confidential commercial arbitration between private parties, the legitimacy of the investor–State dispute settlement system is now challenged (UNCTAD, 2018). By mid-2019, investors had brought more than 980 investor–State dispute settlement cases against 118 countries, including 117 cases against at least 30 African countries.[55] With more than half a century having passed since the first bilateral investment treaty was concluded (between Germany and Pakistan in 1959), international investment agreements have gone through a significant evolutionary process (UNCTAD, 2018:14). A system that was originally developed to foster legal predictability in investment relations between countries has today become a source of legal uncertainty, debate and controversy (El-Kady, 2016; El-Kady and De Gama, 2019:1).

Disputes over international taxation have been increasing in response to rising international trade and investment. Resolving such disputes is, however, problematic, as tax treaties generally do not provide direct access to arbitration. The main instruments for dispute resolution for international taxation issues are the mutual agreement procedures (OECD, 2007). Under such a procedure, taxpayers can submit a request to the competent authority in their resident State if they consider that the actions of the contracting States have resulted in taxation in disaccordance with the provisions of the underlying convention. If no solution is found, the case can be submitted for

[54] Ibid.
[55] See https://investmentpolicy.unctad.org/investment-dispute-settlement.

arbitration, which is non-binding and only imposes on the parties the obligation to negotiate (Chaisse, 2016). This highlights the limitations of the process. On one hand, the process is largely dependent on the decisions of the local tax authority and, on the other hand, the outcome is non-binding.

In light of the void in dispute settlement mechanisms on taxation, investor–State dispute settlement mechanisms were originally designed to resolve disputes on international investment issues and in some instances, investors can challenge the tax policy and tax measures of host States through this mechanism in international arbitration tribunals. This possibility arises if measures implemented by host States to address BEPS issues increase the tax obligations of investors and violate concepts for which international investment agreements offer protection to the investor, such as expropriation or violation of national treatment, most-favoured nation treatment and fair and equitable treatment. Investors therefore may claim that these measures are in breach of international investment agreements, while possibly in line with the spirit of double tax treaties and other international taxation cooperation regimes (Chaisse, 2016).

Over time, the need for systematic reform of the global international investment agreement regime has become evident. A shared view has emerged on the necessity of ensuring that the investment treaty regime works for all stakeholders. The UNCTAD publications *UNCTAD's Reform Package for the International Investment Regime* (UNCTAD, 2018) and *Investment Policy Framework for Sustainable Development* (UNCTAD, 2015b) offer policymakers more than 100 options for treaty drafting and the pros and cons of each. Concerns about the functioning of investor–State dispute settlements under investment treaties have been summarized in UNCTAD (2013). These concerns pertain to the following issues: legitimacy; transparency; consistency of arbitral decisions; erroneous decisions; arbitrators' independence and impartiality; financial stakes; and nationality planning. With regard to the latter, investors may gain access to investor–State dispute settlement procedures using corporate structuring, that is, by channelling an investment through a company established in an intermediary country with the sole purpose of benefiting from an international investment agreement concluded by that country with the host State (UNCTAD, 2013).

The UNCTAD reform package includes provisions on taxation that are of relevance to the regulation of tax-related IFFs. Key reform options, from a tax perspective, relate to carving out taxation policies (including double taxation treaties) from the scope of the treaty (UNCTAD, 2015b:94, policy option 2.3.1), from the treaty's non-discrimination clauses (UNCTAD, 2015b:96, policy options 4.1.3 and 4.2.2) or from the treaty's dispute settlement clause (UNCTAD, 2015b:106, policy option 6.2.1).

Reform of international investment agreements is also well under way in African countries, including on ways to address taxation issues. At present, African countries are taking a more active approach in the formulation of their international investment commitments, at the national, bilateral and regional levels. Africa is becoming a "laboratory for innovative and sustainable development-oriented investment policymaking" (El-Kady and De Gama, 2019). Some of the innovative reform features found in new African international investment agreements explicitly address, in different manners and to varying degrees, taxation matters. To cite a few examples, the Brazil–Ethiopia bilateral investment treaty carves out measures related to taxation from the scope of the treaty (article 3); the recently adopted model bilateral investment treaty in Morocco, in addition to excluding tax measures from the application of the treaty, further provides that in the event of a conflict between the bilateral investment treaty and a tax convention, the latter shall prevail (article 24); and the draft pan-African investment code stipulates that taxation is not subject to the most-favoured nation and national treatment principles (articles 8 and 10).

Home State, third State law and framework for mutual legal assistance

In Africa, MNEs are also subject to the legislation of their home States. Regulations from third States can play a crucial role in FDI projects, even in cases where there is no physical presence of an investor in the host country. While systematic studies on the volume of investment made through these "secrecy jurisdictions" are limited, as stated in chapter 3, a substantial share of global FDI is made through networks of offshore shell companies. Projects that involve the use of OFCs need to comply with the regulations of the corresponding jurisdictions on financing, taxation, anti-money-laundering and the like.

Furthermore, the laws of the home State can have legal effect beyond their territorial scope. For example, the Foreign Corrupt Practices Act of the United States prohibits companies issuing stock in the United States for bribing foreign officials for government contracts and other business. Breach of this Act may lead to hundreds of millions of dollars in penalty or criminal charges.[56] The examination of the list of the United States Securities and Exchange Commission enforcement actions shows that the Act has affected a wide range of sectors and has allowed the conviction of both individuals and companies.

Bilateral arrangements in the context of frameworks for mutual legal assistance play a critical role in the case of frozen assets held abroad. In Switzerland, for example, the

---

[56] For examples of rulings, see https://www.sec.gov/spotlight/fcpa/fcpa-cases.shtml.

Federal Council provides regular updates on the application of the 2016 Federal Act on the Freezing and the Restitution of Illicit Assets held by Foreign Politically Exposed Persons. For example, the closure of mutual legal assistance procedures reduced the prospects for the restitution of assets from Egypt held in Switzerland within the framework of mutual legal assistance and will not result in the release of assets worth approximately SwF430 million; these assets will remain sequestered within the framework of criminal proceedings in Switzerland for the purpose of determining whether or not their origin is licit.[57]

4.6 Entrenched inequalities in the international economic system

As argued in the conceptual framework of the report (chapter 1), the root causes of IFFs originate in structural inequalities in the international legal and economic system. In this section, the review of the historical attempts to address inequities in the international trading system is aimed to inform forthcoming engagement on IFFs at the multilateral level, including during the fifteenth session of the United Nations Conference on Trade and Development. The section also provides a highlight of the literature on gender inequality and IFFs.

Unequal terms of engagement in international trade

The imbalance in terms of engagement between African countries and investors in extractive industries and in most international engagements of relevance to IFFs partly originates in long-standing inequalities in international trade. The struggle of commodity-exporting developing countries for fairer rules of engagement in international trade is the most emblematic of efforts to reverse structural imbalances in the global economy. In 1947 and 1948, as world leaders met during the opening of the United Nations Conference on Trade and Employment in Havana to deliberate on a post-war economic order, concern for the "special difficulties" that developing countries faced and how these affected international trade in primary commodities was on the agenda. To address these difficulties and what has become known as the "commodity problematique" or commodity problem, the Havana Charter recognized that "a special treatment of the international trade in such commodities through intergovernmental agreement" may at times be necessary (United Nations Conference on Trade and Employment, 1948). However, the Havana Charter was never ratified.

---

[57] See https://www.admin.ch/gov/en/start/documentation/media-releases.msg-id-69322.html.

A confluence of factors, inter alia, the impact of the cold war and decolonization, opened opportunities for developing countries to organize themselves around issues of common interest within the United Nations and at the global level. During the 1950s, Raúl Prebisch[58] played a central role in creating a pathway for commodities on both the research and international relations agenda. Working under the aegis of the United Nations, Raúl Prebisch and Hans Singer identified the secular decline in the prices of primary goods relative to the prices of manufactured goods as the major development problem of countries dependent on the exports of primary commodities (Prebisch, 1950; Singer, 1950).

In the context of a continued downward trend in the terms of trade for commodity-exporting countries, combined with instability in commodity prices and revenues, and pressure from developing countries, the United Nations General Assembly approved the recommendation of the Economic and Social Council to convene a United Nations conference on trade and development in 1962.[59] The commodity problem was a priority item on the agenda of the first session of the United Nations Conference on Trade and Development in 1964. The Conference provided a forum for deliberations by the international community to develop a viable international commodity policy. By 1976, at the fourth session of the United Nations Conference on Trade and Development, as part of a new international economic order – a more equitable system of trading relations between the global South and North – the Conference adopted the Integrated Programme for Commodities. Negotiations were launched on a basket of commodities. The idea was to negotiate commodity agreements with economic clauses that would be able to finance buffer stocks in order to reduce price fluctuations and stabilize prices at levels remunerative to producers.

However, due to a combination of factors, including the global recession in the 1980s, falling commodity prices, scepticism regarding the efficiency of the instruments, sector-specific politics and power imbalance in the negotiations, the only new international commodity agreement containing economic clauses negotiated within the context of the Integrated Programme for Commodities at UNCTAD was the International Rubber Agreement (UNCTAD, 2003; Gilbert, 2011; UNCTAD, 2014a; Gayi, 2020). Notwithstanding, the pre-eminence of commodities in the international development discourse has not been matched by concerted action. At the global level, this situation has led to an institutional and political vacuum at worst, or a diffused and incoherent policy agenda for commodities at best (Gayi and Chérel-Robson, forthcoming).

---

[58] Raúl Prebisch (1901–1986) was an Argentinian economist and Secretary-General of UNCTAD from 1964 to 1969.
[59] For a detailed account of the developments leading to this resolution and subsequently to the formation of UNCTAD, see UNCTAD (2014a).

Long after the "Prebisch–Singer thesis", most African countries are still heavily dependent on the export of primary commodities (UNCTAD, 2019d). Furthermore, it is established that power in global value chains is strongly asymmetrical, with MNEs and other private companies controlling critical points along the chains (Fitter and Kaplinsky, 2001; Gibbon, 2001; Gibbon and Ponte, 2005). Analysis based on OECD and WTO trade in value-added data shows that: OECD countries capture 67 per cent of value created in global value chains; the economies of Brazil, China, India, the Russian Federation and South Africa and a handful of economies from East and South-East Asia capture 25 per cent; and the remaining 100 plus developing, mostly commodity-dependent, countries are left to divide among them the balance of 8 per cent of value-added in global value chains (Banga, 2013). Furthermore, although primarily meant to demonstrate the benefits of integrating into global value chains, the analysis reported in *World Development Report 2020* (World Bank, 2020) also provides evidence of the inequality in rules of engagement between developed and developing country actors. The report alludes to the exacerbated market power and large profit rates that "superstar firms" benefit from due to the disproportionate bargaining power that they may have over their suppliers. The report shows that there is a negative relationship between markups and forward participation for developing countries in the same value chain. It further stipulates that "although buyer firms in developed countries are seeing higher profits, supplier firms in developing countries are getting squeezed" (World Bank, 2019:85). In addition to the expansion of global value chains, the financialization of commodity markets has increased the role of trading companies and financial institutions in global commodities trade, and increased market concentration with associated oligopolistic tendencies (UNCTAD, 2013).

Gender inequality and illicit financial flows

As alluded to in chapter 3, it is impossible to ascertain a direct causality link between the poor records of gender balance in institutions within which IFFs are facilitated and IFF prevalence. Yet the Goals of the 2030 Agenda for Sustainable Development suggest that reversing this trend would lead to better outcomes on all fronts. With regard to IFFs, gender inequality is prevalent across many dimensions: at the roots of the structure of economic rights that underline the dominant international economic system; at the institutional level within MNEs across sectors; at the sources of IFFs; and at the distributional impact of the development outcomes of the resulting limited public funds. These are now examined in turn.

A review by the United Nations Human Rights Council on progress on women's human rights and participation in power and decision-making found that, 20 years after the

Beijing Declaration and Platform for Action, women still do not have equal enjoyment of the right to economic and political participation due to "deep-seated patriarchal structures" in both the public and private spheres (Office of the High Commissioner for Human Rights, 2015).

Specifically, many reports on gender equality highlight poor gender representation at the management level across all sectors (see McKinsey Global Institute, 2015, 2019; Crédit Suisse, 2019). Studies also show that women are less represented in key segments of value chains due to gender-based discrimination in access to credit and opportunities (McKinsey Global Institute, 2019). With regard to Africa, progress has stagnated across all indicators, except in legal protection and in political representation. Paradoxically, due to the excellent performance of a small sample of countries (Botswana, Kenya, Rwanda, Uganda and South Africa), Africa has the highest representation of women at the board level of any region, at 25 per cent, whereas the global average is at 17 per cent (McKinsey Global Institute, 2019). Women's representation is also marginally higher than the average representation on executive committees, at 22 per cent.

The gender-related aspects of IFFs are also apparent in their sources. With regard to trafficking in persons and migrant smuggling, for example, 49 per cent of trafficking victims are women and 23 per cent are girls, at the global level (UNODC, 2018). The Financial Action Task Force–Asia Pacific Group on Money-Laundering (2018) uses International Labour Organization estimates to show that human trafficking and associated sexual and labour exploitation generates $150.2. billion per year. Terrorist organizations have also been shown to use human trafficking to fund their activities and organizations. UNDOC (2018) states that trafficking victims from sub-Saharan Africa were reported in 69 countries between 2012 and 2014. The harm caused to victims has many dimensions. In addition to labour bondage and sexual exploitation, for example, a case study based in Nigeria shows that victims are debt bonded to their traffickers for up to €70,000 through the use of illicit money transfer mechanisms (Financial Action Task Force–Asia Pacific Group on Money-Laundering, 2018).

Trafficking in persons and migrant smuggling
is an important source of IFFs.
Globally,
72% of trafficking victims are women and girls.

On the development outcome side, the negative impact of IFFs is also gendered. Tax evasion affects the allocation of scarce government funds and reduces budgetary allocations for public services of which women and girls are the majority beneficiaries. Governments also tend to choose to prioritize certain areas, such as security over social services, creating a further gap in services offered (Waris, 2017). In addition to the widely substantiated feminization of poverty, women also often constitute the largest contingent of victims of health crises. Up to 75 per cent of victims of Ebola virus disease in West Africa, for example, were women (Alliance Sud et al., 2016). In this report, a coalition of civil society organizations argued that budget shortfalls in the health services, exacerbated by tax abuse and illicit financial outflows, worsened the situation. Furthermore, the broadening of the tax base, in order to compensate for revenue shortfalls, is also likely to disproportionately hurt women. Consumption taxes levied on goods and services highly consumed by poor households disproportionately hurt poor women-headed households (Capraro, 2014; Waris, 2017).

4.7 Concluding remarks

This chapter discusses the most prominent features of the regulatory environment of tax-related IFFs in the extractive and other sectors in Africa. In addition to the specifics of these sectors, the discussion also uncovered the broader complex layers of legislation that both countries and investors have to navigate, with the particular dominance of bilateral investment treaties. As in the case of tax treaties discussed in chapter 3, investment treaties tend to be of greater value to investors than to host countries. Furthermore, the chapter's discussion of corruption and anti-money-laundering regulations and the evidence of various rulings on this matter also demonstrate that, overall, neither the domestic nor the international legal systems provide sufficient disincentives against illicit practices. Finally, the gendered impact of IFFs on socioeconomic indicators provide cause for concern. The association between IFFs and sustainable development indicators is further explored in chapters 5 and 6.

Chapter 5

Quantifying the impact of illicit financial flows on sustainable development

This chapter explores the potential relationship between IFFs, structural transformation and sustainable development. It examines how IFFs may be negatively associated with productivity increases across sectors and highlights the role of institutions in channelling such effects. Over the past decade, in most countries in Africa, productivity increases have been low, despite relatively high economic growth rates. The findings indicate how curbing IFFs could contribute to achieving higher levels of economic productivity (target 8.2), supporting productive capacities (target 8.3) and improving resource efficiency (target 8.4) in Africa.

**IFFs UNDERCUT
LABOUR PRODUCTIVITY**

**THE EXTRACTION OF NATURAL
RESOURCES**

consumes large amounts of energy,
increasing climate risks

Section 5.1 describes the methodological approach and model used to quantify the potentially harmful effects of IFFs. Section 5.2 presents the results of the model to show the association with inferior outcomes in sustainable development, followed by a discussion in section 5.3 of how inclusive institutions can reduce the harmful impact of IFFs. Sections 5.4 and 5.5 explore how IFFs can be harmful with regard to environmental performance in extractive sectors and agricultural productivity. Section 5.6 summarizes the key findings.

5.1 Channels of impact of IFFs: Empirical challenges and methodological approach

The analysis in this chapter builds on the existing evidence of the investment-inhibiting effect of IFFs on economic growth (Ndiaye, 2009; Fofack and Ndikumana, 2010; Ndikumana and Boyce, 2011; Mevel et al., 2013; Salandy and Henry, 2013; Dachraoui and Smida, 2014; Ndikumana, 2014; Nkurunziza, 2014; Ndiaye and Siri, 2016). However, it takes a more nuanced approach, focusing on the potential of curbing IFFs to increase productivity. In contrast to high economic growth rates, structural transformation and productivity increases have been insufficient to boost human development. Structural transformation is a complex process that requires a mix of human and physical capital accumulation and institutional quality (North, 1994; Hall and Jones, 1999). Institutional quality refers to, on one hand, the rules of a society that provide certainties for investments and, on the other hand, a system of institutions that sets rules, norms and the environment "within which individuals accumulate skills and firms accumulate capital and produce output" (Hall and Jones, 1999:84; see North, 1994; Vitola and Senfelde, 2015). Various concepts of structural transformation exist. Recent literature has stressed the role that productivity growth plays in achieving structural transformation within sectors. New concepts of structural change that consider the allocation of labour towards productive sectors have been discussed in the literature (McMillan et al., 2014; Martins, 2019; Mühlen and Escobar, 2020). In fact, few studies consider the role of IFFs in decreasing investments that promote productivity increases across and within sectors. Usman and Arene (2014), for example, show that capital flight can be negatively associated with agricultural growth and that it is impacted by macroeconomic and political instability.

The key channels through which IFFs have an impact on value-added growth, productivity increases and socioeconomic development as identified in the literature are capital accumulation, investments and Government revenue. The investment channel is at the centre of the analysis presented in this chapter to explain productivity levels across countries in Africa. The potentially negative impact on social development through the lack of Government revenue and limited domestic resource mobilization is central to the analysis presented in chapter 6. Based on the conceptual framework of this report and the findings presented in the previous chapters, two additional channels are included as cross-cutting elements in explaining the impact of IFFs on sustainable development, namely, institutional harm and environmental sustainability.

IFFs lower the rate of capital accumulation through reductions in private investment that could have financed new production technologies, machinery and innovative production processes needed to increase labour productivity (see, for example, Ndiaye, 2009, 2014; Fofack and Ndikumana, 2010; Ndikumana, 2014; Nkurunziza, 2014). Slany et al. (2020) initially test the link between capital formation and capital flight as established in the literature, providing evidence of a negative correlation. However, this relationship seems to be subject to other variables that affect both capital formation and capital flight. A shortage of capital caused by IFFs increases the domestic interest rate and could put additional pressure on the high levels of external debt service in many countries in Africa. In addition, a potential depreciation of the national currency from capital outflows also increases the costs of investments and lowers the levels of productive investments and productivity growth (Ampah and Kiss, 2019). This chapter does not estimate the relationship between external debt and IFFs, but rather draws on existing literature to assess its developmental impact (Ndikumana and Boyce, 2018; Ampah and Kiss, 2019). In addition, the potentially negative impact on imports due to lower incomes could increase balance of payment pressures and reduce the rate of capital accumulation.

IFFs can affect Government revenue by lowering the tax base, which reduces public expenditure on soft and hard infrastructure, research and development, environmental protection and institutional development (Ndikumana and Boyce, 2011; Mevel et al., 2013; on the relationship with domestic resource mobilization, showing that IFFs can be associated with lower expenditures on health and education, see chapter 6). The accumulation of human capital is critical to increasing labour productivity through the acquisition of skills and knowledge. Public expenditure reductions have potential gender-unequal impacts, in particular if cuts affect expenditures on education and health (Musindarwezo, 2018).[60] Higher levels of public expenditures on education and health potentially reduce the time women spend caring for their families, giving them more time for decent work (Ndikumana and Boyce, 2011). A higher level of education among women boosts productivity growth, in particular in low productivity sectors with a large share of women's employment (Trenczek, 2016).

---

[60] See https://www.brettonwoodsproject.org/2019/04/debt-and-gender-equality-how-debt-servicing-conditions-harm-women-in-africa/.

IFFs with regard to criminal activities, bribery and corruption are likely to undermine the domestic rule of law and to harm institutional quality, as they tend to weaken mechanisms of accountability (Ndikumana, 2014). Good governance and strong institutions provide a more conducive environment for investment, increase economic efficiency and, thereby, help raise productivity (McMillan and Harttgen, 2014; McMillan et al., 2014; Martins, 2019).

In the analysis in this chapter, a fourth channel of impact is assumed that is important in explaining the link between IFFs and sustainable development. IFFs can originate in the illicit exploitation of environmental resources and are associated with the unsustainable use of finite natural resources, which can reduce economic growth (Nordhaus, 1974, 2014). Violations of environmental legislation may result in harm to human health and the environment and thereby reduce labour productivity. Environmental damage such as soil erosion may cause lower soil productivity, which impacts agricultural productivity. In particular, the estimate of IFFs in extractive industries may be associated with the illicit extraction of resources, leading to environmentally harmful impacts (chapter 2).

This report uses an integrated framework addressing economic, social, institutional and environmental harms due to IFFs. This framework is considered in the empirical analysis in this chapter. The methodology and results are based on Slany et al. (2020), showing that the relationship between IFFs and structural transformation is driven by the combined effect of different channels, rather than each channel separately. The analysis uses total labour productivity as the main indicator of productive capacity (data availability does not allow for measurement of sector-specific total factor productivity). In order to provide a quantitative analysis of the negative association between IFFs and sustainable development, the econometric approach takes into account different channels and types of IFFs (chapter 1). The applied econometric panel data approach is described in box 5. The quantitative analysis focuses on capital flight, the residual in the balance of payments method (Ndikumana and Boyce, 2010), as a proxy for IFFs. In addition, the empirical findings are discussed with regard to the trade-related estimates of IFFs (partner-country trade gaps, in which export underinvoicing is indicative of IFFs) that, in 2000–2015, accounted, on average, for 70 per cent of capital flight.

Institutions can be enablers of IFFs (chapters 3 and 4). By contrast, transparent and strengthened institutions can help provide an enabling environment for increases in productivity. Motivated by the interrelationship between IFFs, institutional quality and economic development, the extent of the harmful effects of IFFs depend to some extent on institutional quality (Slany et al., 2020). Therefore, a stable and transparent institutional environment increases the efficiency of economic transactions through the reduction of transaction costs. Illicit capital outflows affect socioeconomic development, depending on the overall level of transaction efficiency.

The lack of enforcement of laws makes a quantitative assessment of the quality of institutions difficult, but the use of a range of indices, for example showing the perception of good governance, provides a reasonable perspective of institutional quality. The choice of institutional variables is guided by the literature on IFFs (see, for example, Ndiaye, 2014; Ndikumana, 2014) and includes the following:

(a) Limited State capacity to ensure security and political stability is proxied by the State fragility index of the Centre for Systemic Peace: High levels of uncertainty due to political instability increase the marginal impact of each unit of lost capital;[61]

(b) The indicator on the perception of the control of corruption is obtained from the world governance indicators of the World Bank: High levels of corruption increase the costs of information and risks and reduce the efficiency of capital spending;

(c) The indicator for financial sector institutions is the financial sector rating in Country Policy and Institutional Assessment (CPIA) subindex No. 7 of the World Bank,[62] which serves as the proxy for financial stability and access to financial resources, beyond the measure of credit to the private sector: Loss of an additional unit of capital is expected to be less harmful given a greater spectrum of alternative financial resources.

The econometric panel data approach is supplemented by comparative statistics. In this chapter, countries for which data is available are classified into two groups with regard to the continental average of 5 per cent of GDP in 2000–2015, as follows: States with estimated low levels of capital flight; and States with estimated relatively high estimates of capital flight (table 8). The grouping of resource-dependent countries in table 8 refers to the following commodity exports: energy products and minerals, ores and metals (Schuster and Davis, 2020; for a comparison between resource-dependent and non-resource dependent countries to show how resource dependency and limited economic diversification are associated with developmental harm, see chapter 6).

---

[61] "A country's fragility is closely associated with its State capacity to manage conflict, make and implement public policy and deliver essential services, and its systemic resilience in maintaining system coherence, cohesion and quality of life, responding effectively to challenges and crises" (see https://www.systemicpeace.org/inscrdata.html).

[62] The index includes financial stability (vulnerability to shocks), efficiency and strength of the financial sector (competition, interest rates, capitalization and concentration of liquidity) and access to financial services (savings, credits, payments and insurance), and is based on qualitative and quantitative information drawn from a number of different sources (see https://databank.worldbank.org/reports.aspx?source=country-policy-and-institutional-assessment).

Due to methodological challenges in estimating the magnitude of IFFs and the multidimensional relationship with sustainable development, the magnitude of the results should not be treated as a definitive estimate, nor should the analysis be considered as establishing causality. Instead, the findings illustrate the negative association between IFFs and sustainable development indicators, rather than providing specific estimates of the magnitude of the relationship.

Table 8

Capital flight and natural resource dependency: Country groups

Capital flight estimates		Natural resource dependency	
High: >5 per cent of GDP	Low: <5 per cent of GDP	Non-dependent	Dependent
Benin, Burundi, Comoros, Congo, Djibouti, Eswatini, Ethiopia, Gabon, Guinea, Lesotho, Mali, Mauritius, Rwanda, Sao Tome and Principe, Senegal, Seychelles, Sierra Leone, Togo, Uganda	Algeria, Angola, Botswana, Burkina Faso, Cabo Verde, Cameroon, Côte d'Ivoire, Democratic Republic of the Congo, Egypt, Ghana, Guinea-Bissau, Kenya, Madagascar, Malawi, Mauritania, Morocco, Mozambique, Namibia, Nigeria, South Africa, Sudan, Tunisia, United Republic of Tanzania, Zambia, Zimbabwe	Benin, Cabo Verde, Central African Republic, Comoros, Côte d'Ivoire, Djibouti, Egypt, Eswatini, Ethiopia, Gambia, Guinea-Bissau, Kenya, Lesotho, Madagascar, Malawi, Mauritius, Morocco, Sao Tome and Principe, Senegal, Seychelles, Sierra Leone, Somalia, South Africa, Tunisia, Uganda, Zimbabwe	Algeria, Angola, Botswana, Burkina Faso, Burundi, Cameroon, Chad, Congo, Democratic Republic of the Congo, Equatorial Guinea, Eritrea, Gabon, Ghana, Guinea, Libya, Mali, Mauritania, Mozambique, Namibia, Niger, Nigeria, Sudan, Liberia, Rwanda, Sierra Leone, Togo, United Republic of Tanzania, Zambia

Source: UNCTAD secretariat.

Box 5

Estimating the marginal effects of illicit financial flows on cross-sector labour productivity

The main model discussed in this chapter is guided by a review of the existing literature and is described in the following equation:

$$\ln\left(\frac{\text{value added}}{\text{employment}}\right)_{itk} = f(\text{illicit financial flows}_{it-1}; \text{institutions}_{it-1}; \text{illicit financial flows}_{it-1} \# \text{institutions}_{it-1}; \text{control variables}_{it-1}; \text{set of fixed effects})$$

where i is the country level, t refers to the period 2000–2015 and k to the following sectors: agriculture, mining and quarrying, manufacturing, construction, wholesale and retail trade, transport services and other services. The equation is estimated at the sector *itk* level. The set of fixed effects in the main specification includes country-sector (μ_{ik}) and sector-year (γ_{tk}) fixed effects. The sensitivity of the results to a different set of fixed effects is discussed in Slany et al. (2020). Considering within-sector productivity increases as the main contributor to overall productivity levels, the dependent variable is value added in sector k, divided by sectoral employment in country i at time t (2000–2015). This approach allows for an estimate of sector-specific effects. Sectoral productivity is a function of the variables of interest (IFFs, institutions and interactions between institutions and IFFs) and control variables (macroeconomic variables, education levels and vulnerability to natural disasters).

Variables used in the econometric analysis and expected signs of estimated coefficients

Variable	Description	Data source	Expected sign
IFFs	Capital flight as percentage of current GDP; total trade export underinvoicing (extraregional) as percentage of current GDP	Balance of payments method from the Political Economy Research Institute	-
Institutional quality and interaction terms			
State fragility index	The index measures State performance with regard to effectiveness and legitimacy in addressing shocks and crises: 1=low level of fragility; 25=high level of fragility	Centre for Systemic Peace	-
Interaction of IFFs State fragility index*			
Control of corruption	The indicators are based on variables showing the perception of corruption: -2.5=high corruption; 2.5=low corruption	World Bank world governance indicators	+
*Interaction of IFFs*control of corruption*			
Financial sector rating in CPIA subindex No. 7	The subindex assesses financial stability and access to financial resources: 1=low financial sector rating; 6=high financial sector rating	World Bank	+
*IInteraction of IFFs*financial sector rating*			
Control variables			
Resource dependency	Share of value added in the mining and utilities sectors as percentage of total value added	UNCTAD Statistics	-
Gross capital formation	Gross capital formation as percentage of GDP	World Bank world governance indicators	+
Inflation	Change in annual consumer price index (percentage)	World Bank world governance indicators	-
Primary enrolment rate	Net enrolment rate in primary education	UNESCO	+
Natural disasters	Number of occurrences each year	Emergency events database	-

Negative values of capital flight estimates are deleted. In order to allow for an easier interpretation of the variables of interest, IFFs and the conditional effect on institutions (all independent variables) are centred at the mean. Endogeneity caused by omitted variable bias is partially controlled by the set of fixed effects and the control variables. Endogeneity from reverse causality is addressed in the first lag of all of the independent variables. Additional robustness checks with a higher lag are discussed in Slany et al. (2020). The equation is estimated using a fixed effects estimator, controlling for autocorrelation and correlation across panels (Driscoll-Kraay standard errors). The results with regard to a selection bias (lack of or biased estimate of IFFs, low quality of data and low capacity to collect data) are discussed in Slany et al. (2020). All relevant results with regard to different interaction terms are shown in table 9. The results cover the period 2000–2015 and are only reported for a sample of 24 countries.

Source: UNCTAD secretariat.

Table 9
Regression results for fixed-effects estimation: Total cross-sectoral productivity, 2000–2015

	1	2	3	4	5	6
	State fragility		Control of corruption		Financial sector rating	
	No interaction	Interaction with State fragility	No interaction	Interaction with control of corruption	No interaction	Interaction with financial sector rating
Capital flight (percentage of GDP)	-0.00164***	-0.000995	-0.00202***	-0.00247**	-0.00224***	-0.00216**
	(0.000540)	(0.000736)	(0.000571)	(0.000901)	(0.000594)	(0.000706)
State fragility	-0.0202**	-0.0193**				
	(0.00937)	(0.00899)				
Interaction of capital flight with State fragility		-0.000528**				
		(0.000202)				
Control of corruption			0.157***	0.164***		
			(0.0325)	(0.0333)		
Interaction of capital flight with control of corruption				0.00233		
				(0.00203)		
Financial sector rating					0.152*	0.153*
					(0.0765)	(0.0768)
Interaction of capital flight with financial sector rating						-0.000624
						(0.00165)
Share of mining and utilities value added (percentage of total)	-0.000739	-0.00104	-1.78e-05	0.000188	0.00271	0.00253
	(0.00139)	(0.00144)	(0.00167)	(0.00166)	(0.00349)	(0.00384)
Gross fixed capital formation (percentage of GDP)	0.00267*	0.00300**	0.00239**	0.00233*	0.00403**	0.00400*
	(0.00141)	(0.00138)	(0.00109)	(0.00109)	(0.00179)	(0.00183)
Inflation (percentage change)	-0.00223	-0.00275	-0.00103	-0.00128	-0.00450	-0.00449
	(0.00264)	(0.00245)	(0.00355)	(0.00331)	(0.00349)	(0.00346)
Primary enrolment rate	0.00198	0.000443	0.00275*	0.00233	0.000651	0.000867
	(0.00145)	(0.00156)	(0.00145)	(0.00146)	(0.00107)	(0.00123)

135

Table 9

Regression results for fixed-effects estimation: Total cross-sectoral productivity, 2000–2015 *(continuation)*

	1	2	3	4	5	6
	State fragility		Control of corruption		Financial sector rating	
	No interaction	Interaction with State fragility	No interaction	Interaction with control of corruption	No interaction	Interaction with financial sector rating
Number of natural disasters	-0.0137*	-0.0135**	-0.0120*	-0.0121*	-0.00803	-0.00793
	(0.00701)	(0.00632)	(0.00635)	(0.00607)	(0.00922)	(0.00906)
Constant	7.939***	7.921***	7.831***	7.824***	8.376***	8.374***
	(0.0248)	(0.0193)	(0.0332)	(0.0277)	(0.0140)	(0.0172)
Observations	1 393	1 393	1 344	1 344	784	784
Number of groups	168	168	168	168	126	126
Adjusted R-squared	0.626	0.630	0.585	0.587	0.378	0.378

Source: UNCTAD secretariat.
Note: All independent variables are centred at the mean; country sector and sector year fixed effects are always included; robust Driscoll-Kraay standard errors are shown in parentheses; *, ** and *** indicate a 10, 5 and 1 per cent significance level, respectively.

5.2 Illicit financial flows associated with inferior outcomes in sustainable development

Lower productive investments for structural transformation
The regression results for the impact of capital flight on the dependant variable of productivity, showing the inclusion of the proxies for institutional quality and the interaction terms, are provided in table 9. An interaction term captures the effect on a dependent variable of a change in the variable of interest and is dependent on the level of a third explanatory variable. The results suggest that the loss of productive investments through all-inclusive capital flight significantly reduces productivity across sectors in Africa. This finding is robust across model specifications and the inclusion of different interaction terms. Resource dependency, measured by the share of value added in the mining and utilities sectors as a share of total value added, itself does not influence the magnitude of the harmful impact of IFFs, although IFFs are most pronounced in the extractive industries (Slany et al., 2020). The institutional environment is more important in explaining the extent to which IFFs are harmful for investments in productive capacities. The lower the level of State fragility, the more stable is the overall business environment and the less is the direct negative impact of IFFs on productivity (table 9, column 2). Lower State fragility, better

control of corruption and a higher quality of financial sector institutions directly promote productivity through a reduction of the transaction costs of economic activities and higher levels of economic efficiency. A comparison with export underinvoicing as a proxy for IFFs, accounting for the trade channel of capital flight, shows that corruption plays an important role in explaining the harmful effects of IFFs on productivity because of bribery and smuggling (Slany et al., 2020).

IFFs have multiplier effects on labour productivity through the investment inhibiting channel and the Government spending channel. Higher levels of both capital formation and primary education significantly promote productivity. However, the control of corruption plays a stronger role in explaining productivity levels, indicated by a greater statistical significance. The regression is able to explain 40–60 per cent of the variation in labour productivity; the model therefore captures a significant share of labour productivity changes over time (for a discussion of the extent to which curbing IFFs can be directly associated with better outcomes in education and health, accelerating human capital, see chapter 6). Moreover, with regard to additional indicators of IFFs, criminal activity in extractive industries (proxied by the indicator on non-renewable resource crimes in the organized crime index of the Enhancing Africa's Ability to Counter Transnational Organized Crime) is also closely related to lower levels of gross fixed capital formation.

The empirical results also indicate that the number of natural disasters that negatively affect human and physical capital reduces productivity. The unsustainable exploitation of natural resources, linked to IFFs, can contribute to the scarcity and finiteness of resources, eroding the productive base of an economy (Nordhaus, 1974, 2014). The loss of capital through IFFs creates a further challenge for the mobilization of resources in countries in Africa with regard to adapting to climate change (chapter 6).

The coefficient estimates for capital flight are somewhat lower when the empirical findings are compared with the literature on IFFs in Africa (Ndiaye, 2009; Fofack and Ndikumana, 2010; Ndikumana, 2014). First, the absolute increase in labour productivity has been much less than GDP growth. Second, a relatively low estimated correlation suggests that private and public investments (capital accumulation and public spending) have been less able to translate into structural transformation (Grigoli and Kapsoli, 2013; Gaspar et al., 2019; Kharas and McArthur, 2019).

Economic sectors are also impacted differently by drivers of structural transformation and IFFs, depending on the initial level of productivity. For example, sectors in which access to capital is crucial to boosting value addition in productive processes, such as agriculture and manufacturing, depend more on financial stability, access to finance and stronger institutions to boost economic efficiency (section 5.5). The harmful impacts of IFFs are seen in the lack of private and public investment and are, on average, greater in lower productivity sectors such as agriculture and manufacturing (Usman and Arene, 2014; Slany et al., 2020).

Undermined progress on poverty reduction

Higher levels of output per worker are associated with poverty alleviation, in particular in the case of agricultural productivity. Productivity growth can reduce food prices, increase real wages and yield diversification as well as potential employment growth in the non-farm sector (Thirtle et al., 2001; Byerlee et al., 2005; Schneider and Gugerty, 2011; Asfaw et al., 2012).

IFFs imply an unequal distribution of wealth, which leads to higher levels of poverty and inequality (AfDB et al., 2012; Nkurunziza, 2014). Only a small share of the population has the power to engage in capital flight-related activities (AfDB et al., 2012). The negative impact on economic development arising from lower levels of investment and reduced Government spending is most keenly felt by the poor. The channels through which IFFs undermine efforts to reduce poverty mainly relate to a loss of Government revenue, leading to lower levels of expenditure on education, health and infrastructure, but also to negative externalities on labour productivity arising from export underinvoicing in extractive industries (section 5.5).

Higher levels of poverty are, on average, observed in countries with a higher level of resource dependency. In countries with high levels of capital flight, limited economic diversification and a large proportion of the population living below the poverty line (in the group of countries with high levels of capital flight, a poverty rate of 33 per cent of the population living below the poverty line of $1.90 per day is observed), only a small group benefit from natural resource extraction, which further drives inequality (AfDB et al., 2012; inequality measures between countries are not compared because of the lack of sufficient data). One of the key determinants as to whether natural resources are "a blessing or a curse" appears to be the efficacy of governance, in particular the existence of sufficiently good institutions, whereby the main channels of the curse are high levels of public and private consumption, low and often inefficient investment and an overvalued (strong) currency (Dutch disease; Collier and Goderis, 2008). However, the significant aspect is that all of these channels can be neutralized or ameliorated through appropriate policies and strategies and the resource curse can become a blessing through the deployment of resource rents towards enhancing productive capacities and diversifying the economy.

Some have questioned the resource curse hypothesis, highlighting examples of commodity exporting countries that have done well and stating that resource endowments and booms are not exogenous (Frankel, 2010). The existence of a potential resource curse has continued to be discussed, with some studies finding some positive linkages between mining activities and local development, yet also raising the point that this strongly depends on specific economic linkages to the regional economy.[63] For example, in Zambia, such linkages from mining companies can be confirmed, despite the absence of fiscal revenue or dividend income for the population of Zambia (Lippert, 2014). For example, von der Goltz and Barnwal (2019) show, for a sample of developing countries, that mining can boost local wealth, yet often have negative health and pollution-related impacts. Negative externalities arising from air pollution and water contamination may negatively affect agricultural productivity and increase inequalities, as not everyone can benefit from higher levels of investment (Amundsen, 2017). Among the most resource-dependent countries, Angola and Chad have experienced higher levels of inequality; the opposite is observed in Algeria, and Nigeria is also characterized by high levels of inequality between states (Amundsen, 2017). Onyele and Nwokocha (2016) show that there was a significantly negative impact of capital flight on poverty in Nigeria in 1986–2014. The persistent outflow of capital contributes to poor capital formation, lower levels of investment in infrastructure and domestic production that traps large parts of the economy in poverty. Taxation and redistribution policies can have a significant impact on the distribution of income (for the role of capital flight in domestic resource mobilization, see chapter 6).

5.3 How inclusive institutions can reduce the harmful impact of illicit financial flows

Section 5.2 provides evidence of how IFFs impact structural transformation through lower levels of productive investment. Domestic resources are one vehicle for sustainable development, yet good governance and inclusive institutions are crucial for deploying financial resources to meet development needs and boost the efficiency of financial resources. In this chapter, the models include institutional quality and interaction with IFFs, showing that capital flight harms economic development, in particular when institutional development and transparency are not adequate.

---

[63] Findings range from negative cross-country correlations between resource exports and economic development (Sachs and Warner, 1995; Sachs and Warner, 2001) to negative impacts on institutions and rent seeking (Mehlum et al., 2006; Besley and Persson, 2010) and evidence of increased conflict (Collier and Hoeffler, 2004), with all of the results subject to some endogeneity bias (Collier and Hoeffler, 2004).

Financial transparency and regulation

The findings detailed in this chapter suggest that improvements in financial stability and access to financial resources, proxied by the financial sector rating in CPIA subindex No. 7, promote higher productivity (table 9, columns 5 and 6). Strong financial sector institutions may make a country less vulnerable to the negative effects of capital flight. When companies and self-employed people such as farmers have better access to other financial resources, illicit financial outflows may be less of a constraint to capital accumulation and building productive capacity. Transparency in the financial sector and inclusive access to finance is key in tackling IFFs and economic development.

Financial transparency and regulation are a global multilateral task. For example, to increase financial transparency in States vulnerable to conflict, the United States has provisions that require companies to produce a compliance report on the use of minerals, namely, tin, tungsten, tantalum and gold, from the Democratic Republic of the Congo and any neighbouring countries.[64] However, companies often face difficulties in complying with these regulations and Parker and Vadheim (2017) and Stoop et al. (2018), for example, question whether the regulations have achieved their goals (chapter 4).

Financial transparency is important in monitoring money-laundering activities[65] and may be partially associated with higher levels of capital accumulation, proxied in the model by gross fixed capital formation. The anti-money-laundering initiative and the counter-financing of terrorism initiative, implemented by IMF,[66] require the preparation of suspicious transaction reports, used to detect, fight and prevent IFFs from criminal activities (Braun et al., 2016). The Intergovernmental Action Group against Money-Laundering in West Africa supports countries in Western Africa in complying with these initiatives. In 2018, countries in West Africa with a high number of suspicious transaction reports related to money-laundering, terrorism financing and other economic crimes (for example, Benin, Ghana and Nigeria) also tended to score highly on the index of non-renewable resource crimes (figure 13). Although such reports are considered an important identifier of criminal activity, of the 2,755 cases recorded in 2018, only 145 cases were juridically investigated (Intergovernmental Action Group against Money-Laundering in West Africa, 2018).

---

[64] See https://www.csis.org/analysis/dodd-frank-1502-and-congo-crisis.
[65] The ranking of a country on the anti-money-laundering index of Enhancing Africa's Ability to Counter Transnational Crime can serve as a proxy for the ability to monitor money-laundering.
[66] See https://www.imf.org/external/np/leg/amlcft/eng/.

Figure 13

Western Africa: Number of suspicious transaction reports received and non-renewable resource crimes, 2018

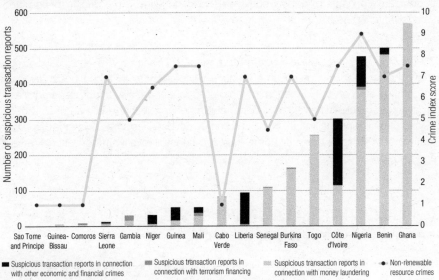

Source: UNCTAD calculations based on Intergovernmental Action Group against Money-Laundering in West Africa (2018) and the organized crime index of Enhancing Africa's Ability to Counter Transnational Crime.
Note: The index includes the incidence of illicit extraction, smuggling, mining and bunkering of a country's key resources, such as oil, gold, gas, diamonds, other gemstones and precious metals

Peace and security and control of corruption

Limited State capacity to ensure security and social and economic efficiency, as measured by the State fragility index, leaves a country highly vulnerable to capital flight from the proceeds of crime and money-laundering. Cobham and Janský (2018) provide evidence of how different indicators of IFFs impact State funds and State effectiveness. An increase in a country's fragility also lowers the level of productivity. Moreover, capital flight appears to be more detrimental to productivity at higher levels of State fragility (table 9, column 2).

Better control of corruption is associated with higher levels of productivity (table 9, columns 3 and 4). High levels of corruption create uncertainties about the institutional environment and reduce private investment, with harmful effects on productivity across sectors. Corruption has been a major factor in enabling capital to cross borders illicitly and, at the same time, IFFs allow for the proceeds of corruption to be hidden. The negative impact of IFFs on productivity channelled through corruption is greater in the trade-related channel of capital outflows (export underinvoicing) due to bribery and smuggling (chapter 2).

In order to fight corruption and promote transparency in extractive value chains, 23 countries in Africa have implemented the EITI initiative. The empirical findings show that greater transparency can reduce vulnerability to IFFs and boost levels of productivity (section 5.2). Freedom of the press, gender equality and transparency are, on average, greater when there is better control of corruption (Kaufman et al., 2005). Recent literature on the impact of the EITI framework provides some evidence of the fact that membership has a weakly positive effect on non-oil revenue mobilization (Mawejje and Sebudde, 2019).

5.4 Illicit financial flows and environmental performance in extractive sectors

The impact of extractive industries and natural resource dependency has been widely discussed, yet the association of IFFs with environmental performance has received little attention. The world atlas of illicit flows notes that environmental crime is an important dimension of IFFs, through the illicit mining of minerals and the smuggling of fuel. Estimates on overall environmental crime, defined as "activities that breach environmental legislation and cause significant harm or risk to the environment, human health or both" range from $110 billion to $281 billion annually, of which illegal mining totals $12 billion to $48 billion (International Criminal Police Organization et al., 2018).[67] Environmental crime inhibits the ability of countries to achieve environmental goals such as with regard to biodiversity and to achieve sustainable development.

IFFs are most prevalent in energy-intensive extractive industries. The link between the sustainable use of resources, energy security and the supply of food and water, called the water-energy-food nexus, is shown in figure 14 (World Economic Forum, 2011; Biggs et al., 2015). A large-scale extraction of natural resources requires prohibitive amounts of energy, which can lead to the depletion of capital stocks and increase climate-related risks (Biggs et al., 2015). Higher levels of energy production require greater amounts of water, which can impact water quality and availability. Water is an essential input to

---

[67] See https://www.europol.europa.eu/crime-areas-and-trends/crime-areas/environmental-crime.

agricultural production, and limited access to water and/or poor quality water threatens food security. Extractive industry activity is not only energy intensive but can also create pollution and contaminate the soil, groundwater and surface water (Aragón and Rud, 2016; Woodroffe and Grice, 2019). Poor environmental performance, in particular with regard to water quality, negatively impacts human health, agricultural output and food security.

Figure 14
The water-food-energy nexus in resource extraction

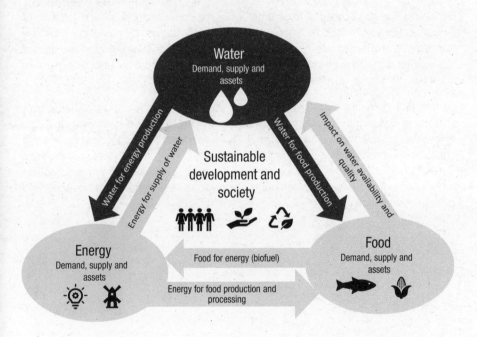

Source: UNCTAD secretariat based on World Economic Forum (2011) and Biggs et al. (2015).

Chapter 2 provides a measure of commodity-specific export underinvoicing that may be associated with the unsustainable use of natural resources. The relationship is twofold. A low level of enforcement and control of environmental standards may facilitate the illicit exploitation and trade of natural resources. In addition, illegal logging, for example, can increase the proceeds of crime and money-laundering, with often hazardous and severe environmental impacts (OECD, 2019c). Countries in which export underinvoicing in extractive industries is less pronounced perform better, on average, with regard to environmental policies, as shown by different indices for environmental performance.

The environmental performance index combines a number of indicators on environmental health and economic vitality, including the risk of exposure to air pollution and lead poisoning, which are closely related to mining activities.[68] In 2018, countries with higher values of commodity-specific export underinvoicing were associated with lower levels of environmental performance, for example, Angola, Benin and Burundi (figure 15). In contrast, as indicated by a simple linear regression of export underinvoicing and environmental sustainability (figure 15, blue line), countries with relatively higher scores in national environmental sustainability commitments and achievements had lower levels of commodity-specific export underinvoicing (figure 15, lower right-hand quadrant).

Stricter environmental standards and better enforcement of existing standards over time is proxied by the environmental sustainability rating in CPIA subindex No. 12.[69] IFFs are linked to environmental sustainability in two directions, as follows: inadequate environmental policies and weak enforcement of existing commitments may increase the incidence of illicit resource exploitation and capital outflows in extractive industries; and the loss of capital undermines public expenditures with regard to biodiversity and climate change mitigation.

---

[68] The construction of the index acknowledges the tensions between environmental health (a lower level of environmental risk exposure), which is positively influenced by higher income levels, and ecosystem vitality (biodiversity and sustainable resource use), which is negatively impacted by industrialization and urbanization; and notes that good governance institutions are a critical factor in the overall performance of sustainability (Wendling et al., 2018; see https://epi.envirocenter.yale.edu/epi-downloads).

[69] The subindex assesses the extent to which environmental policies foster the protection and sustainable use of natural resources and the management of pollution (see https://databank.worldbank.org/reports. aspx?source=country-policy-and-institutional-assessment).

Figure 15

Commodity-specific export underinvoicing and environmental performance index, 2018

(Percentage of gross domestic product)

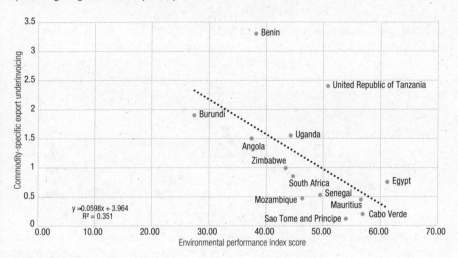

Source: UNCTAD calculations based on the environmental performance index.

Environmentally sustainable production processes that are less resource and energy intensive require a high level of investment and high-level technical capability. IFFs in the energy intensive mining and utilities sectors may divert capital away from countries in Africa in which financial resources are needed to reduce vulnerability to climate change through investments in climate change adaptation and mitigation (chapter 6). In addition, given limited energy supply in most countries in Africa, the high level of energy used in the mining sector may imply a lack of energy supply in other sectors. Energy represents 30–35 per cent of the operational costs of mining (Zharan K and Bongaerts, 2018; UNCTAD, 2019a). Negative externalities from the poor management of natural resources, causing competition over land use, greater air pollution, a high level of energy use and a loss of capital have adverse impacts across sectors and are particularly associated with negative outcomes in the agricultural sector (Aragón and Rud, 2016; Ouoba, 2018).

5.5 Poor resource management and negative externalities on agricultural productivity

The relatively low level of agricultural productivity in Africa is a major obstacle to poverty reduction, food security and gender equality (Nin-Pratt, 2015). Women farmers tend to have lower levels of productivity than men farmers due to lower levels of access to finance and agricultural inputs (UN-Women, 2019). Lack of access to land and access to capital are among the main reasons for why farmers are prevented from graduating from subsistence to higher productivity farming.

Countries with high IFFs
have only **1/3**
of the agriculture productivity levels
of countries with low IFFs

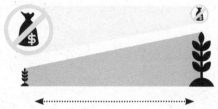

Poor management and an environmentally unsustainable use of natural resources negatively impacts agricultural productivity (Aragón and Rud, 2016). The simple mean comparison of agricultural productivity across countries by high versus low levels of capital flight suggests that countries with greater IFFs experience, on average, lower agricultural productivity (figure 16; for further econometric evidence of the negative relationship, see Slany et al., 2020). There are several channels related to environmental sustainability and access to capital, as follows:

(a)   Mismanaged extractive industries, in combination with low environmental standards, can have a negative impact on water resources and soil productivity and also increase air pollution. Aragón and Rud (2016), using household-level data, estimate that in Ghana, large-scale gold mining has reduced agricultural productivity by 40 per cent in areas closer to a mine. The effect is mainly driven by high levels of pollution rather than the lack of inputs. The statistically negative impact of export underinvoicing in extractive industries on agricultural productivity is correlated with overall resource dependency (Slany et al., 2020);

(b)   Negative externalities due to the activities of extractive industries that may impact agricultural productivity can arise from competition over land use, changes in land prices and expropriation (UNECA and African Union, 2011; Kotsadam and Tolonen, 2016; Ouoba, 2018). Furthermore, this may also be linked to a deterioration in peace and security (Berman et al., 2017);

(c)   The lack of investment and financial resources potentially reduces the availability of funds for agricultural activities. Inability to secure finance to raise productivity or innovate has been a major impediment to growth for smallholding farmers (McMillan et al., 2017);

(d)   Financial outflows that can lead to a devaluation in local currencies further increase the relative price of imports. Imported fertilizer as an important source of enhanced productivity is, as a consequence, relatively low. This may also be due to rising international fertilizer prices.

Figure 16
Africa: Agricultural sector labour productivity by estimated level of capital flight
(Constant 2010 dollars)

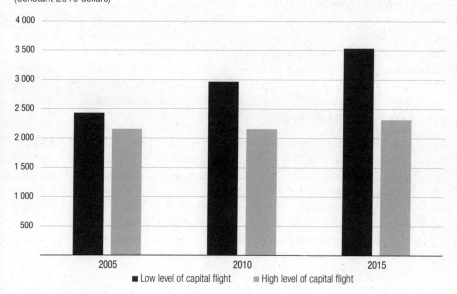

Source: UNCTAD calculations.
Note: For the classification of low and high levels of capital flight, see table 8; labour productivity is defined as value added divided by employment.

In order to restore used land that has been damaged by mining activities, referred to as site rehabilitation, sufficient financial resources must be set aside by domestic and international mining operators. If sound policies and regulations, including for rehabilitation, are lacking, companies may shift profits abroad through export underinvoicing, rather than investing in rehabilitation, which can severely impact agricultural productivity in the long term (International Finance Corporation, 2014). In some developing countries, regulations already require companies to provide a financial fund for site rehabilitation. With greater requirements for compensation schemes and other regulatory standards, companies in extractive industries are required to increase local savings and investments, which could potentially lower the amount of capital outflow. Tackling IFFs and investing in sustainable development could have a positive impact on and improve environmental performance.

5.6 Concluding remarks

This chapter provides evidence of the relationship between IFFs and sustainable development. It highlights the interlinkages between economic, institutional and environmental development and how curbing IFFs could enhance prospects for productivity increases in Africa. The empirical findings provide evidence of how capital flight can reduce productive investment, impacting institutional capacity to control corruption, weaken institutions with regard to environmental standards and lower financial sector ratings. Improving institutional settings can potentially boost productivity through efficiency increases. In addition, it can help reduce the marginal vulnerability of State development due to IFFs.

In light of the literature on environmental crime, the chapter further assesses the relationship between IFFs and environmental sustainability. Agricultural productivity, as output per worker, is particularly vulnerable to poor natural resource management and environmental performance. Countries with high levels of IFFs experience, on average, lower agricultural productivity. Higher estimated levels of export underinvoicing are negatively associated with lower levels of environmental sustainability. By contrast, good policies with regard to environmental sustainability and better enforcement of existing environmental laws can reduce the harmful effect of IFFs on productivity

Domestic resource mobilization and financing for the Sustainable Development Goals

One of the main motivations for tackling IFFs originates in concerns about the capacity of countries in Africa to raise sufficient revenue to invest in achieving the Sustainable Development Goals (Goal 17). This highlights the importance of increasing tax revenue, to help curb IFFs and recover stolen assets. The direct impact of IFFs on social development is mainly channelled through lower levels of domestic resource mobilization, which adversely affect capacity in Africa to finance the achievement of the Goals.

**CURBING
CAPITAL FLIGHT**
could contribute almost

50%

of the investment needed for
climate change adaptation
and mitigation
in Africa

PER PERSON, COUNTRIES WITH HIGH IFFs
spend

75%
on health

42%
on education

compared to countries with low IFFs

This chapter highlights some of the detrimental impacts of IFFs on social development and aims to provide a better understanding of the potential opportunity costs due to IFFs with regard to public finance and social expenditure in countries in Africa (Moore, 2012; Herkenrath, 2014; Carbonnier and de Cadena, 2015). Section 6.1 focuses on recent domestic resource mobilization. Sections 6.2 and 6.3 provide an assessment of Goals-related outcomes and how capital flight relates to the financing gap impeding the achievement of the Goals in Africa. The analysis is complemented by a discussion in section 6.4 on climate change-related financing needs in countries in Africa. Section 6.5 highlights the potential for multilateral cooperation in curbing IFFs and a case study of taxation in the gold mining industry. Section 6.6 provides a case study from Nigeria and discusses country-specific instruments for tackling IFFs. Section 6.7 summarizes the key points.

6.1 Illicit financial flows and Government revenue in Africa

The state of Government revenue

Governments in Africa raise taxes equivalent to 16 per cent of GDP, a figure that has been increasing steadily since 2010. Although the recent trend is upward, this increase largely reverses a decline that took place in the 1980s and 1990s, as structural adjustment reforms significantly reduced tax revenue from international trade. ODA and revenue from a boom in natural resources mitigated the reduction in tax revenue during this period. If natural resource revenue is included, countries in Africa raise taxes amounting to 18 per cent of GDP. Income generated only from resources (tax and non-tax) amounts to 10 per cent of GDP, on average, in countries in Africa (figure 17). As revenue from taxes on international trade has declined, there has been a broadening of the revenue base. Personal income tax and, significantly, value-added tax have both become more important sources of revenue in Africa, enough to offset the decline due to lower tariff revenue. Personal income tax has nonetheless doubled as a share of GDP in countries in Africa in the past two decades. According to data from ICTD and UNU-WIDER, corporate income tax amounts to around 3 per cent of GDP in nearly all countries of the world, including countries in Africa.

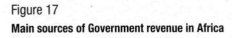

Figure 17

Main sources of Government revenue in Africa

(Percentage of gross domestic product)

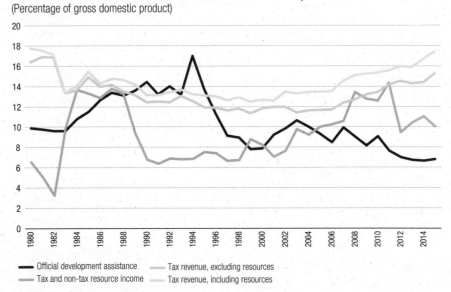

— Official development assistance   — Tax revenue, excluding resources
— Tax and non-tax resource income   — Tax revenue, including resources

Source: UNCTAD calculations based on the ICTD and UNU-WIDER government revenue database and the World Bank world development indicators.

Countries in Africa, as do other developing countries, raise less total revenue than developed countries (33 per cent of GDP). The only taxes with regard to which countries in Africa raise more as a share of GDP than OECD member countries are those related to international trade. The large share of the informal sector and the number of small-scale firms limit the ability to raise a large amount of taxes. In addition, a taxation system that favours MNEs that exploit natural resources and pay taxes in the countries in which their headquarters are located narrows the tax base, in particular in resource-dependent countries (UNCTAD, 2019a; chapter 3).

Tax revenue and illicit financial flows

Revenue losses from corporate tax avoidance are significant. Developing countries lose a greater share of their tax revenue in this way than do developed countries, yet their performance in raising corporate tax, measured as a share of GDP, is already similar to that of developed countries (Hearson, forthcoming). The level of corporate tax raised may be expected to increase because statutory corporate tax rates in developing countries tend to be higher yet, by contrast, effective rates may be lower than the statutory tax rates as a result of tax incentives. However, the diversity of the tax base in developing countries suggests that dramatically increasing the overall revenue raised will require efforts across a range of sources including, but not limited to, corporate income tax.

The magnitude of overall capital flight and estimated tax avoidance is compared by region in figure 18. Revenue loss from tax avoidance is on average highest in Middle Africa, Northern Africa and Eastern Africa (2.7 per cent of GDP), compared with Southern Africa (nearly 2 per cent of GDP) and Western Africa (2.3 per cent of GDP). Estimates of high levels of capital flight, ranging from a median of 10.3 per cent in Western Africa to 2.7 per cent in Northern Africa, are also associated with lower levels of domestic revenue. Some of the key challenges in increasing tax revenue relate to compliance with laws and administrative capacity to collect taxes. Across countries, there are large tax-related gaps, namely, the difference between potential and actual value-added tax, ranging from 92 per cent in the Central African Republic to 13 per cent in South Africa (UNECA, 2019). These gaps may arise due to the prevalence of special provisions or exemptions for value-added tax laws or limitations in administering the collection of value-added tax, including issues related to inefficiency, limited capacity, fraud and unreliable consumption data. Coulibaly and Gandhi (2018) estimate that improving tax efficiency and closing the average tax-related gap of 20 per cent could raise tax revenue by 3.9 per cent of GDP. Improving governance through the better control of corruption and effective enforcement of existing laws could largely reduce inefficiencies and could help raise an additional $110 billion per year. Total capital flight amounted to roughly $88.6 billion per year on average in 2013–2015.

Figure 18

Capital flight and revenue loss from tax avoidance, median by region, 2013–2015
(Percentage of gross domestic product)

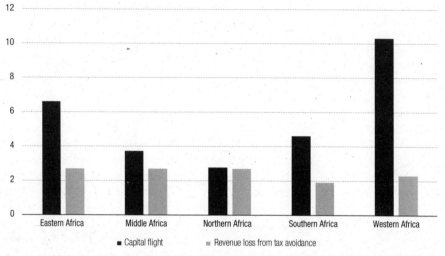

Source: UNCTAD calculations based on Cobham and Janský (2018) and Political Economy Research Institute database.

Note: Negative values are deleted; not all countries have data on capital flight and averages are therefore biased towards countries for which there is data available and high levels of capital flight; average values of capital flight as a percentage of GDP in 2013–2015 are 3.0 (Northern Africa), 5.9 (Southern Africa), 9.2 (Eastern Africa), 12.9 (Middle Africa) and 34.9 (Western Africa).

6.2 How illicit financial flows impair Goals-related outcomes

Efforts to increase domestic resource mobilization are crucial in achieving the Goals but are not a panacea. At the same time, it is equally important to increase the efficiency of spending on Goals-related outcomes. This section considers both with regard to estimates of capital flight and expenditure, in relation to current estimates of Goals-related financing needs. The estimates do not imply causality and are driven by national characteristics that affect both macroeconomic performance and institutional quality. Countries with high levels of IFFs spend 75 per cent of the amount that countries with relatively low levels of IFFs spend on per capita expenditure on health and, with regard to education, 42 per cent (figure 19). Restraints on higher levels of public spending are also determined by the overall composition of Government expenditure. According to the IMF government finance statistics, fragile States in particular may have higher levels of expenditure on defence and general public services, which includes debt service.[70] In 2015, countries in Africa spent, on average, $354 per capita on Goals-related outcomes, compared with a global average of around $3,000 per capita (Kharas and McArthur, 2019).

Figure 19
Africa: Total health and education expenditure, median by level of capital flight
(Dollars per capita)

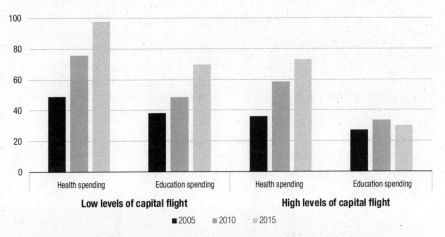

Source: UNCTAD calculations based on World Bank world development indicators.
Note: For the classification of low and high levels of capital flight, see table 8.

Can lower levels of expenditure be directly associated with inferior outcomes in health and education? In order to project what re-investing IFFs into social development could mean, the analysis uses available data on the under-5 mortality rate, current expenditure on health as a share of total Government expenditure and an estimated health-outcome elasticity of increases in public expenditure of -0.19 and -0.09 in countries in Africa from Makuta and O'Hare (2015). Achieving target 3.2, aimed at reducing under-5 mortality to at least as low as 25 per 1,000 live births, is strongly linked to other health indicators such as malnourishment. The best data coverage is also available for this variable.

In 2018, the under-5 mortality rate in countries with relatively high levels of capital flight was, on average, 59, down from 66 in 2015 (figure 20). Countries with lower levels of capital flight relative to GDP had the slightly lower rate of 55, down from 61 in 2015. Assuming an ambitious scenario in which the health sector is prioritized and curbed capital

[70] See https://data.imf.org/?sk=5804C5E1-0502-4672-BDCD-671BCDC565A9.

flight leads to increases in health expenditure as a share of GDP by the same amount, countries with high levels of capital flight could reduce the mortality rate to 20 and achieve target 3.2. In a more realistic scenario in which the share of health expenditure in total expenditure is kept constant at 6 per cent of Government revenue, there may be limited improvement through tackling capital flight and, due to low elasticities of health outcomes from spending increases, curbing capital flight would have only a marginal impact on reducing the mortality rate (Grigoli, 2015; Moulemvo, 2016; Manuel et al., 2018; Kharas and McArthur, 2019). Countries in Africa can come closer to achieving target 3.2 only if all curbed capital flight is devoted to health expenditure. For example, in the Congo, while social expenditure would largely increase from investing capital flight into the local economy, "it would enable only a marginal effect on the primary school competition rate [and] on the mortality rate of children below one year of age" (Moulemvo, 2016:121). A country-level comparison suggests that countries in Northern Africa and Southern Africa are on track to achieve target 3.2 and that Middle Africa and Western Africa are not.

Figure 20

Projections on achieving target 3.2, by level of capital flight and region

(Under-5 mortality per 1,000 live births)

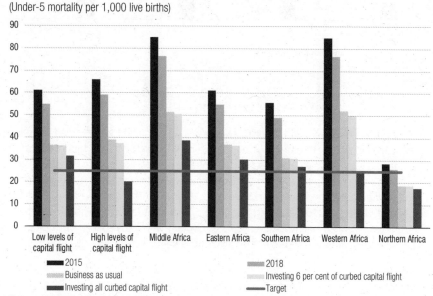

Source: UNCTAD calculations based on World Bank world development indicators.

Note: Average values of capital flight as a percentage of GDP in 2013–2015 are 3.0 (Northern Africa), 5.9 (Southern Africa), 9.2 (Eastern Africa), 12.9 (Middle Africa) and 34.9 (Western Africa); for the classification of low and high levels of capital flight, see table 8.

Compared with health-related outcomes, differences in education outcomes are less pronounced with regard to estimates of capital flight, which can be related to greater opportunity costs and the personal transaction costs of attending school (figure 21). Higher levels of investment in education and an improved quality of education benefit productivity through the acquisition of knowledge. In the analysis, the rate of enrolment in primary education serves as the proxy for educational performance, as the best data coverage over time and across countries is available for this variable. The possibility of acquiring an education strongly depends on household income levels and microeconomic factors not related to macroeconomic measures of capital flight. Higher levels of Government spending could, however, not only finance more teachers and schools but also provide for better infrastructure to allow for greater access to educational facilities.

Figure 21

Africa: Primary net enrolment rate, by level of capital flight

(Percentage of age group)

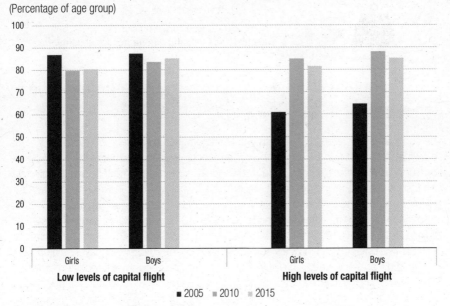

■ 2005   ■ 2010   ■ 2015

Source: UNCTAD calculations based on UNESCO Institute for Statistics data and World Bank world development indicators.
Note: UNESCO defines the net primary enrolment rate as the total number of students in the theoretical age group for a given level of education enrolled in that level, expressed as a percentage of the total population in that age group; for the classification of low and high levels of capital flight, see table 8.

Grigoli (2015) and Ihugba et al. (2019) note that increased expenditure on education is inefficiently deployed in many countries in Africa. Such inefficiencies tend to be more pronounced in countries with a large rural population and point to difficulties in accessing education due to poor rural infrastructure, high income inequalities and inefficient institutions. Lower levels of capital flight positively impact productivity levels and income generation and thereby lead to multiple opportunities to boost private and public investment in education. Public investment in early childhood education can also have positive impacts on productivity and gender equality because women as primary caregivers can spend more time engaging in higher paid work (Alfers, 2016).[71] Gender equality in education can also spur productivity growth and structural transformation and at higher levels improves institutional quality and, inter alia, potentially contributes to reducing IFFs (Klasen, 2002; Klasen and Lamanna, 2009; Trenczek, 2016).

Tax evasion and avoidance
particularly impacts women,
undermining efforts
to close the financing gap for gender equality.

6.3 Curbing illicit financial flows can help finance the achievement of the Goals

The comparison of levels of IFFs with Goals-related financing needs is based on Kharas and McArthur (2019), in which the multiplier effects of various dimensions – agriculture and rural development, health, education, social spending, infrastructure, biodiversity and justice – are considered and it is noted that none of the Goals can be treated in isolation. In order to estimate country-specific Goals-related financing needs, Kharas and McArthur (2019) build on existing literature for 10 different related sectors (UNCTAD, 2014b; UNESCO, 2015; Stenberg et al., 2017; Manuel et al., 2018) and the estimation of Goals-related spending in 2025 considers each country's spending level as a share of GDP in 2015 and applies a 1.13 multiplier relative to each country's forecasted growth in GDP per capita until 2025. In estimating financing needs in 2025, Kharas and McArthur (2019) acknowledge that higher levels of Goals-related spending do not guarantee greater outcomes. Inefficiencies due to poor access to health and education facilities and a lack of quality infrastructure can be addressed when public spending is distributed across various dimensions of the Goals. Therefore, using the term "needs gap" instead of "financing

---

[71] See https://www.brettonwoodsproject.org/2017/10/imf-gender-equality-labour/.

gap", Kharas and McArthur (2019) emphasize that there is not only a lack of finance but also a lack of efficiency. Section 6.2 addresses this aspect in the discussion of low efficiency in social expenditure for increasing health and education outcomes (for further empirical evidence of low spending efficiency in Africa, using cross-country estimates, see Grigoli and Kapsoli, 2013; Gaspar et al., 2019).

The estimate of the financing gap by region is compared with per capita estimates of capital flight (figure 22; estimates are displayed for illustrative purposes and should not be taken as exact numbers). The estimated Goals-related financing needs are greatest in Middle Africa ($289 per capita) and Western Africa ($274 per capita). In the Middle Africa region, the needs gap is highest in the Central African Republic and the Congo. Curbing the high level of capital flight across countries in Africa, estimated at $78 per capita, could close the financing gap by 33 per cent. In Southern Africa and Western Africa, in which the estimated capital flight relative to the population is greatest ($159 and $107 per capita, respectively), curbing capital flight could reduce the estimated Goals-related financing gap by 75 and 40 per cent, respectively.

Figure 22
Total financing gap and capital flight, by region, 2013–2015
(Dollars per capita)

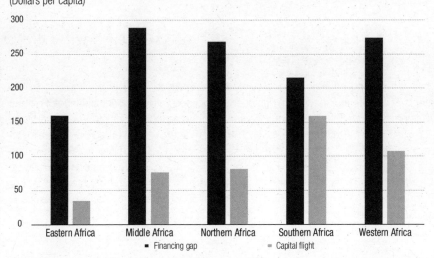

Source: UNCTAD calculations based on Kharas and McArthur (2019) and Political Economy Research Institute database.
Note: Regional estimates are derived from the sum of the Goals-related financing gap per region, divided by total regional population; only positive estimates are included.

The needs gap differs between countries even with similar per capita GDP and is subject to uncertainties due to data limitations. Significant differences arise from differences in income distribution, the local disease burden, soil suitability for agriculture, exposure to droughts and floods, migration patterns and ease of access to trading partners, among others (Kharas and McArthur, 2019). Country-specific estimates of Goals-related financing needs are required to yield a better understanding of the challenges and financial possibilities in each country. In some countries, the Goals have been directly integrated into national development plans, aimed at providing estimates on sectoral needs. For example, in Rwanda, the Goals and targets have been integrated into the National Strategy for Transformation 2017–2024 and sectoral initiatives have been implemented to estimate sectoral needs for achieving the strategy.

This section considers estimates of Goals-related spending by the public sector, yet the private sector also has a key role, as it both generates and can help ameliorate the negative effects of IFFs. Some MNEs have initiatives within value chains for investing in local human capital accumulation in health and education, as well as in infrastructure, to boost firm-level productivity.

6.4 Special case of climate change-related financing needs and illicit financial flows

Many developing countries, including countries in Africa, are highly vulnerable to the effects of climate change, which has been associated with a higher incidence of natural disasters. Occurrences of natural disasters and the associated costs have significantly increased since 2005 (figure 23). Such trends place a heavy burden on sustainable development in Africa. Total reported costs amounted to $796 million in 2018 and rose to $2.4 billion in 2019. Such costs do not include the long-term costs of lower levels of productivity. There is a significant negative effect from natural disasters on labour productivity in Africa (chapter 5). The mobilization of significant financial resources is required in each country to adapt to climate change.

Figure 23
Africa: Number of natural disasters and related costs
(Millions of dollars)

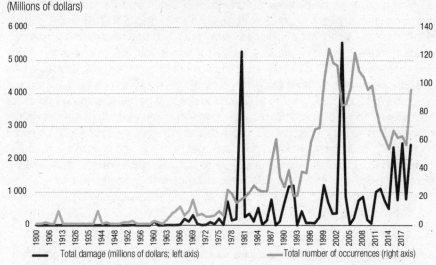

Total damage (millions of dollars; left axis) ━━━ Total number of occurrences (right axis)

Source: UNCTAD calculations based on the emergency events database, available at https://www.emdat.be/.
Note: Total estimated damages are calculated as a value of all damage and economic losses directly or indirectly related to each disaster; natural disasters (occurrences and costs per year) include all subgroups (climatological, geophysical, biological, hydrological and meteorological).

Measuring the level of financing needed to achieve the goals of the Paris Agreement is challenging. Kharas and McArthur (2019) refer to levels of required Government spending with regard to biodiversity conversation, which relates to environmental protection expenditure but does not include the costs of climate change mitigation and adaptation. In order to assess the magnitude of capital flight in relation to financing needs with regard to climate change mitigation and adaptation, two estimates are compared, namely, investment needs for climate change mitigation and adaptation; and capital flight.

Investment needs for climate change mitigation and adaption are based on intended nationally determined contributions under the Paris Agreement that have been submitted by all parties except Libya, although commitments vary widely with regard to details of the sectors targeted, whether commitments are conditional based on financial needs and whether financial needs have been quantified. With regard to sectoral coverage, 38 countries include commitments with regard to climate change mitigation or adaptation in agriculture and two countries, the Congo and Guinea, in mining (for a discussion of nationally determined contributions, see UNCTAD, 2019a). Financial needs in developing countries are rarely quantified at the country level, mainly due to uncertainties and difficulty in estimating the impact of climate change. For example, UNEP (2016) estimates that adaptation costs will be between $280 billion and $500 billion per year by 2050 and mitigation costs will be between $140 billion and $175 billion. Shimizu and Rocamora (2016) state that, to achieve climate change mitigation and adaptation by 2030, financing needs in sub-Saharan Africa are $2,457 billion or, on average, $60 billion per country, as well as an estimated $71 billion per country in North Africa and the Middle East, for a total of $356 billion. In sub-Saharan Africa, to meet the costs of climate change mitigation and adaptation by 2030, an estimated $153.5 billion needs to be mobilized each year. In per capita terms, this is around $152 per year until 2030 (country-specific estimates are not possible due to a lack of data and per capita estimates are only for comparative purposes and should not be interpreted as a population weighted estimate of financing needs). A comparison of estimated climate change-related financing needs with total annual capital flight in sub-Saharan Africa suggests that curbing capital flight could contribute almost 50 per cent to the total climate change mitigation and adaptation needs of countries in sub-Saharan Africa (figure 24).

Figure 24
Sub-Saharan Africa: Annual climate change-related finance needs by 2030 and capital flight
(Millions of dollars)

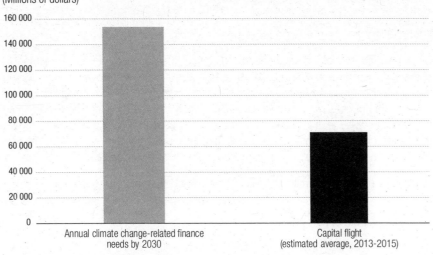

Source: UNCTAD calculations based on Shimizu and Rocamora (2016).
Note: The estimated financing needs of $2,457 billion in sub-Saharan Africa until 2030 are divided by 16 (2015–2030) to allow for a comparison with total annual capital flight.

6.5 Initiatives to promote domestic resource mobilization and tackle illicit financial flows

Multilateral cooperation for resource mobilization: Reclaiming stolen assets
Following the adoption by the General Assembly of resolution 58/4 and the United Nations Convention against Corruption in 2003, StAR was launched in 2007 as a joint project of UNODC and the World Bank (Ajayi and Ndikumana, 2014). Article 53(b) of the United Nations Convention against Corruption states that each State Party shall, in accordance with its domestic law, "take such measures as may be necessary to permit its courts to order those who have committed offences established in accordance with this Convention to pay compensation or damages to another State Party that has been harmed by such offences". Stolen assets are the proceeds of corruption and countries in Africa face significant legal and practical constraints in dealing with stolen assets and reclaiming them. Through StAR, a total of $1.53 billion has been recovered and returned to countries in Africa, but this amount is not significant, compared with the high level of capital flight.

Through the StAR initiative,
African countries have recovered
$1.5 billion
equivalent to only
0.5% of capital flight

As at January 2020, the database of the initiative reported 79 claims, yet only 17 countries had an ongoing or complete case; 22 cases have been completed but only 10 of these have resulted in stolen assets being reclaimed. The most active jurisdiction of asset recovery is Switzerland, followed by the United Kingdom and the United States. With regard to the number of cases and success with regard to recovered assets, at up to $1.48 billion in total, Nigeria is the most active country (figure 25).

Figure 25
Returned stolen assets, by country
(Sum in dollars)

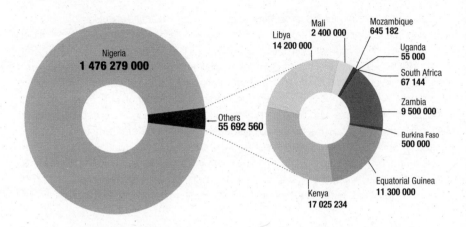

Source: UNCTAD calculations based on the database of StAR.

The database of StAR also shows the length of time required for proceedings; many cases opened before 2010 are still ongoing. In addition, the amount of assets returned are less than the assets that were frozen, indicating the level of difficulty in reclaiming stolen assets (Gray et al., 2014). This is closely related to the difficult process of gathering information and converting it into actionable evidence. The case that has seen the greatest amount reclaimed, namely, $723 million from Switzerland to Nigeria, provides an example of how returned assets can be used in sustainable development, as the agreement states that projects in the sectors of health, education, water, electricity and roads should be funded, with the World Bank responsible for monitoring.[72]

It is necessary to undertake multilateral efforts to strengthen asset recovery policies, standards and actions. StAR is the leading institution in the global network of initiatives, which include the Asset Recovery Inter-Agency Network for Southern Africa, founded in 2009; the Asset Recovery Inter-Agency Network for East Africa, founded in 2013;

---

[72] See https://www.worldbank.org/en/news/factsheet/2017/12/04/world-bank-monitoring-of-repatriated-abacha-funds.

and the Asset Recovery Inter-Agency Network for West Africa, founded in 2014. The secretariat of the Camden Asset Recovery Inter-Agency Network and the European Union Agency for Law Enforcement Cooperation organize annual meetings for training, exchanging knowledge and sharing information (for further information on other regional networks and the Global Focal Point Network on Asset Recovery, see StAR, 2019). Current projects to tackle IFFs show how greater cooperation in capacity-building can facilitate stolen asset recovery. For example, as part of a German Corporation for International Cooperation project, multi-agency teams were established to conduct financial investigations in Kenya and, in 2016–2017, the national Ethics and Anti-Corruption Commission was able to increase its conviction rate by over 50 per cent and recovered a total of $27 million in stolen assets in the first four months of 2019 alone.[73] This approach has been promoted within the Asset Recovery Inter-Agency Network for East Africa.

The need for more effective tax regimes: Taxation in the gold mining industry
As noted, most trade-related IFFs originate in extractive industries, in which rents are created from the exploitation and export of non-renewable resources that constitute national assets, and the extractive sector is typically dominated by MNEs. This section discusses in more detail effective tax regimes for extractive industries to estimate the share of rents that should be collected by Governments, building on the discussion of tax regulatory frameworks and domestic legislation for extractive industries (chapter 4). This section uses data from a database developed by the Fondation pour les Études et Recherches sur le Développement to highlight the special case of taxation in the gold mining industry in Africa, which allows for an evaluation of revenue losses from unequal taxation resulting from exemptions, with data for 21 countries.[74] The database combines all of the juridical sources from the selected countries, to provide the legal framework for tax regimes applicable to gold mining companies, including mining codes, implementation decrees, tax laws, annual finance laws and other fiscal laws. This permits the calculation of the share of rents that should theoretically go to the State, using a cash flow model developed by the IMF. The average effective tax rate is simulated for different representative mining projects, depending on the grade of a mine and the gold selling price. The mining tax rate may decrease with the grade of a mine, which indicates that there is a regressive tax rate applied to companies when a mining project is more profitable (Laporte et al., 2017). In 2018, countries

[73] See https://www.giz.de/en/worldwide/39748.html.
[74] Benin, Burkina Faso, Chad, Congo, Côte d'Ivoire, Cameroon, Democratic Republic of the Congo, Gabon, Ghana, Guinea, Kenya, Madagascar, Mali, Mauritania, Niger, Nigeria, Senegal, Sierra Leone, South Africa, United Republic of Tanzania, Zimbabwe.

with the most regressive tax schemes for high-grade mines included Gabon, Mali, the Niger, Nigeria and Zimbabwe. A regressive tax scheme tends to increase inequalities when companies with low levels of profitability pay higher taxes and are less able to allocate an appropriate amount to economic savings and investments, worsening the economic situation (UNECA, 2019). Widespread tax evasion not only exacerbates the challenge faced by tax authorities in Africa in providing basic public services, but also limits efforts to address urgent institutional reforms (Prichard and Bentum, 2009; Herkenrath, 2014; chapter 4). Kharas and McArthur (2019) state that greater royalties from mineral taxation would potentially reduce profit shifting and IFFs, but such tax benefits might still be low in terms of scale. In contrast, corporate income taxes that are higher in terms of scale could also have negative effects on tax revenue due to incentive diversion.

Figure 26 shows the composition of the average effective tax rate and the relative importance of different tax elements based on legal origins. The elements include profit-based taxes such as dividend and interest tax (a withholding tax), corporate income tax (an income tax on the profits of companies) and resource rent tax (a direct tax on net cash flow that is rarely applied due to the difficulty of administration); free State equity (shareholding); and production-based taxes such as mining royalty (an ad valorem tax on the value of the ore when it is sold or exported) and fixed and ground fees (usually related to the surface and/or property of a mine). The most common profit-based instrument is corporate income tax and almost all production-based instruments involve mining royalties (Laporte et al., 2017; Bouterige et al., 2019). Since 2002, French-speaking countries have tended to rely more on mining royalties and free State equity than corporate income tax (Bouterige et al., 2019). The definition of mining royalties varies across countries and this may also result in different tax rates, which can be fixed, variable or progressive; most countries apply a fixed rate (Laporte et al., 2017). In contrast, English-speaking countries remain reliant on corporate income tax, with almost no use of free State equity until 2017.

Figure 26
Africa: Composition of average effective tax rates
(Share of total average effective tax rate)

(a) English-speaking countries

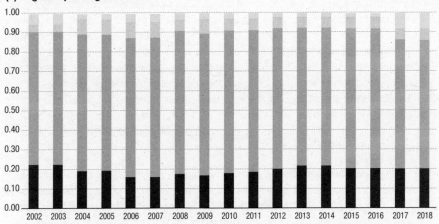

■ Mining royalties and fixed and ground fees ■ Corporate income and resource rent tax ■ Dividend and interest tax ■ Free State equity

(b) French-speaking countries

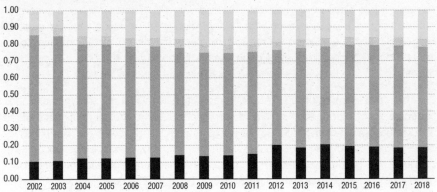

■ Mining royalties and fixed and ground fees ■ Corporate income and resource rent tax ■ Dividend and interest tax ■ Free State equity

Source: UNCTAD calculations based on the Fondation pour les Études et Recherches sur le Développement database
Note: The average effective tax rate shown is that for high-grade mines and a gold selling price of $1,400 per ounce.

The use of corporate income tax has been declining, indicating that profit-based taxes have been less utilized, which could be a missed opportunity if the demand for gold increases. Corporate income tax is sometimes accompanied by a minimum tax to provide a floor for State revenue, mostly in French-speaking countries (the minimum tax applies to turnover and ranged between 0.5 and 2.5 per cent in 2018; Bouterige et al., 2019). Applied corporate income taxes range from 20 to 35 per cent in the 21 countries included in the database. Moreover, a tax on mineral resource rents could be a neutral tax, yet clearly defining the tax base has been a challenge (Bouterige et al., 2019). Based on the data, in 2018, countries using mining royalties the most as a share of all instruments (with levels above 20 per cent) were the Niger, Zimbabwe, Mali, Mauritania and Senegal. With the exception of Zimbabwe, these are French-speaking countries in Western Africa. However, some countries, although they are also French-speaking countries, have had the lowest shares (less than 10 per cent) of mining royalties, such as Benin, Chad and Madagascar.

In 2016–2018, the average effective tax rate remained relatively stable in most countries, but decreased in Cameroon and increased in Chad, the Democratic Republic of the Congo, Kenya, Senegal, South Africa and the United Republic of Tanzania. The increases in some of these countries can be attributed to the implementation of different tax rates. For example, the Democratic Republic of the Congo, Senegal, Sierra Leone and the United Republic of Tanzania increased mining royalties and Chad, the Democratic Republic of the Congo and Sierra Leone introduced a tax on mineral resource rents. The use of free State equity has also increased, to allow States increased access to information and to receive direct dividends. Among the countries with the greatest increases in average effective tax rates, mining acts have been implemented in Chad, the Democratic Republic of the Congo, Kenya, Senegal and the United Republic of Tanzania.

With the establishment of AfCFTA, the complexities of mining tax schemes and their treatment are of importance for many Governments in Africa. Greater continental efforts through national implementation of AMV are required, to address the complexity of different aspects of taxing extractive industries and how tax reforms and mining contracts may be improved in order to increase the average effective tax rate and boost Government revenue from natural resources (chapter 3). The selection of profit-based or production-based instruments also remains a complex issue, which requires further research beyond the scope of this report. The public finances of States are likely more affected by the business cycle if tax schemes are less regressive. To maximize commodity revenues for the financing of sustainable development, Governments could use profit-based instruments such as corporate income tax during periods of sustained economic expansion. When commodity prices are high, using profit-based instruments is beneficial to Governments because they can capture a greater share of the financial gain. However, when commodity prices are low, it may be better for Governments to use production-based instruments such as mining royalties. The taxation of profits, particularly in extractive industries, has the disadvantage that the tax base can be manipulated in numerous ways. Therefore, Governments could consider, for example, shifting to taxation methods that are easier to administer.

6.6 Policy instruments to tackle illicit financial flows: Case study from Nigeria

Nigeria has the largest economy in Africa and is the main oil producer. The experience of Nigeria presents an interesting case study of how tackling IFFs can improve domestic resource mobilization and promote sustainable development. The country remains highly dependent on oil, which, during most of the past 55 years of its commercial exploitation, has contributed around 80 per cent of annual export earnings and 70 per cent of the revenue of the Government, with little variation over the years. However, this oil wealth has long been associated with internal conflicts, Dutch disease, environmental damage and economic mismanagement (Sala-i-Martin and Subramanian, 2003). By 2015, following a significant drop in oil prices, Nigeria was facing one of the worst economic crises in its history. Nigeria accounts for an estimated 46 per cent of the capital flight on the continent, based on average estimates for 2013–2015, and 80 per cent of the capital flight in Western Africa. In 2013, estimated capital flight peaked at $45.5 billion, or roughly $264 per capita. Capital flight in Nigeria increased to roughly 8.8 per cent of GDP in 2013 and, in 2015, despite some reduction, mainly due to declining oil prices, capital flight remained a significant problem (figure 27). In the same period, capital formation fell continuously, from 34 per cent of GDP to 15 per cent of GDP in 2015 and Government revenue declined from 27.6 per cent of GDP to 7.6 per cent of GDP. This trend presents a challenge in promoting structural transformation, economic diversification and social development and in reducing poverty and inequalities. Capital flight may be negatively associated with economic growth in the long term (Uguru, 2016; Ogbonnaya and Ogechuckwu, 2017). The literature on IFFs and economic development in Nigeria provides a diverse picture, yet there are more studies identifying a significantly negative impact (Olatunji and Oloye, 2015; Uguru, 2016; Ogbonnaya and Ogechuckwu, 2017; Nelson et al., 2018).

Figure 27
Nigeria: Capital flight, capital formation and Government revenue
(Percentage of gross domestic product)

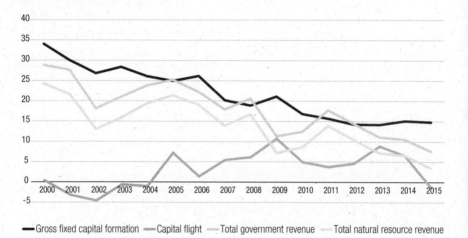

Source: UNCTAD calculations based on UNCTAD statistics, the ICTD and UNU-WIDER government revenue database and the Political Economy Research Institute database.

Tackling IFFs in Nigeria has been a challenge. Significant efforts have been made to implement the necessary instruments to increase transparency in the oil and gas sector and to deal with IFFs.

Extractive industry transparency initiative

In 2003, Nigeria was the first country in Africa to join EITI and, in 2007, through an act of the National Assembly, established the Nigeria Extractive Industries Transparency Initiative as a transparency, accountability and anti-corruption initiative. The Initiative, an agency of the Government, is an autonomous self-accounting body with statutory reporting requirements to the President and the National Assembly. It is led by an executive secretary and overseen by a chair of the board. The Initiative is built on the principles and criteria of EITI and Nigeria was the first English-speaking country in Africa to be awarded satisfactory status by the board of EITI for implementing all requirements in the latter's standards. The Initiative has been effective in strengthening public debate and promoting policy options with regard to signing bonuses, unpaid royalties and the theft of crude oil and refined products. It has identified $9.8 billion owed to the Government, of which $2.4 billion has been recovered through the efforts of the Initiative (Tan and Faundez, 2017). The Initiative discloses data on the allocation of licences, the administration of oil and gas subnational transfers and crude oil sales within the Nigerian National Petroleum Corporation.

In February 2019, the report of the Board of EITI on the second validation of Nigeria cited information and data from reports of the Nigeria Extractive Industries Transparency Initiative and noted that around $3 billion in mostly illicit payments had been recovered.[75] In 2020, the Nigeria Extractive Industries Transparency Initiative established a beneficial ownership register for extractive industries, which shows the beneficial owners of assets in the oil and gas sector; through the portal, the Government aims to track the origin of such funds that leave the country and to detect tax evasion, cases of money-laundering and drug financing.[76] However, the registry may not have the desired comprehensive effect, as the legal instruments to make it enforceable may be lacking. A petroleum industry bill that seeks to unbundle the Nigerian National Petroleum Corporation and make the oil and gas sector more transparent may be passed by the National Assembly in 2020, attracting more investment into the sector.[77]

Tax reforms and financial transparency

Nigeria has signed international treaties and agreements to tackle international tax avoidance and evasion. In 2017, Nigeria signed the Multilateral Convention to Implement Treaty-Related Measures to Prevent Base Erosion and Profit Shifting and the Common Reporting Standard Multilateral Competent Authority Agreement, which forms part of the Multilateral Convention on Mutual Administrative Assistance in Tax Matters. Several national initiatives have been undertaken by the Government to tackle IFFs, as follows:

(a) Finance Act 2020, which came into force on 13 January and replaces Finance Act No. 30 of 1999 and is aimed at improving sustainable increases in public revenue and ensuring that tax law provisions are consistent with national tax policy objectives;

(b) Voluntary assets and income declaration scheme, introduced in 2017 to give defaulting taxpayers an opportunity to fulfil outstanding tax obligations from 2011–2016 without liability to penalty, interest or criminal prosecution. The limited success of this scheme can be related to the inadequate structure and processes for collaboration between regional tax authorities and the absence of a credible threat of post-amnesty proceedings;[78]

[75] See https://eiti.org/news/nigeria-uses-eiti-to-reform-industry-build-accountability.
[76] See https://allafrica.com/stories/201912090630.html.
[77] See www.oilreviewafrica.com/events/event-news/nigeria-set-to-take-leap-forward-on-petroleum-industry-bill.
[78] See https://www.accaglobal.com/an/en/member/member/accounting-business/2019/06/insights/tax-amnesty.html.

(c)   Bank verification number scheme, introduced by the Central Bank in 2014 as a centralized biometric identification system for account holders that provides a unique identity for each account holder and protects the accounts of customers from unauthorized access; as at 2 February 2020, more than 40 million account holders had obtained bank verification numbers.[79] The Government stated that it would freeze the accounts of those that did not obtain numbers.[80] The scheme has achieved a high rate of compliance by account holders.

Another notable development in tackling IFFs through financial transparency is the improved inter-agency relationship between regulators, which has led to the recovery of funds for the Government. For example, the Economic and Financial Crimes Commission has established a dedicated tax investigation team to work with the Federal Inland Revenue Services and the Revenue Mobilization Allocation and Fiscal Commission in identifying and prosecuting tax evaders. The partnership involves information-sharing to arrest and prosecute tax defaulters in the country, in particular following the conclusion of the voluntary assets and income declaration scheme.[81] Collaborative efforts by the agencies in the collection of outstanding value-added tax and withholding taxes led to the recovery of ₦28 billion ($77.56 million) in 2017.[82]

Nigeria is among the most active countries in recovering stolen assets and engaging with multilateral stakeholders. Practical steps taken by the Government to address IFFs include the signing of bilateral agreements with Switzerland, the United Arab Emirates, the United Kingdom and the United States for the return of stolen assets, with the expectation that such bilateral agreements will act as a disincentive to the sending of illicit funds from Nigeria to these countries.[83] The outcomes will depend in part on how the agreements are enforced and whether they dissuade corrupt practices. Most recently, the Government announced that it will reclaim $311 million in misappropriated funds, as part of an agreement with the United States and Jersey.[84] The Financial Intelligence Unit is a central independent body within the Central Bank, responsible for requesting, receiving, analysing and disseminating financial intelligence reports, and its efforts have led to improvement in detecting cases of money-laundering, financing related to terrorism and other economic and financial crimes.[85]

---

[79]   See https://nibss-plc.com.ng/bvn/.
[80]   See https://www.theafricancourier.de/africa/nigeria-federal-government-to-freeze-all-bank-accounts-without-bvn/.
[81]   See https://thenationonlineng.net/firs-teams-up-with-efcc-to-tackle-high-profile-tax-defaulters/.
[82]   See https://punchng.com/efcc-recovers-n28bn-from-tax-defaulters/.
[83]   See https://infotrustng.com/combatting-corruption-and-illicit-financial-flows-in-nigeria/.
[84]   See https://nairametrics.com/2020/01/30/fg-to-repatriate-fresh-321million-abacha-loot-to-be-spent-on-road-construction/.
[85]   See https://placng.org/wp/wp-content/uploads/2018/07/Nigerian-Financial-Intelligence-Unit-Act-2018.pdf.

According to reports by the Intergovernmental Action Group against Money-Laundering in West Africa on the implementation of the IMF Anti-Money-Laundering and Combating the Financing of Terrorism framework by member States, Nigeria has made notable progress, improved financial institutions and enhanced supervision, yet deficiencies remain in countering the financing of terrorism, investigating suspicious transaction reports, freezing funds or other property and convicting the financing of terrorism. Money-laundering is mostly conducted through investment in real estate and cross-border cash movements and through bank transactions. In 2014, the Financial Intelligence Unit received 1,442 suspicious transaction reports, but there were a low number of prosecutions (Intergovernmental Action Group against Money-Laundering in West Africa, 2014). Of the 477 cases detected through the suspicious transaction reports in 2018, 383 were related to money-laundering; none of the cases reported were processed (Intergovernmental Action Group against Money-Laundering in West Africa, 2018).

Federal Ministry of Finance whistle-blower programme

Nigeria introduced a whistle-blower policy in 2016 through an executive order of the Government, which seeks to incentivize the exposure of stolen funds in Nigeria and abroad and to reward whistle-blowers for tips that lead to the successful recovery of illicit funds (Gholami and Salihu, 2019). This anti-corruption programme encourages the voluntary disclosure to the Federal Ministry of Finance of information about fraud, bribery, financial misconduct and any other form of corruption or theft. Anyone responsible for providing the Government with information that directly leads to the return of stolen or concealed public funds or assets may be entitled to anywhere between 2.5 and 5.0 per cent of the amount recovered. The policy has led to some success.[86] As at November 2019, the Government had saved ₦594 billion ($1.65 billion) through the policy since its introduction.[87]

However, the policy has fallen short of its full potential given the absence of a statutory framework (Onuegbulam, 2017). Whistle-blowers are concerned about the risk of retaliation from employers if they provide information to the Government (Ifejika, 2018). The Government states that it deals with reports in a confidential manner and discourages retaliation against whistle-blowers, yet there is no legal protection for whistle-blowers (Omojola, 2019). In addition, there are no established penalties for those who retaliate against whistle-blowers and some have lost their jobs after reporting to the Government.[88] Citizens are reluctant to become involved due to the lack of effective protection, as whistle-

[86] See https://www.premiumtimesng.com/news/top-news/240339-whistle-blower-policy-one-buharis-main-achievements-adeosun.html.
[87] See https://allafrica.com/stories/201911220105.html.
[88] See https://www.pplaaf.org/country/nigeria.html.

blowers have faced a number of reprisals, ranging from suspension from work and the withholding of salaries and promotions to threats to their lives. To address such issues, in 2017, the African Centre for Media and Information Literacy launched Corruption Anonymous, a platform for protecting whistle-blowers and expanding the frontiers of whistleblowing as a mechanism for tackling corruption in Nigeria.

Despite recent efforts and improvements, in 2019, Nigeria ranked as the twelfth most vulnerable country on the Basel anti-money-laundering index with regard to money-laundering and terrorist financing risks, out of 125 countries, down from a rank of sixteenth in 2018. Nigeria has made some improvements, and progress is observed in voice and accountability, as efforts to increase transparency and freedom of speech seem to have been fruitful and, after 2014, some progress was observed in the control of corruption, yet Nigeria ranks among the lowest in political stability. Security is crucial to socioeconomic development and insurgency and terrorist activities remain serious threats (Yagboyaju and Akinola, 2019).

6.7 Concluding remarks

Countries in Africa raise less tax revenue as a share of GDP than countries in other regions. In light of high levels of capital flight and tax avoidance and a relatively high level of dependence on corporate income tax, countries in Africa face significant limitations in increasing tax bases. The significant financing gap related to achieving the Sustainable Development Goals cannot be closed solely through Government revenue. Within the context of AfCFTA and regional economic communities, enhanced regional cooperation among countries in Africa could potentially have an important role in raising greater tax revenue from extractive industries in the following ways:

(a) Intra-African coordination and cooperation by tax administrations and cross-border prosecution of crimes;

(b) Elaboration of regional positions and proposals as a contribution to global tax cooperation efforts in existing institutional contexts;

(c) Joint programmes and mutual support towards capacity-building in tax administration and enforcement.

The comparison in this chapter between estimated financing needs and levels of capital flight suggests that countries in Africa could contribute to closing the financing gap by tackling IFFs. An integrated financing approach targeting several sectors, considering multiplier effects across various Goals and related targets, is crucial to increasing the effectiveness of current spending on health and education. Country-specific evaluations are necessary in order to identify national Goals-related needs, financial requirements and leakages, to improve spending efficiency. In order to tackle IFFs, transparency in extractive industries, multilateral cooperation in stolen asset recovery, financial investigations and dealing with corruption have shown some measure of successful results.

Chapter 7
Recommendations

Analytical contributions are provided in this report on tackling IFFs at the multilateral, regional and domestic levels in Africa. Addressing this topic falls within the mandate of UNCTAD and reflects its history as the institution that was first established to promote fairer rules of engagement in international trade for exporters of primary commodities. This is important to underline, setting out on the road to the fifteenth session of the United Nations Conference on Trade and Development in Barbados.

10-POINT PLAN
FOR TACKLING IFFs IN AFRICA

SOCIAL

ECONOMIC

- Engage on IFFs and ethics

- Protect civil society, whistle-blowers and journalists

- Devote more resources to the recovery of stolen assets

- Strengthen African engagement in international taxation reform

- Intensify the fight against corruption and money-laundering

2030
Agenda for
Sustainable
Development

- Strengthen domestic regulatory frameworks

- Rekindle trust in multilateralism to fight IFFs

- Invest in data infrastructure and transparency

- Engage MNEs on taxation and sustainable development

- Invest in research on IFFs and climate change

INSTITUTIONS

ENVIRONMENT

Analytically, the main focus of the report has been on understanding the breadth of channels and mechanisms through which IFFs are conducted and how they affect sustainable development in Africa. In this chapter, recommendations are made for the multilateral community and for African Governments. The recommendations build on the landmark Mbeki report (UNECA, 2015) and aim at contributing to global efforts to address key issues highlighted in the recent General Assembly resolution, on the promotion of international cooperation to combat IFFs, and strengthening good practices on the return of assets to foster sustainable development and the achievement of the 2030 Agenda for Sustainable Development.

7.1 Main findings

Critically, in the report, it is argued that IFFs are a shared responsibility between developed and developing countries, at the core of multilateralism. Illicit financial flows appear to be large, but irrespective of their scale, they need to be tackled as a significant impediment to the economic development of Africa. High levels of illicit financial flows, as shown by the prevalence of misinvoicing and capital flight, indicate that many African Governments do not benefit from a significant portion of their international trade transactions and experience significant losses in capital and foreign exchange. Key stylized facts, resulting from the models developed in this report, include:

- In Africa, IFFs linked to the export of primary extractive resources were estimated as being as high as $40 billion in 2015 and $278 billion (cumulative) over the past decade. This is a conservative estimate and should be taken as a lower bound (chapter 2).

- In Africa, on average, extractive export underinvoicing is equivalent to 16 per cent of merchandise exports of the commodities covered in this report (chapter 2).

- Generally, commodities show a similar pattern across countries: at 77 per cent, gold is the largest contributor in total African extractive export underinvoicing, and other precious metals, such as platinum (6 per cent) and diamonds (12 per cent), are also persistent positive contributors (chapter 2).

- Capital flight, which captures trade misinvoicing and other balance-of-payment transactions, was estimated at $88.6 billion, on average, during 2013–2015 or around 3.7 per cent of African GDP. Capital flight between 2000–2015 was

$836 billion or 2.6 per cent of GDP. In terms of capital flight, the largest positive absolute outliers are Nigeria ($41 billion), Egypt ($17.5 billion) and South Africa ($14.1 billion), on average, during 2013–2015.

- IFFs are negatively associated with target 8.2, on achieving higher levels of economic productivity. As indicated by the econometric analysis in chapter 5, labour productivity, as an indicator for productive capacity, is inversely related to IFFs. This suggests that an increase in illicit financial flows is decreasing domestic productive capacity. The effect is likely however to be low in Africa due to the continent's relatively low productive growth.

- As IFFs were found to be negatively correlated to poor financial sector regulation, improvement in the latter could stimulate productivity growth. It could also reduce capital outflow through stronger compliance with the Financial Action Task Force and capacity to track financial flows.

- Curbing IFFs is an avenue for improved prospects for environmental, social and economic development in Africa. The impact of IFFs on environmental sustainability has hardly been assessed in the literature, although environmental damage in the extractives sector is a major concern. Countries with high IFFs may be more vulnerable to climate change and appear to have the lowest ability to leverage investments for health, education and climate change mitigation.

- Public expenditure reductions potentially have unequal impacts on gender, especially if cuts affect health and education expenditures. A negative impact of IFFs is prevalent where tax evasion affects the allocation of scarce government funds and reduces fiscal expenditure on public services where women and youth are the majority beneficiaries.

7.2 Strengthen African engagement in international taxation reform

Aim for an intergovernmental African position on Organization for Economic Cooperation and Development/Group of 20 proposals
African countries should aim for an intergovernmental position to be reflected given the current momentum for international taxation reforms. The negotiations on the second wave of the OECD secretariat proposals on the BEPS initiative, labelled pillar one and

pillar two, began in early 2019 and are planned to be held through multiple meetings until the end of 2020. In effect, though the consultation process is inclusive, as of March 2020, there were no official statements on an intergovernmental African position on the negotiation of the Inclusive Framework, raising questions about the extent of engagement of the African members in the Inclusive Framework.

The proposal for a unified approach under pillar one primarily focuses on the reallocation of taxing rights to market jurisdictions. On scope, the document explicitly states that "the approach covers highly digital business models but goes wider – broadly focusing on consumer-facing businesses with further work to be carried out on scope and carve-outs. Extractive industries are assumed to be out of the scope" (OECD, 2019d: 5). The proposal further reiterates that sectors "such as commodities and extractives" (labelled as such) would be carved out (OECD, 2019d: 7). While acknowledging the need for an "administrable" simplification of the arm's length principle, especially for emerging and developing countries, the proposal also stipulates that "it would retain the current rules based on the arm's length principle in cases where they are widely regarded as working as intended, but would introduce formula-based solutions in situations where tensions have increased – notably because of the digitalization of the economy" (OECD, 2019d: 6). The pillar two proposal, titled Global Anti-Base Erosion Proposal, focuses on tax challenges arising from the digitalization of the economy (OECD, 2019e).

As they stand, with their focus on tax and digitalization, these proposals do not sufficiently address the specific loopholes that limit the taxation rights of African countries. This point is also corroborated by the Independent Commission for the Reform of International Corporate Taxation for developing countries at large.[89] The gaps in the OECD proposals underline the urgency of strong political leadership from Africa on international taxation reforms.

Increase space for other multilateral engagement and alternative views

Unless the underlying distribution of taxing rights is addressed, African countries will continue to be vulnerable to significant revenue losses. African interests must be defended in spaces where the concerns of countries are fully heard and where alternative and substantiated views on international corporate taxation can be elaborated. As shown in the report, the dichotomy that arises from the location of real economic activity and of permanent establishment status lies at the core of the perceived injustices. At the global level, it could be argued that only the United Nations, with its near universal

---

[89] See https://www.icrict.com/press-release/2020/2/13/the-oecds-proposed-reform-will-fail-to-generate-meaningful-additional-tax-revenue-especially-for-developing-countries.

membership and democratic structure, can provide a truly global tax body (Independent Commission for the Reform of International Corporate Taxation, 2018). Reflecting these concerns, as of March 2020, OECD proposals did not fully address the priorities of African countries. Other spaces where taxation issues are discussed include the Platform for Collaboration on Tax, a joint effort of the IMF, World Bank, OECD and the United Nations, and in academic research undertaken by entities supporting the interests of developing countries.

Africa's voice in these spaces is carried by ATAF. From 25 members at the time of its creation in 2009 to 38 members in November 2019, ATAF has increasingly gained legitimacy and capacity in defending African interests on taxation issues. Building on the expertise of ATAF representatives, political leadership at the highest level is needed to take Africa's multilateral engagement on proposals for international reforms to the next level. African academic institutions should receive greater support in developing Africa-based taxation expertise and data-sharing initiatives, such as that initiated by the multi-disciplinary team of the Committee on Fiscal Studies.[90] Ezenagu (2019), for instance, puts forward proposals for taxation reforms that would be more appropriate to the administrative capacity of African countries.

Finally, concerns that parallel negotiations on trade in digital services at WTO, where African countries are more united, may constrain their taxing rights (James, 2019) warrant further research and feature on a new agenda on international trade and taxation issues.

Review tax treaties and aim for more taxing rights
Countries should avoid signing tax treaties that impinge greatly on taxing rights. Tax treaties that include anti-abuse clauses make tax avoidance through treaty shopping harder. For example, withholding taxes is a strong frontline protection against profit-shifting for countries with limited administrative capacity (see chapter 3 and Hearson, forthcoming). In this regard, countries should not accept having them lowered to a very large degree by tax treaties. Similarly, tax treaties often exempt some types of income earned in the source State from taxation in that State altogether (see, for example, chapter 4, box 4, on tax dispute on capital gains). Countries should assess the costs of removing these taxing rights against the expected benefits in FDI attraction. Current evidence does not support the argument on expected benefits in FDI attraction (chapter 4). In this regard, it is recommended that African countries keep and expand their taxing rights.

[90] See https://cfs.uonbi.ac.ke/.

Countries are best protected by a combination of specific anti-abuse rules, applying to individual treaty clauses, and a general anti-abuse rule, covering the whole treaty, along with an anti-avoidance rule in domestic law. Such clauses are becoming increasingly common and are now found in the main model treaties used for negotiations (chapter 4).

Considering the continent's revenue losses to tax havens and secrecy-based jurisdictions (chapter 3), African countries should be among those leading the charge to pressure tax havens to sign treaties with all countries. Progress on this is critical, taking account of the evidence that tax havens complied with the minimum number of tax treaties by signing many treaties among themselves (Zucman, 2014). Zucman's findings further suggest that the signing of bilateral treaties providing for exchange of bank information led to a relocation of bank deposits between tax havens rather than to significant repatriations of funds, concluding that "the least compliant havens have attracted new clients, while the most compliant ones have lost some, leaving roughly unchanged the total amount of wealth managed offshore".

Make tax competition consistent with protocols of the African Continental Free Trade Area

In addition to such engagement, African countries need to incorporate international taxation matters in relevant regional and continental initiatives. Without a harmonized taxation system at the continental level, African countries should aim at defining ways to curtail tax competition. Related efforts should include context-based analytical assessments of the welfare effects of falling headline tax rates and the proliferation of tax incentives across the continent and leverage the AfCFTA as a platform to avoid a race to the bottom. UNCTAD continues provision of technical assistance, in the context of ongoing and forthcoming negotiations on phase 2 of the AfCFTA on investment, competition and intellectual property rights.

More critically, African countries should build on the formidable negotiations forum that the continent has established in the context of AfCFTA. For now, the governance mechanisms of negotiations include senior officials of trade ministries and ministers of trade. There should be mechanisms to bridge the gap between these trade-focused groups, ministers of finance and the High-Level Panel on Illicit Financial Flows, while considering negotiations on phase 2. These include the protocols on investment, competition and intellectual property rights. There are also proposals either to give ATAF an intergovernmental dimension or, as argued by other authors, for the creation of an African tax body (Ezenagu, 2019).

7.3 Intensify the fight against corruption and money-laundering

Support and scale up African anti-money-laundering initiatives
In addition to being party to global level initiatives and subject to third-party legislation on corruption and money-laundering, African countries should collectively intensify initiatives to fight these problems on the continent. In this regard, good practices, such as those of the Intergovernmental Action Group against Money-Laundering in West Africa, should be supported and further developed. Initially created by the Economic Community of West African States in 2000 to combat the financing of terrorist groups, over the years, the Intergovernmental Action Group has provided assessment and capacity-building on anti-money-laundering and counter-financing of terrorism of countries located in the region. The initiative has improved countries' capacity to identify suspicious transactions related to anti-money-laundering. However, performance varies greatly across countries, with some countries showing worse results than in previous years. In addition, assessment reports show that successful records of financial intelligence units of tracking suspicious transactions are poorly matched by adequate action of investigative authorities (Intergovernmental Action Group against Money-Laundering in West Africa, 2014; ibid., 2018). This highlights the need for all African countries to strengthen their capacity to track suspicious transactions and ensure that the latter are properly investigated.

In the same vein, the African Peer Review Mechanism – a voluntary self-monitoring mechanism for African Union member states – should be given a clear mandate to devise binding legislative tools to address matters related to corruption and money-laundering. In addition to cross border movements of funding, the increase in the prevalence of real-estate transactions in money-laundering methods in West Africa (Intergovernmental Action Group against Money-Laundering in West Africa, 2018), for instance, warrants greater capacity in identifying and regulating specific characteristics of anti-money-laundering at the continental level.

7.4 Invest in data infrastructure and transparency (including gendered data)

Good data play a critical role in allowing an effective fight against IFFs. The vast literature on profit-shifting by MNEs of the United States, for example, is due to United States data being particularly good (Zucman, 2019). As custodian agencies of Sustainable Development Goal indicator 16.4.1 (total value of inward and outward IFFs, in current United States dollars), UNODC and UNCTAD are leading the work to develop a statistical methodology and a measurement standard to estimate IFFs. This will be critical to developing a set of methodological guidelines that can be used at the national and international levels to estimate the total value specified by the indicator. In the context of analysing the impact of IFFs on African communities and the Sustainable Development Goals, more and better data on gender in financial services, trade, employment and taxation are required to generate new insights to inform policy interventions on the economic, social and environmental pillars of sustainable development.

Collect better and greater trade data

Alleviation of trade misinvoicing in African countries will require better trade data, including where appropriate at the gender-disaggregated level, for risk-exposure analysis and enhanced regional cooperation on common reporting standards for firm-level tax and commercial information. Critically, there needs to be a greater exchange of information on trade data with trade partners to identify anomalies and discrepancies that warrant further investigation. The analysis in chapter 2 aimed at the detection of systemic customs fraud linked to the export of primary extractive resources shows that, while the analysis of macro trade data can be a useful indicator, it has its limitations. Such limitations can be addressed with better access to and use of transaction-level trade data. This could be done through several platforms, including the UNCTAD Mineral Output Statistical Evaluation System.[91] This platform has already shown its beneficial results at the domestic level. In the case of Zambia, for example, the System allows for mineral value chain monitoring of the country's mineral exports. It includes a mineral production reporting and export permit tool, which allows companies to submit their mandatory monthly production export and request export permits online. This replaces the manual process which required companies to travel to Lusaka. Since its implementation in 2017, the Mineral Output Statistical Evaluation System delivered the following for the Government of Zambia:

- Revenue recuperation due to the System audits reached around $910,000 (since 2018).

- Grading of minerals is more accurate.

- Zambia started collecting non-mineral-related royalties.

- Penalties collected have reached more than $50,000 (since 2018).

- Export permits increased 66 per cent after implementation of the System.

Governments with access to transaction-level trade data can also implement a price-filter analysis. The price-filter analysis relies on a single country's transaction-level data by product and compares the value/price on a customs invoice to past prices or the free market price, to distinguish between normal and abnormal pricing (Carbonnier and Mehrotra, 2019). Though both the partner-country trade gap and price filter methods have their flaws, they can be useful and intuitive tools for customs fraud detection. Global Financial Integrity has also developed its "GFTrade" tool based on the interquartile range price filter method, which provides direct feedback to customs officials. Prototype software based on blockchain technology is also being developed to provide transparency of global trade logistics and global value chains (McDaniel and Norberg, 2019) from which Africa may usefully benefit in tackling trade misinvoicing. African countries should also look to leverage the provisions of article 12 of the WTO Agreement on Trade Facilitation[92] to improve the exchange of trade data to better monitor IFFs.

Accelerate progress on tax reporting

African Governments should explore innovative means of utilizing voluntary tax reporting, for revenue mobilization purposes, and strengthen related initiatives. In this regard, increased goodwill of MNEs to voluntarily publish their tax data for global reporting initiatives should be matched by similar enthusiasm for public country-by-country reporting (Tax Justice Network, 2020).

7.5 Strengthen regulatory frameworks at the domestic level through a multi-track approach

Design a specific policy and regulatory framework on illicit financial flows

The prevalence of IFFs in Africa and the diversity in their origins, mechanisms and impact are such that countries should have their own national policy framework for combating these flows. Such a framework should include a full assessment of existing policies and legislation across countries.

In addition, countries should strengthen the set of standard legislations and regulatory measures of relevance to IFFs. These should also include strengthening of local judiciary

[92] See https://www.tfafacility.org/article-12.

systems, increase capacity for dispute resolution and consider adoption of UNCTAD reforms on international investment agreements (UNCTAD, 2018).

Domesticate the African Mining Vision

The AMV was adopted by the African Union in 2009 to promote equitable, broad-based development through prudent exploitation and utilization of the continent's mineral wealth. The AMV aims at setting the path to broad-based sustainable growth and socioeconomic development, including through the adoption of global norms for the equitable governance of the natural resources sector. Its objectives are far-reaching and actions of intervention are spread across six major areas, namely: improving the quality of geological data, as a bargaining tool for fairer deals and more equitable returns on mining investments; contract negotiation capacity; resource governance; management of mineral wealth; tackling infrastructure constraints; and recognizing the developmental role of artisanal and small-scale mining.

Considering the comprehensive coverage of the AMV, countries should use existing guidelines to enact policies and regulations aimed at its implementation (UNECA, 2014). The expectations of mineral-rich countries in Africa on development benefits from the extractive sector are justified by its status as a key generator of export revenues and foreign exchange in mineral-exporting economies. To fulfil these expectations and considering the magnitude of the extractive sector as a source of IFFs, African countries should build on lessons learned from past engagement on international commodity governance (chapter 4).

Establish cross-institutional collaboration

The multi-dimensional nature of IFFs requires coordinated multi-institutional actions at the domestic level. In this regard, a combination of interministerial actions and strengthening of lead institutions in the fight against tax avoidance, money-laundering and other crimes is needed. On interministerial actions, in Nigeria, for example, the interministerial committee on anti-money-laundering is co-chaired by the ministers of finance, justice and interior, to fulfil its mandate of national cooperation and coordination of other national stakeholders (Intergovernmental Action Group against Money-Laundering in West Africa, 2018). As part of this cross-institutional collaboration, a pre-evaluation workshop gathered more than 20 agencies, including regulators, tax authorities, financial and non-financial institutions.

Efforts to invest in strengthening the capacity of the range of domestic institutions involved in monitoring, identifying and regulating IFFs should be supported. National financial intelligence units are public agencies that play a central role as receivers of notifications about large and/or suspicious transactions. They analyse and forward them to law enforcement bodies, where appropriate. Tax authorities should have the capacity to scrutinize company contracts and accounts and tax declarations, identify accurate product prices and combat abusive practices. Customs authorities are responsible for monitoring and evaluating the veracity of export and import prices and quantities, while judicial authorities are responsible for law enforcement. Designing policies and laws to combat IFFs is the responsibility of policymakers. This underscores the importance of supporting institutional capacity-building across all levels of national authorities in Africa.

More specifically, in many African countries, tax authorities are in urgent need of additional resources and capacity-building activities and training. They are understaffed and lack the required expertise. For example, in a survey of Nigeria, 62 per cent of firms expressed concern with the lack of knowledge of tax authorities during audits (AndersenTax, 2019). To build its domestic capacity in revenue collection, an issue for many African countries, as shown in chapter 4, the Government of the United Republic of Tanzania, for example, invested resources in auditing capacity after a decade of private investment in the mining sector and persistently low revenue collection. It created the Tanzania Mineral Audit Agency as an autonomous agency under its Ministry of Energy and Minerals in 2009. The Agency is responsible for monitoring the quality and quantity of minerals that mining companies produce and export, and for conducting financial audits. Owing to sufficient funding and staffing, including tax experts, environmental scientists, information technology analysts, engineers and gemmologists, the Tanzania Mineral Audit Agency has been successful in financial auditing and addressing transfer pricing. Thanks to the effective cooperation between the Tanzania Revenue Authority and the Tanzania Mineral Audit Agency, tax authorities collected an additional $65 million in corporate income tax between 2009 and 2015, accounting for about 7 per cent of mining tax receipts in that period (Redhead, 2017).

7.6 Devote more resources to the recovery of stolen assets

The slow pace of progress on the recovery of stolen assets emphasizes the need for greater capacity at the domestic and international levels to quicken the pace for recovery in the context of the Decade for Action. In this regard, the international community should provide greater support to initiatives, such as StAR of the World Bank–UNODC, in efforts to offer practical advice on the strategy and management of asset recovery efforts. The multilateral nature of the organizations leading the project makes it an appropriate platform for dialogue and collaboration on specific cases as they often involve different jurisdictions, spanning developed and developing countries.

7.7 Protect and support civil society organizations, whistle-blowers and investigative journalists

Civil society organizations, whistle-blowers and investigative journalists have played a critical role in revealing the magnitude of IFFs and the mechanisms that support them in Africa and beyond. As part of this chain of actors, transparency initiatives must be encouraged and supported, including in their use of new technologies. In the United Republic of Tanzania, for example, Jamii Forums is a news and social networking platform for whistle-blowing and has exposed several national corruption scandals. It has more than 3 million Facebook followers and, as of 2015, had 28 million mobile subscribers.[93] In Kenya, the Action for Transparency application, produced by Transparency International–Kenya, provides information on money promised for school and hospital funding versus money actually disbursed.[94]

At the global level, organizations such as Open Ownership and the Financial Transparency Coalition work on ending secrecy legislation that is holding back full beneficial ownership transparency. In addition to the central leading role played by ATAF on taxation issues, other organizations such as the Tax Justice Network–Africa also provide capacity-building initiatives. For instance, in 2015 the Tax Justice Network successfully campaigned for renegotiating the tax treaty of Zambia with Ireland and the Netherlands to include anti-abuse provisions. Similarly, Action Aid and partners have been vigorously supporting campaigners in Malawi in their fight against existing tax treaties, which made use of the country's weak taxation frameworks, with loopholes that offered ample opportunities for tax avoidance.[95]

Whistle-blowing comes with enormous risks, but as it can serve the public interest, it should be protected by law. For instance, in October 2019, the Council of Ministers of the European Union adopted new rules to ensure that member countries change domestic laws to protect insiders who report on misconduct. The impact of the Panama papers

[93]   See https://thelawmarket.com/anti-corruption-and-anti-bribery-apps-2dc578efad6e.
[94]   See https://actionfortransparency.org/.
[95]   See https://mwnation.com/treasury-reviewing-double-taxation-pacts/.

on the design of legislation illustrates the powerful reach of whistle-blowing. Following the press revelations, many countries, including Australia and France, for example, established parliamentary commissions to consider actions to tackle tax evasion. Some of these measures were the catalysts for legislative change on multinational anti-avoidance laws. It is estimated, for instance, that, as a result, AU$7 billion a year in sales by 44 MNEs will be returned to Australia.[96]

7.8 Build bridges between multinational enterprises, taxation and the 2030 Agenda for Sustainable Development

Curbing illicit financial flows for structural transformation
African countries should communicate to all actors, including MNEs, the primacy of the role that curbing IFFs would play in the financing of sustainable development on the continent (chapter 5). In addition, Governments and MNEs should focus on constructive engagement with a view to eliminating tax evasion and curbing tax avoidance. Doing so is likely to help addressing the effects of IFFs on economic, political and social stability in Africa and beyond (introduction and chapter 1).

Include taxation… in environmental, social and governance reporting
The review of the international corporate taxation regime and of the associated theoretical economic literature on MNEs and transfer pricing provides justification that they provide for developmentally harmful tax practices among MNEs (chapter 3). Furthermore, international guiding principles for better practices are soft laws and not legally binding, while domestic regulatory systems are insufficiently developed. As a result, African countries have become dependent on mining contracts and case-specific community development agreements (chapter 4). Considering increasing interest in sustainability issues among private sector stakeholders, African countries should build on the rise in environmental, social and governance reporting to identify links between these reporting mechanisms and the objectives of curbing IFFs for sustainable development. Progress in the Sustainable Stock Exchanges Initiative shows that there is an increasing number of stock exchanges mandating environmental, social and governance disclosure for listed companies, which provides good grounds for pioneering greater consideration

---

[96] See www.theguardian.com/australia-news/2019/apr/05/tax-office-may-apply-40-tax-against-multinationals-for-diverting-profits.

of taxation components.[97] In this regard, efforts to strengthen the capacities of Governments to measure and monitor private-sector contribution to the 2030 Agenda for Sustainable Development should be encouraged. Examples of such efforts include an UNCTAD project on enabling policy frameworks for enterprise sustainability and Sustainable Development Goal reporting in Africa and Latin America.[98] Other examples include transparency pacts between Governments and the private sector, such as Publish What You Pay.[99]

Pioneering of the inclusion of taxation in environmental, social and governance reporting should be done with recognition of the mixed performance of private-sector engagement in sustainability initiatives. Key business analysts, recognize, for example, that neither the 2008 crisis nor corporate social responsibility nor sustainability initiatives have changed the current status quo of a world "where people and the planet are in the service of business. Business, in turn, is in the service of finance, and finance is primarily in the service of itself" (Saïd Business School, 2019).

7.9 Invest in research to account for links between illicit financial flows, environmental sustainability and climate change

The review of sources of IFFs highlights the magnitude of environmentally harmful activities, such as illegal logging, illegal fishing, illegal mining and illegal waste trafficking (chapter 1). Similarly, as shown in the report's empirical analysis (chapter 5), negative externalities from the extractive industry not only have ripple effects on other sectors, such as agriculture, but also affect critical water resources at the community level. However, challenges related to the dominant features of established economic models of structural transformation and data constraints make it difficult to establish causality links in econometric models on IFFs and sustainable development.

In light of these findings, there should be greater research on integrating the value of environmental damage caused by dominant sources of illicit flows into ongoing initiatives on the measurement of IFFs. Such efforts could allow African Governments to strengthen the case for bridging negotiation agendas on curbing IFFs and making claims on climate finance (chapter 5).

---

[97] For more information on the Sustainable Stock Exchanges Initiative, see https://sseinitiative.org/.
[98] See https://unctad.org/en/Pages/DIAE/ISAR/UNDA-Project-1819H.aspx.
[99] See https://www.pwyp.org/.

7.10 Rekindle trust in multilateralism through tangible actions in the fight against illicit financial flows

Support multilateralism to curb illegal financial flows at the Economic and Social Council and United Nations General Assembly

Multilateralism implies use of international cooperation to attempt to find solutions to transnational problems. Globalization has brought a new set of challenges to multilateralism, as globalization is associated with the spread of problems of a transnational dimension and involving many non-State actors (Newman et al., eds., 2006). IFFs are part of such transnational problems and, hence, could be resolved through multilateral means. Such efforts could benefit from lessons learned from multilateral engagement on the international commodity agenda (chapter 4).

Beyond the multiple United Nations resolutions on IFFs, recent initiatives, such as a joint initiative to establish a high-level panel on financial accountability, transparency and integrity under the President of the General Assembly and the President of the Economic and Social Council, provide hope of moving towards more concrete action on addressing IFFs through inclusive multilateral action. The joint initiative is set in the context of the Decade of Action to help promote faster progress towards achieving the 2030 Agenda on Sustainable Development. The panel is expected to produce an interim report in July 2020 and a final report with recommendations in January 2021.

Walk the talk: Put more resources in international cooperation on illicit financial flows

More resources are needed to amplify the work of various agencies and donors to enhance the capacity of local revenue authorities in Africa. OECD and UNDP, for example, set up the Tax Inspectors Without Borders programme which delivers technical assistance predominantly on auditing multinational taxpayers. The programme claims to have contributed to an additional $220 million in tax revenue in Africa between 2013 and 2018 (OECD and UNDP, 2018). Several donors committed to double their aid for tax capacity-building between 2015 and 2020 through the Addis Tax Initiative. This initiative aims at increasing the volume and quality of technical assistance to enhance domestic resource mobilization in partner countries. Furthermore, OECD along with three countries (Germany, Italy and Kenya) launched the pilot programme, Africa Academy for Tax and Financial Crime Investigation, at the Group of 20 Africa Conference held in Berlin in June 2017. This programme will cover all aspects of conducting and managing financial investigations, including complex money-laundering and the role of tax investigators, investigative techniques, identifying, freezing and recovering assets, managing international investigations and specialty topics, such as value added tax/goods and services tax fraud.

Enhance cooperation on tackling illicit financial flows in relation to achieving health-related Sustainable Development Goals and building resilience to shocks

The current coronavirus disease outbreak is first and foremost a health crisis. Second, it is an impediment to progress towards achieving health-related Sustainable Development Goals. Third, it is fast becoming the starting point of a global economic and financial crisis with severe economic and social consequences for the world's poorest countries. Tackling the crisis will not be easy in a context of inadequate funds for health services globally (Glied and Miller, 2015), including in Africa. Though the first to reach a global scale, this coronavirus outbreak is not the first health crisis with international dimensions. The Ebola crisis triggered debates on the creation of an international health emergency fund (Ooms and Hammond, 2014). The Ebola crisis also underlined the critical role that global governance for health could play, through partnership and financial and technical assistance and the reduction of health inequalities (Waris and Latif, 2015). These issues remain relevant today and missed opportunities in fiscal revenue due to tax avoidance and tax evasion should be addressed (ibid.). Although the current epidemic appears to affect fewer women than men, it is likely that women will be affected by the socioeconomic impact of the crisis as core care providers for their families. Achievement of the Sustainable Development Goals in the context of the emerging implications of the current coronavirus disease crisis will likely be more challenging and depend critically on the capacity of African countries to tackle IFFs, which hinder the mobilization of sufficient resources to finance development.

Identify win–win solutions

In addition to engagement through existing mechanisms of information exchange, despite difficulties in avoiding tax competition, developing countries can jointly decide to identify common areas of interest. These could include, for example, an agreement not to give tax incentives on profits, but rather provide incentives on actual business activities based on a set of indicators pertaining to the real economy. Similarly, greater resources could be pooled in undertaking capacity-building initiatives with dual objectives: (a) exchanges of experiences and capacity and (b) coalition building in areas of common interest.

In this regard, African countries could engage in exchanges on negotiation tactics on the combination of multiple agendas with other countries from the global South. The

Republic of Korea, for example, successfully used a request for the restitution of cultural heritage as part of their leverage in 2010 in bilateral trade negotiations with France (Savoy, 2018).[100]

However, given differing economic interests, achieving consensus on tackling IFFs among countries will be difficult, but should be fully considered. Indeed, small island developing States, for example, feature prominently among the top list of financial secrecy jurisdictions. In such cases, finding common areas of interest would be more challenging and would necessitate greater investments in preliminary assessments of areas of convergence and compromise.

7.11 Engage on illicit financial flows and ethics

In many ways, addressing IFFs is a matter of ethics. These ethical concerns are recognized by all stakeholders, including MNEs, involved in the fight against IFFs.[101] In the African context, the emphasis on ethics is apparent in the African Peer Review Mechanism. The Mechanism's methodology includes a corporate governance thematic area and an objective on ensuring ethical conduct within organizations, which seeks to address corruption and illicit flow of funds (African Union Commission, 2019: 130).

7.12 Conclusion

The role of multilateralism in reducing the harm from IFFs and encouraging greater participation by African countries in global governance on the matter is clear. The expectation is that the recommendations drawn from the analysis presented in this report will strengthen the policy approaches taken to tackle the incidence and impact of IFFs. A stronger and more resilient Africa, as a result, would be better situated to tackle the current coronavirus disease pandemic, as well as future challenges.

---

[100] See https://www.theartnewspaper.com/comment/the-restitution-revolution-begins.
[101] The World Bank, for example, states that "a potentially more far-reaching development is the increased attention the private sector is paying to adherence to ethical compliance across all business practices. Increased legal and market risks connected to being associated with corruption have spurred firms to establish ethics and compliance programmes" (available at https://www.worldbank.org/en/topic/financialsector/brief/illicit-financial-flows-iffs).

References

Abotsi KE, Galizzi P and Herklotz A (2015). Wildlife crime and degradation in Africa: An analysis of the current crisis and prospects for a secure future. *Fordham Environmental Law Review*. 27(3):394–441.

ActionAid (2016). Mistreated: The tax treaties that are depriving the world's poorest countries of vital revenue. Available at https://actionaid.org/sites/default/files/actionaid_-_mistreated_tax_treaties_report_-_feb_2016.pdf.

Adam S (2019). How high are our taxes, and where does the money come from? Briefing Note 259. The Institute for Fiscal Studies.

AfDB, OECD, UNDP and UNECA (2012). *African Economic Outlook 2012: Promoting Youth Employment*. OECD Publishing. Paris.

AfDB (2015). International anti-corruption day: AfDB calls for stronger measures in Africa. Available at https://www.afdb.org/en/news-and-events/international-anti-corruption-day-afdb-calls-for-stronger-measures-in-africa-15205.

Africa Renewal (2020). Promotion of international cooperation to combat illicit financial flows. Available at https://www.un.org/africarenewal/news/promotion-international-cooperation-combat-illicit-financial-flows.

African Union Commission (2019). *Domestic Resource Mobilization: Fighting Against Corruption and Illicit Financial Flows*. Addis Ababa.

Ahene-Codjoe AA and Alu A (2019). Commodity trade-related illicit financial flows: Evidence of abnormal pricing in commodity exports from Ghana. Working Paper No. 3. University of Ghana.

Ajayi SI and Khan MS, eds. (2000). *External Debt and Capital Flight in Sub-Saharan Africa*. IMF. Washington, D.C.

Ajayi SI and Ndikumana L, eds. (2014). *Capital Flight from Africa: Causes, Effects and Policy Issues*. Oxford University Press. Oxford.

Alfers L (2016). Our children do not get the attention they deserve: A synthesis of research findings on women informal workers and childcare from six membership-based organizations. Women in Informal Employment: Globalizing and Organizing. Cambridge, United States.

Alliance Sud, Centre for Economic and Social Rights, Global Justice Clinic, New York University School of Law, Public Eye and Tax Justice Network (2016). Swiss responsibility for the extraterritorial impacts of tax abuse on women's rights. Report submitted to the sixty-fifth session of the Committee on the Elimination of Discrimination against Women. Geneva. 24 October–18 November.

Allingham MG and Sandmo A (1972). Income tax evasion: A theoretical analysis. *Journal of Public Economics*. 1(3):323–338.

Alstadsæter A, Johannesen N and Zucman G (2018). Who owns the wealth in tax havens? Macro evidence and implications for global inequality. *Journal of Public Economics*. 162(C):89–100.

Ampah IK and Kiss GD (2019). Economic policy implications of external debt and capital flight in sub-Saharan Africa's heavily indebted poor countries. *Society and Economy*. 41(4):523–542.

Amundsen I (2017). Nigeria: Defying the resource curse. In: William A and Le Billon P, eds. *Corruption, Natural Resources and Development: From Resource Curse to Political Ecology*. Edward Elgar Publishing. Cheltenham and Northampton, United Kingdom.

AndersenTax (2019). Review of transfer pricing development in Africa: A study of key sub-Saharan African countries. Available at https://andersentax.ng/docs/review_ of_transfer_pricing_development_in_africa_10042019.pdf.

Anderson B and Jooste J (2014). Wildlife poaching: Africa's surging trafficking threat. Security Brief No. 28. Africa Centre for Strategic Studies.

Aragón FM and Rud JP (2016). Polluting industries and agricultural productivity: Evidence from mining in Ghana. *The Economic Journal*. 126(597):1980–2011.

Ariyoshi A, Kirilenko A, Ötker I, Laurens B, Canales Kriljenko J and Habermeier K (2000). Capital controls: Country experiences with their use and liberalization. Occasional Paper No. 190. IMF.

Asfaw S, Kassie M, Simtowe F and Lipper L (2012). Poverty reduction effects of agricultural technology adoption: A micro evidence from rural [United Republic of] Tanzania. *The Journal of Development Studies*. 48(9):1288–1305.

ATAF (2019). ATAF high-level tax policy dialogue: Ensuring Africa's place in the taxation of the digital economy. Available at https://events.ataftax.org/media/documents/42/ documents/OUTCOMES_STATEMENT_-_3rd_HLPD_Zimbabwe_FINAL.pdf.

Auty RM (1993). *Sustaining Development in Mineral Economies: The Resource Curse Thesis*. Routledge. London.

Ayogu MD and Gbadebo-Smith F (2014). Governance and illicit financial flows. In: Ajayi SI and Ndikumana L, eds. *Capital Flight from Africa: Causes, Effects and Policy Issues*. Oxford University Press. Oxford.

Baker RW (2005). *Capitalism's Achilles' Heel: Dirty Money and How to Renew the Free-Market System*. John Whiley and Sons. Hoboken, United States.

Banga R (2013). Measuring value in global value chains. Regional Value Chains Background Paper No. 8. UNCTAD.

Barthel F, Busse M and Neumayer E (2010). The impact of double taxation treaties on foreign direct investment: Evidence from large dyadic panel data. *Contemporary Economic Policy*. 28(3):366–377.

Bates RH (2006). Institutions and development. *Journal of African Economies*. 15(1):10–61.

Beer S and Loeprick J (2018). The cost and benefits of tax treaties with investment hubs: Findings from sub-Saharan Africa. Policy Research Working Paper 8623. World Bank.

Beja jr. EL (2006). Revisiting the revolving door: Capital flight from Southeast Asia. Working Paper No. 16. United Nations Department of Economic and Social Affairs.

Benk S, McGee RW and Yuzbasi B (2015). How [do] religions affect attitudes toward ethics of tax evasion? A comparative and demographic analysis. *Journal for the Study of Religions and Ideologies*. 14(41):202–223.

Bensassi S, Jarreau J and Mitaritonna C (2016). Determinants of cross-border informal trade: The case of Benin. Working Paper. International Food Policy Research Institute.

Bergstrand JH and Egger P (2007). A knowledge-and-physical-capital model of international trade flows, foreign direct investment and multinational enterprises. *Journal of International Economics*. 73(2):278–308.

Berman N, Couttenier M, Rohner D and Thoenig M (2017). This mine is mine! How minerals fuel conflicts in Africa. *American Economic Review*. 107(6):1564–1610.

Besley T and Persson T (2010). State capacity, conflict and development. *Econometrica*. 78(1):1–34.

Bhagwati J (1964). On the underinvoicing of imports. *Bulletin of the Oxford University Institute of Economics and Statistics*. 27(4):389–397.

Bhagwati J (1967). Fiscal policies, the faking of foreign trade declarations and the balance of payments. *Bulletin of the Oxford University Institute of Economics and Statistics*. 29(1):61–77.

Bicaba Z, Brixiová Z and Ncube M (2015). Capital account policies, IMF programmes and growth in developing regions. Working Paper Series No. 217. AfDB.

Biggs EM, Bruce E, Boruff B, Duncan JMA, Horsley J, Pauli N, McNeill K, Neef A, Van Ogtrop F, Curnow J, Haworth B, Duce S and Imanari Y (2015). Sustainable development and the water-energy-food nexus: A perspective on livelihoods. *Environmental Science and Policy*. 54:389–397.

Birdsall N and Londono JL (1997). Asset inequality matters: An assessment of the World Bank's approach to poverty reduction. *The American Economics Review*. 87(2):32–37.

Birdsall N, Ross D and Sabot R (1995). Inequality and growth reconsidered: Lessons from East Asia. *The World Bank Economic Review*. 9(3):477–508.

Blankenburg S and Khan M (2012). Governance and illicit flows. In: Reuter P, ed. *Draining Development? Controlling Flows of Illicit Funds from Developing Countries*. World Bank. Washington, D.C.:21–68.

Bolwijn R, Casella B and Rigo D (2018). An FDI-driven approach to measuring the scale and economic impact of BEPS. *Transnational Corporations*. 25(2):107–144.

Boston Consulting Group, the Sutton Trust (2014). Pathways to banking: Improving access for students from non-privileged backgrounds. Available at https://eric. ed.gov/?q=SERVICES+AND+BANKING&id=ED559276.

Bouterige Y, de Quatrebarbes C and Laporte B (2019). Mining taxation in Africa: What recent evolution in 2018? Working Paper P257. Fondation pour les Études et Recherches sur le Développement.

Braun J, Kasper M, Majdanska A and Somare M (2016). Drivers of suspicious transaction reporting levels: Evidence from a legal and economic perspective. *Journal of Tax Administration*. 2(1):95–125.

Bridge G (2004). Mapping the bonanza: Geographies of mining investment in an era of neoliberal reform. *The Professional Geographer*. 56(3):406–421.

Brink J (2018). South Africa's first transfer pricing case? South African Institute of Tax Professionals. Available at https://www.thesait.org.za/news/409156/South-Africas-first-transfer-pricing-case-.htm.

Brugger F and Engenbretsen R (2019). Value chain risk maps. R4D-IFF Working Paper Series. Available at https://curbingiffsdotorg.files.wordpress.com/2019/02/r4d_iff_valuechainriskmaps-1.pdf.

Bundhoo-Jouglah S, Kochen A and Williams T (2005). Bilateral analysis of asymmetries in foreign trade statistics between Germany and the United Kingdom. Edicom Report 200453202016. Her Majesty's Revenue and Customs. Southend-on-Sea, United Kingdom.

Byerlee DR, Jackson CP and Diao X (2005). Agriculture, rural development and pro-poor growth: Country experiences in the post-reform era. Agriculture and Rural Development Discussion Paper No. 21. World Bank.

Campos JE and Pradhan S, eds. (2007). *The Many Faces of Corruption: Tracking Vulnerabilities at the Sector Level*. World Bank. Washington, D.C.

Capraro C (2014). Taxing men and women: Why gender is crucial for a fair tax system. Christian Aid. London.

Carbonnier G and de Cadena AZ (2015). Commodity trading and illicit financial flows. *Revue internationale de politique de développement*.

Carbonnier G and Mehrotra R (2018). Trade-related illicit financial flows: Conceptual framework and empirical methods. Working Paper No. R4D-IFF-WP01-2018. The Graduate Institute of International and Development Studies

Carbonnier G and Mehrotra R (2019). Abnormal pricing in international commodity trade: Empirical evidence from Switzerland. Discussion Paper No. R4D-IFF-WP01-2019. The Graduate Institute of International and Development Studies.

Cardoso EA and Dornbusch R (1989). Foreign private capital flows. In: Chenery H and Srinivasan TN, eds. *Handbook of Development Economics*. Elsevier:1387–1439.

Carr DL, Markusen JR and Maskus KE (2001). Estimating the knowledge-capital model of the multinational enterprise. *American Economic Review*. 91(3):693–708.

Carter P (2017). Why do development finance institutions use offshore financial centres? Overseas Development Institute.

Cathey J, Hong KP and Pak SJ (2018). Estimates of undervalued import of EU[European Union] countries and the US[United States] from the Democratic Republic of [the] Congo during 2000–2010. *International Trade Journal*. 32(1):116–128.

Chaikin D and Sharman JC (2009). Corruption and money-laundering. *Journal of Law and Society*. 36(4):589–591.

Chaisse J (2016). The E15 initiative: Strengthening the global trade and investment system for sustainable development. International Centre for Trade and Sustainable Development and World Economic Forum. Available at http://e15initiative.org/publications/international-investment-law-taxation-coexistence-cooperation/.

Chalendard C, Raballand G and Rakotoarisoa A (2016). The use of detailed statistical data in customs reform: The case of Madagascar. Policy Research Working Paper No. 7625. World Bank.

Chérel-Robson M (2017). Is local content a catalyst for development? The case of oil in Nigeria. Background document to the *Commodities and Development Report 2017*.

Chibundu MO (2010). Tensions between international law and domestic responsibilities. *International Law Studies Journal of International Law*. 1:1–9.

Cobham A and Janský P (2018). Global distribution of revenue loss from corporate tax avoidance: Re-estimation and country results. *Journal of International Development*. 30(2):206–232.

Cobham A and Janský P (2019). Measuring misalignment: The location of US[United States] multinationals' economic activity versus the location of their profits. *Development Policy Review*. 37(1):91–110.

Collier P (2007). *The Bottom Billion: Why the Poorest Countries are Failing and What Can Be Done About It*. Oxford University Press. Oxford

Collier P and Goderis B (2008). Commodity prices, growth and the natural resource curse: Reconciling a conundrum. Munich Personal Research Papers in Economics Archive. University Library of Munich, Germany.

Collier P and Hoeffler A (2004). Greed and grievance in civil war. *Oxford Economic Papers*. 56(4):563–595.

Collier P, Hoeffler A and Pattillo C (2001). Flight capital as a portfolio choice. *World Bank Economic Review*. 15(1):55–80.

Coulibaly BS and Gandhi D (2018). Mobilization of tax revenues in Africa: State of play and policy options. Policy Brief. Brookings.

Crédit Suisse (2017). Global Wealth Report 2017: Where are we 10 years after the crisis? Available at https://www.credit-suisse.com/about-us-news/en/articles/news-and-expertise/global-wealth-report-2017-201711.html.

Crédit Suisse (2019). The Crédit Suisse gender 3000 report 2019: The changing face of companies. Available at https://www.credit-suisse.com/about-us-news/en/articles/news-and-expertise/cs-gender-3000-report-2019-201910.html.

Crivelli E, de Mooij RA and Keen MJ (2015). Base erosion, profit shifting and developing countries. Working Paper No. 15/118. IMF.

Cumby R and Levich R (1987). On the definition and magnitude of recent capital flight. Working Paper No. w2275. National Bureau of Economic Research.

Dachraoui H and Smida M (2014). Measurement of capital flight and its impact on domestic investment in emerging countries. Munich Personal Research Papers in Economics Archive. University Library of Munich, Germany.

Daurer V (2014). *Tax Treaties and Developing Countries*. Series on International Taxation No. 44. Kluwer Law International.

De Wulf L (1981). Statistical analysis of under- and overinvoicing of imports. *Journal of Development Economics*. 8(3):303–323.

Devereux MP and Griffith R (1998). Taxes and the location of production: Evidence from a panel of US[United States] multinationals. *Journal of Public Economics*. 68(3):335–367.

Devereux MP and Griffith R (2003). Evaluating tax policy for location decisions. *International Tax and Public Financing*. 10(2):107–126.

DLA Piper (2012). Mining in Africa: A legal overview. Available at https://www.dlapiper. com/en/global/insights/publications/2018/08/mining-in-africa/.

Douglas LR and Alie K (2014). High-value natural resources: Linking wildlife conservation to international conflict, insecurity and development concerns. *Biological Conservation*. 171:270–277.

Eckstein D, Hutfild M-L and Winges M (2019). Global climate risk index: Who suffers most from extreme weather events? Weather-related loss events in 2017 and 1998 to 2017. Briefing paper. German Watch.

EITI Togo (2013). Report on the reconciliation of extractive payment and revenues for the year 2013. Available at https://itietogo.org/rapport-itie/.

Elborgh-Woytek K, Newiak M, Kochhar K, Fabrizio S, Kpodar KR, Wingender P, Clements BJ and Schwartz G (2013). Women, work and the economy: Macroeconomic gains from gender equity. Staff Discussion Notes No. 13/10. IMF.

El-Kady H (2016). Towards a more effective international investment policy framework in Africa. *Transnational Dispute Management*. 4.

El-Kady H and De Gama M (2019). The reform of the international investment regime: An African perspective. *International Centre for Settlement of Investment Disputes Review – Foreign Investment Law Journal*. 34(2):482–495.

European Commission (2017). The EU[European Union] new conflict minerals regulation: A quick guide if you're involved in the trade in tin, tungsten, tantalum or gold. Available at https://trade.ec.europa.eu/doclib/docs/2017/march/tradoc_155423. pdf.

European Parliament (2017). Report A8-0357/2017. Available at https://www.europarl. europa.eu/doceo/document/A-8-2017-0357_EN.html.

Ezenagu A (2019). Safe harbour regimes in transfer pricing: An African perspective. ICTD Working Paper No. 100. Available at https://www.ictd.ac/publication/safe-harbour-regimes-in-transfer-pricing-an-african-perspective/.

Feld L and Frey B (2006). Tax evasion in Switzerland: The roles of deterrence and tax morale. Working Paper. Centre for Research in Economics, Management and the Arts.

Financial Action Task Force (2003). *Financial Action Task Force: 40 Recommendations*. Available at https://www.fatf-gafi.org/media/fatf/documents/FATF%20Standards%20-%2040%20Recommendations%20rc.pdf.

Financial Action Task Force (2015). *Annual Report 2015–2016*. Available at www.fatf-gafi.org/media/fatf/documents/reports/FATF-annual-report-2015-2016.pdf.

Financial Action Task Force–Asia Pacific Group on Money-Laundering (2018). *Financial Flows from Human Trafficking*. Paris.

Fitter R and Kaplinsky R (2001). Who gains from product rents as the coffee market becomes more differentiated? A value chain analysis. *Institute of Development Studies Bulletin*. 32(3):69–82.

Fofack H and Ndikumana L (2010). Capital flight repatriation: Investigation of its potential gains for sub-Saharan African countries. *African Development Review*. 22(1):4–22.

Forstarter M (2017). Gaps in trade data ≠ criminal money-laundering. Available at https://www.cgdev.org/blog/gaps-trade-data-criminal-money-laundering.

Forstarter M (2018). Illicit financial flows, trade misinvoicing and multinational tax avoidance: The same or different? Policy Paper No. 123. Centre for Global Development

France, Assemblée Nationale (2019). Mission d'information commune relative au bilan de la lutte contre les montages transfrontaliers. Available at http://www.assemblee-nationale.fr/dyn/15/dossiers/bilan_lutte_montages_transfrontaliers_mi.

Francophone LIC[Low-Income Country] Finance Ministers Network (2014). LIC[Low-Income Country] Ministers demand their fair share of global tax revenues. Available at http://www.oecd.org/dac/OIF%20Recommendations.pdf.

Frankel JA (2010). The natural resource curse: A survey. Working Paper No. 15836. National Bureau of Economic Research.

Fukuda-Parr S (2003). The human development paradigm: Operationalizing Sen's ideas on capabilities. *Feminist Economics*. 9:301–317.

Fukuda-Parr S and Kumar S, eds. (2006). *Readings in Human Development: Concepts, Measures and Policies for a Development Paradigm*. Oxford University Press. Oxford.

Gaspar V, Amaglobeli D, Escribano MG, Prady D and Soto M (2019). Fiscal policy and development: Human, social and physical investments for the SDGs[Sustainable Development Goals]. Staff Discussion Notes No. 19/03. IMF.

Gayi S (2020). Illicit financial flows and commodities in Africa. Background paper. UNCTAD.

Gayi S and Chérel-Robson M (forthcoming). International commodity governance and illicit financial flows. UNCTAD. Geneva.

Gholami H and Salihu HA (2019). Combating corruption in Nigeria: The emergence of whistle-blowing policy. *Journal of Financial Crime*. 26:131–145.

Gibbon P (2001). Upgrading primary production: A global commodity chain approach. *World Development*. 29(2):345–363.

Gibbon P and Ponte S (2005). *Trading Down: Africa, Value Chains and the Global Economy*. Temple University Press. Philadelphia, United States.

Gilbert C (2011). International agreements for commodity price stabilization: An assessment. Food, Agriculture and Fisheries Working Papers No. 53. OECD.

Glied SA and Miller EA (2015). Economics and health reform: Academic research and public policy. *Medical Care Research and Review*. 72(4):379–394.

Global Financial Integrity (2017). Illicit financial flows to and from developing countries: 2005–2014. Available at www.gfintegrity.org/wp-content/uploads/2017/05/GFI-IFF-Report-2017_final.pdf.

Global Financial Integrity (2019). Illicit financial flows to and from 148 developing countries: 2006–2015. Available at https://gfintegrity.org/report/2019-iff-update/.

Godonou A (2007). A propos de l'universalité et du retour des biens culturels. Available at http://africultures.com/a-propos-de-luniversalite-et-du-retour-des-biens-culturels-6752/.

Gray L, Hansen K, Recica-Kirkbride P and Mills L (2014). *Few and Far: The Hard Facts on Stolen Asset Recovery*. World Bank and OECD. Washington, D.C.

Grigoli F (2015). A hybrid approach to estimating the efficiency of public spending on education in emerging and developing economies. *Applied Economics and Finance*. 2(1):19–32.

Grigoli F and Kapsoli J (2013). Waste not, want not: The efficiency of health expenditure in emerging and developing economies. Working Paper No. 13/187. IMF.

GSMA (2019). The mobile economy: Sub-Saharan Africa. Available at https://www.gsma.com/mobileeconomy/sub-saharan-africa/.

Guj P, Marin S, Maybee B, Cawood F, Bocoum B, Gosai N and Huibregtse S (2017). *Transfer Pricing in Mining with a Focus on Africa: A Reference Guide for Practitioners.* World Bank and Minerals and Energy for Development Alliance. Washington, D.C.

Haberly D and Wójcik D (2015). Regional blocks and imperial legacies: Mapping the global offshore FDI network. *Economic Geography.* 91(3):251–280.

Hall RE and Jones CI (1999). Why do some countries produce so much more output per worker than others? *The Quarterly Journal of Economics.* 114(1):83–116.

Hayashi F and Prescott EC (2006). The depressing effect of agricultural institutions on the pre-war Japanese economy. *Journal of Political Economy.* 116(4):573–632.

Hearson M (2016). Measuring tax treaty negotiation outcomes: The ActionAid tax treaties data set. Working Paper No. 47. ICTD.

Hearson M (2018). When do developing countries negotiate away their corporate tax base? *Journal of International Development.* 30(2):233–255.

Hearson M (forthcoming). International tax avoidance in Africa. Background paper for *Economic Development in Africa Report 2020.* UNCTAD.

Hearson M and Kangave J (2016). A review of Uganda's tax treaties and recommendations for action. Working Paper No. 50. Institute of Developmental Studies.

Henry J (2012). The price of offshore revisited. Available at https://www.taxjustice. net/2014/01/17/price-offshore-revisited/.

Herkenrath M (2014). Illicit financial flows and their developmental impacts: An overview. *Revue internationale de politique de développement.*

Hong KP and Pak SJ (2017). Estimating trade misinvoicing from bilateral trade statistics: The devil is in the details. *International Trade Journal.* 31(1):3–28.

Horst T (1971). The theory of the multinational firm: Optimal behaviour under different tariff and tax rates. *Journal of Political Economy.* 79(5):1059–1072.

Hunter M and Smith A (2017). *Follow the Money: Financial Flows linked to Artisanal and Small-Scale Gold Mining in Sierra Leone – A Case Study.* Global Institute against Transnational Organized Crime.

Independent Commission for the Reform of International Corporate Taxation (2018). A road map to improve rules for taxing multinationals. Available at www.dbriefsap.com/bytes/ Feb2018_3.IndependentCommissionforReformofInternationalCorporateTaxreport. pdf.

Ifejika SI (2018). The "other side" of whistle-blowing practice: Experiences from Nigeria. *Rule of Law and Anti-Corruption Centre Journal.* 4.

Ihugba OA, Ukwunna JC and Obiukwu S (2019). Government education expenditure and primary school enrolment in Nigeria: An impact analysis. *Journal of Economics and International Finance*. 11(3):24–37.

IMF (2004). *Financial Intelligence Units: An Overview*. Washington, D.C.

IMF (2008). *Regional Economic Outlook: Sub-Saharan Africa*. Washington, D.C.

IMF (2014). Implementing AML/CFT[Anti Money-Laundering/Combating the Financing of Terrorism] measures in the precious minerals sector: Preventing crime while increasing revenue. Technical Notes and Manuals 14/01.

IMF (2020). IMF and the fight against illicit financial flows. Available at https://www.imf.org/en/About/Factsheets/Sheets/2018/10/07/imf-and-the-fight-against-illicit-financial-flows.

Intergovernmental Action Group against Money-Laundering in West Africa (2014). *2014 Annual Report*. Dakar.

Intergovernmental Action Group against Money-Laundering in West Africa (2018). Summary of countries' activity reports: October 2017–September 2018. Prepared for the thirtieth plenary meeting of the Technical Commission. 12–16 November 2018.

Intergovernmental Forum on Mining, Minerals, Metals and Sustainable Development (2017). Guidance for Governments managing artisanal and small-scale mining. International Institute for Sustainable Development. Winnipeg, Canada.

International Criminal Police Organization, Rhipto Norwegian Centre for Global Analysis and Global Initiative against Transnational Organized Crime (2018). *World Atlas of Illicit Flows*.

International Finance Corporation (2014). *Sustainable and Responsible Mining in Africa: A Getting Started Guide*. Nairobi.

International Labour Organization (2019). *A Quantum Leap for Gender Equality: For a Better Future of Work for All*. Geneva.

Ireland, Ministry of Finance (2015). IBFD[International Bureau of Fiscal Documentation] spillover analysis: Possible effects of the Irish tax system on developing economies. Available at www.budget.gov.ie/Budgets/2016/Documents/IBFD_Irish_Spillover_Analysis_Report_pub.pdf.

James D (2019). Anti-development impacts of tax-related provisions in proposed rules on digital trade in WTO. *Development*. 62(1):58–65.

Janský P and Palanský M (2018). Estimating the scale of profit shifting and tax revenue losses related to foreign direct investment. Working Paper No. 21. UNU-WIDER. Helsinki.

Jerven M (2013). *Poor Numbers: How We Are Misled by African Development Statistics and What To Do About It*. Cornell University Press.

Johannesen N, Tørsløv T and Wier L (2016). Are less developed countries more exposed to multinational tax avoidance? Method and evidence from micro data. Working Paper No. 10. UNU-WIDER. Helsinki.

Kar D and Cartwright-Smith D (2009). Illicit financial flows from developing countries: 2002–2006. Available at DOI:10.2139/ssrn.1341946.

Karl TL (1997). *The Paradox of Plenty: Oil Booms and Petro-States*. University of California Press. Berkeley, United States.

Kaufman D, Kraay A and Mastruzzi M (2005). Governance matters IV: Governance indicators for 1996–2004. Policy Research Working Paper No. 3630. World Bank.

Kharas H and McArthur J (2019). Building the SDG[Sustainable Development Goal] economy: Needs, spending and financing for universal achievement of the Sustainable Development Goals. Working Paper No. 131. Brookings.

Knowles, S (2001). Inequality and economic growth: The empirical relationship reconsidered in the light of comparable data. Credit Research Paper No. 01/03. Centre for Research in Economic Development and International Trade. University of Nottingham, United Kingdom.

Kose MA, Prasad ES, Rogoff K and Wei S-J (2009). Financial globalization: A reappraisal. *Panoeconomicus*. 56(2):143–197.

Kotsadam A and Tolonen A (2016). African mining, gender and local employment. *World Development*. 83(C):325–339.

Kuteesa F, Tumusiime-Mutebile E, Whitworth A and Williamson T, eds. (2010). *Uganda's Economic Reforms: Insider Accounts*. Oxford University Press. Oxford.

Lannen A, Bürgi Bonanomi E, Rist S and Wehrli J (2016). Switzerland and the commodities trade: Taking stock and looking ahead. Factsheet 11(1). Swiss Academies of Arts and Sciences.

Laporte B, de Quatrebarbes C and Bouterige Y (2017). Mining taxation in Africa: The gold mining industry in 14 countries from 1980 to 2015. Working Paper No. 164. Fondation pour les Études et Recherches sur le Développement.

Le Billon P (2011). Extractive sectors and illicit financial flows: What role for revenue governance initiatives? *U4 Issue*. 2011:13.

Lemieux AM and Clarke RV (2009). The international ban on ivory sales and its effects on elephant poaching in Africa. *British Journal of Criminology*. 49(4):451–471.

Letete E and Sarr M (2017). Illicit financial flows and political institutions in Kenya. Working Paper No. 275. AfDB.

Lewis M, Brooks R, Chisanga P, Hearson M, Jordan C, Nshindano K, Tharoor A and Wu P (2013). Sweet nothings: The human cost of a British sugar giant avoiding taxes in Southern Africa. Available at https://www.actionaid.org.uk/sites/default/files/doc_lib/sweet_nothings.pdf.

LEX Africa (2019). *Guide to Mining Regimes in Africa 2019*. Luanda.

Limão N and Venables AJ (2001). Infrastructure, geographical disadvantage, transport costs and trade. *The World Bank Economic Review*. 15(3):451–479.

Lippert A (2014). Spillovers of a resource boom: Evidence from Zambian copper mines. Ox Carre Working Paper No. 131. Oxford Centre for the Analysis of Resource Rich Economies.

Luttmer EFP and Singhal M (2014). Tax morale. *Journal of Economic Perspectives*. 28(4):149–168.

Makuta I and O'Hare B (2015). Quality of governance, public spending on health and health status in sub-Saharan Africa: A panel data regression analysis. *Bio Med Central Public Health*. 15.

Malhotra G (2010). A new dimension of socioeconomic offences: E[lectronic] money-laundering. Available at DOI:10.2139/ssrn.1635651.

Manuel M, Desai H, Samman E and Evans M (2018). Financing the end of extreme poverty. Overseas Development Institute.

Marini M, Dippelsman R and Stanger M (2018). New estimates for direction of trade statistics. Working Paper No. 16. IMF.

Martins PMG (2019). Structural change rediscovered: The role of human and physical capital. Research and Policy Brief No. 24. World Bank.

Marur S (2019). Mirror-trade statistics: Lessons and limitations in reflecting trade misinvoicing. Discussion Paper No. R4D-IFF-WP08-2019. Graduate Institute of International and Development Studies.

Mawejje J and Sebudde RK (2019). Tax revenue potential and effort: Worldwide estimates using a new data set. *Economic Analysis and Policy*. 63(C):119–129.

May C (2017). *Transnational Crime and the Developing World*. Global Financial Integrity.

Mbembe A (2015). Decolonizing knowledge and the question of the archive. Available at https://trafo.hypotheses.org/2413.

McDaniel CA and Norberg HC (2019). Can blockchain technology facilitate international trade? Mercatus Research Paper. Available at https://ssrn.com/abstract=3377708.

McKinsey Global Institute (2015). How advancing women's equality can add $12 trillion to global growth.

McKinsey Global Institute (2019). The power of parity: Advancing women's equality in the United States.

McMillan M, Rodrik D and Sepúlveda C, eds. (2017). *Structural Change, Fundamentals and Growth: A Framework and Case Studies*. International Food Policy Research Institute. Washington, D.C.

McMillan M, Rodrik D and Verduzco-Gallo Í (2014). Globalization, structural change and productivity growth, with an update on Africa. *World Development*. 63:11–32.

McMillan M and Harttgen K (2014). What is driving the "African growth miracle"? Working Paper No. 20077. National Bureau of Economic Research.

Mehlum H, Moene K and Torvik R (2006). Institutions and the resource curse. *The Economic Journal*. 116(508):1–20.

Messina J (2006). The role of product market regulations in the process of structural change. *European Economic Review*. 50(7):1863–1890.

Mevel S, Ofa SV and Karingi S (2013). Quantifying illicit financial flows from Africa through trade mispricing and assessing their incidence on African economies. Presented at the sixteenth Global Trade Analysis Project conference. 12–14 June.

Miao G and Fortanier F (2017). Estimating transport and insurance costs of international trade. Statistics Working Paper No. 04. OECD.

Miyandazi L (2019). The complexities of tackling illicit financial flows in practice. Available at https://ecdpm.org/publications/complexities-of-tackling-illicit-financial-flows-in-practice/.

Miyandazi L and Ronceray M (2018). Understanding illicit financial flows and efforts to combat them in Europe and Africa. Discussion Paper Series. European Centre for Development Policy Management.

Moore M (2012). The practical political economy of illicit flows. In: Reuter P, ed. *Draining Development? Controlling Flows of Illicit Funds from Developing Countries*. World Bank. Washington, D.C.:457–482.

Moore M, Prichard W and Fjeldstad O-H (2018). *Taxing Africa: Coercion, Reform and Development*. Zed Books. London.

Morgenstern O (1963). *On the Accuracy of Economic Observations*. Princeton University Press.

Morrissey O, Lopez RA and Sharma K (2015). *Handbook on Trade and Development*. Edward Elgar Publishing.

Moulemyo A (2016). Impact of capital flight on public social expenditure in Congo-Brazzaville. *African Development Review*. 28(S1):113–123.

Mühlen H and Escobar O (2020). The role of FDI in structural change: Evidence from Mexico. *The World Economy*. 43(3):557–585.

Murphy R (2019). The European tax gap: A report for the Socialists and Democrats Group in the European Parliament. Available at https://www.socialistsanddemocrats.eu/sites/default/files/2019-01/the_european_tax_gap_en_190123.pdf.

Musindarwezo D (2018). The 2030 Agenda from a feminist perspective: No meaningful gains without greater accountability for Africa's women. *Agenda*. 32(1):25–35.

Musselli I and Bürgi Bonanomi E (2020). Illicit financial flows: Concepts and definition. *Revue internationale de politique de développement*.

Ndiaye AS (2009). Capital flight and its determinants in the Franc zone. *African Journal of Economic Policy*. 16(1).

Ndiaye AS (2014). Capital flight from the Franc zone: Exploring the impact on economic growth. Research Paper No. 269. African Economic Research Consortium.

Ndiaye AS and Siri A (2016). Capital flight from Burkina Faso: Drivers and impact on tax revenue. *African Development Review*. 28(S1):100–112.

Ndikumana L (2003). Capital flows, capital account regimes and foreign exchange rate regimes in Africa. Working Paper Series No. 55. Political Economy Research Institute.

Ndikumana L (2014). Capital flight and tax havens: Impact on investment and growth in Africa. *Revue d'économie du développement*. 22(2):113–141.

Ndikumana L and Boyce JK (2010). Measurement of capital flight: Methodology and results for sub-Saharan African countries. *African Development Review*. 22(4):471–481.

Ndikumana L and Boyce JK (2011). *Africa's Odious Debts: How Foreign Loans and Capital Flight Bled a Continent*. Zed Books. London.

Ndikumana L and Boyce JK (2018). Capital flight from Africa: Updated methodology and new estimates. Research Report. Political Economy Research Institute.

Ndikumana L and Boyce JK (2019). Magnitudes and mechanisms of capital flight from Angola, Côte d'Ivoire and South Africa. Capital Flight from Africa Working Paper No. 500. Political Economy Research Institute.

Ndikumana L, Boyce JK and Ndiaye AS (2014). Capital flight: Measurement and drivers. Research Report No. 363. Political Economy Research Institute.

Nelson J, Krokeme O, Markjarkson D and Timipere ET (2018). Impact of capital flight on exchange rate in Nigeria. *International Journal of Academic Research in Accounting, Finance and Management Sciences*. 8(1):41–50.

Netherlands, Ministry of Finance (2013). Government's response to the report from Seo Economics Amsterdam on other financial institutions and the IBFD[International Bureau of Fiscal Documentation] report on developing countries. Available at https://www.government.nl/documents/parliamentary-documents/2013/09/09/government-s-response-to-the-report-from-seo-economics-amsterdam-on-other-financial-institutions-and-the-ibfd-report-on-develop.

Neumayer E (2006). Do double taxation treaties increase foreign direct investment to developing countries? *The Journal of Development Studies*, 43(8):1501–1519.

Newman E, Thakur R and Tirman J, eds. (2006). *Multilateralism Under Challenge: Power, International Order and Structural Change*. United Nations University Press. Tokyo.

Nicolaou-Manias K and Wu Y (2016). Illicit financial flows estimating trade mispricing and trade-based money-laundering for five African countries. Available at www.gegafrica.org/publications/illicit-financial-flows-estimating-trade-mispricing-and-trade-based-money-laundering-for-five-african-countries.

Nin-Pratt A (2015). Inputs, productivity and agricultural growth in Africa south of the Sahara. Discussion Paper No. 01432. International Food Policy Research Institute.

Nitsch V (2011). Trade mispricing and illicit flows. Discussion Papers in Economics No. 206. Darmstadt University.

Nkurunziza JD (2014). Capital flight and poverty reduction in Africa. In: Ajayi SI and Ndikumana L, eds. *Capital Flight from Africa*. Oxford University Press. Oxford:81–110.

Nordhaus WD (1974). Resources as a constraint on growth. *The American Economic Review*. 64(2):22–26.

Nordhaus WD (2014). Estimates of the social cost of carbon: Concepts and Results from the DICE[Dynamic Integrated Climate-Economy]-2013R model and alternative approaches. *Journal of the Association of Environmental and Resource Economists*. 1(1).

North DC (1994). Institutions matter. Economic History No. 9411004. University Library of Munich, Germany.

OECD (2007). *Manual on Effective Mutual Agreement Procedures*. Available at www.oecd.org/ctp/38061910.pdf.

OECD (2013). *Addressing Base Erosion and Profit Shifting*. OECD Publishing. Paris.

OECD (2015). OECD/Group of 20 Base Erosion and Profit Shifting Project explanatory statement: 2015 final reports. Available at www.oecd.org/ctp/beps-explanatory-statement-2015.pdf.

OECD (2016). OECD Secretary-General Angel Gurría welcomes European Commission corporate tax avoidance proposals. Available at https://www.oecd.org/tax/oecd-secretary-general-angel-gurria-welcomes-european-commission-corporate-tax-avoidance-proposals.htm.

OECD (2017). OECD Council approves the 2017 update to the OECD model tax convention. Available at https://www.oecd.org/tax/treaties/oecd-approves-2017-update-model-tax-convention.htm.

OECD (2018a). *A Broken Social Elevator? How to Promote Social Mobility*. OECD Publishing. Paris.

OECD (2018b). Additional guidance on the attribution of profits to a permanent establishment. BEPS Action 7.

OECD (2018c). *Tax Challenges Arising from Digitalization – Interim Report 2018*. OECD Publishing. Paris.

OECD (2019a). *Risks That Matter: Main Findings from the 2018 OECD Risks that Matter Survey*. OECD Publishing. Paris.

OECD (2019b). The Multilateral Convention on Mutual Administrative Assistance in Tax Matters. Update, questions and answers. Available at https://www.oecd.org/tax/exchange-of-tax-information/ENG_Convention_Flyer.pdf.

OECD (2019c). *The Illegal Wildlife Trade in Southeast Asia: Institutional Capacities in Indonesia, Singapore, Thailand and Viet Nam*. OECD Publishing. Paris.

OECD (2019d). Public consultation document: Secretariat proposal for a "unified approach" under pillar one. Available at https://www.oecd.org/tax/beps/public-consultation-document-secretariat-proposal-unified-approach-pillar-one.pdf.

OECD (2019e). OECD and Group of 20 inclusive framework on BEPS: Progress report July 2017–June 2018. Available at www.oecd.org/ctp/inclusive-framework-on-beps-progress-report-june-2017-july-2018.htm.

OECD and UNDP (2018). *Tax Inspectors Without Borders: Annual Report 2017/18.* Available at www.tiwb.org/resources/publications/tax-inspectors-without-borders-annual-report-2017-2018-web.pdf.

Office of the High Commissioner for Human Rights (2015). Joint statement by United Nations human rights experts, the rapporteur on the rights of women of the Inter-American Commission on Human Rights and the special rapporteurs on the rights of women and human rights defenders of the African Commission on Human and Peoples' Rights. Available at https://www.ohchr.org/EN/NewsEvents/Pages/DisplayNews.aspx?NewsID=16490&LangID=E.

Ogbonnaya AK and Ogechuckwu OS (2017). Impact of illicit financial flow on economic growth and development: Evidence from Nigeria. *International Journal of Innovation and Economic Development.* 3(4):19–33.

Olatunji O and Oloye MI (2015). Impact of capital flight on economic growth in Nigeria. *International Journal for Innovation Education and Research.* 3(8):10–46.

Omojola O (2019). Whistle blower protection as an anti-corruption tool in Nigeria. *Journal of Law, Policy and Globalization.* 92:173–179.

Onuegbulam MC (2017). Whistle-blowing policy and the fight against corruption in Nigeria: Implications for criminal justice and the due process. *Nnamdi Azikiwe University Journal of International Law and Jurisprudence.* 8(2).

Onyele KO and Nwokocha EB (2016). The relationship between capital flight and poverty: The case of Nigeria. *Scientific Papers Series: Management, Economic Engineering in Agriculture and Rural Development.* 16(3).

Ooms G and Hammond· R (2014). Financing global health through a global fund for health? Working Group on Financing, Paper 4. Chatham House.

Osiander A (2001). Sovereignty, international relations and the Westphalian myth. *International Organization.* 55(2):251–287.

Ouoba Y (2018). Industrial mining land use and poverty in regions of Burkina Faso. *Agricultural Economics.* 49(4):511–520.

Oxfam (2018). Reward work not wealth. Available at https://www-cdn.oxfam.org/s3fs-public/file_attachments/bp-reward-work-not-wealth-220118-summ-en.pdf.

Oxfam (2019). Off the hook: How the EU[European Union] is about to whitewash the world's worst tax havens. Available at https://policy-practice.oxfam.org.uk/publications/off-the-hook-how-the-eu-is-about-to-whitewash-the-worlds-worst-tax-havens-620625.

Östensson O (2018). Misinvoicing in mineral trade: What do we really know? *Mineral Economics*. 31(1–2):77–86.

Palan R (2002). Tax havens and the commercialization of state sovereignty. *International Organization*. 56(1):151–176.

Parker D and Vadheim B (2017). Resource cursed or policy cursed? US[United States] regulation of conflict minerals and violence in the [Democratic Republic of the] Congo. *Journal of the Association of Environmental and Resource Economists*. 4(1):1–49.

Picciotto S (2013). Is the international tax system fit for purpose, especially for developing countries? Working Paper No. 13. ICTD.

Picciotto S (2018). Problems of transfer pricing and possibilities for simplification. Available at https://www.ictd.ac/publication/problems-of-transfer-pricing-and-possibilities-for-simplification/.

Piketty T (2019). *Capital et idéologie*. Seuil. Paris.

Prebisch R (1950). *The Economic Development of Latin America and its Principal Problems*. United Nations Economic Commission for Latin America (United Nations publication. Sales No. 50.II.G.2. New York).

Preobragenskaya G and McGee RW (2016). A demographic study of Russian [Federation] attitudes toward tax evasion. *Journal of Accounting, Ethics and Public Policy*. 17(1).

Prichard W and Bentum I (2009). *Taxation and Development in Ghana: Finance, Equity and Accountability*. Tax Justice Network. London.

Quentin D (2017). Risk-mining the public exchequer. *Journal of Tax Administration*. 3(2).

Ravallion M (2001). Growth, inequality and poverty: Looking beyond averages. Policy Research Working Paper No. 2558. World Bank.

Redhead A (2017). Improving mining revenue collection: [United Republic of] Tanzania's Mineral Audit Agency. Natural Resource Charter Case Study. Natural Resource Governance Institute.

Reed Q and Fontana A (2011). Corruption and illicit financial flows: The limits and possibilities of current approaches. U4 Issue No. 2. Anti-Corruption Resource Centre, Christian Michelsen Institute.

Reuter P (2012). *Draining Development? Controlling Flows of Illicit Funds from Developing Countries*. World Bank. Washington, D.C.

Reuters (2019). Gold worth billions smuggled out of Africa. Available at https://www. reuters.com/investigates/special-report/gold-africa-smuggling/.

Sachs JD and Warner AM (1995). Natural resource abundance and economic growth. Working Paper No. 5398. National Bureau of Economic Research.

Sachs JD and Warner AM (2001). The curse of natural resources. *European Economic Review*. 45:827–838.

Sahay MR, Cihak M, N'Diaye PM, Barajas A, Kyobe AJ, Mitra S, Mooi YN and Yousefi R (2017). Banking on women leaders: A case for more? Working Paper No. 199. IMF.

Saïd Business School (2019). *Responsible Business Forum – The Economics of Mutuality*. University of Oxford.

Sala-i-Martin X and Subramanian A (2003). Addressing the natural resource curse: An illustration from Nigeria. Working Paper No. 9804. National Bureau of Economic Research.

Salandy M and Henry L (2013). The impact of capital flight on investment and growth in Trinidad and Tobago, 1971–2008.

Sarr F and Savoy B (2018). The restitution of African cultural heritage. Toward a new relational ethics. Available at http://restitutionreport2018.com/.

Sauvant KP and Sachs LE (2009). *The Effect of Treaties on Foreign Direct Investment: Bilateral Investment Treaties, Double Taxation Treaties and Investment Flows*. Oxford University Press. Oxford.

Savoy B (2018). The restitution revolution begins. *The Art Newspaper*. 16 February. Available at https://www.theartnewspaper.com/comment/the-restitution-revolution-begins.

Schjelderup G and Sorgard L (1997). Transfer pricing as a strategic device for decentralized multinationals. *International Tax and Public Finance*. 4(3):277–290.

Schneider K and Buehn A (2013). Estimating the size of the shadow economy: Methods, problems and open questions. Working Paper Series No. 4448. Centre for Economic Studies Institute for Economic Research.

Schneider K and Gugerty MK (2011). Agricultural productivity and poverty reduction: Linkages and pathways. *The Evans School Review*. 1(1).

Schuster C and Davis J (2020). The value of mirror-trade data analysis for the detection of commodity-specific illicit outflows from Africa. Background document for the *Economic Development in Africa Report 2020*. UNCTAD.

Sen A (1992). *Inequality Re-examined*. Harvard University Press.

Sen A (1999). *Development as Freedom*. Anchor Books.

Shimizu N and Rocamora AR (2016). Analysis of financial components of intended nationally determined contributions: Lessons for future NDCs[nationally determined contributions]. Working Paper. Institute for Global Environmental Strategies.

Singer HW (1950). The distribution of gains between investing and borrowing countries. *The American Economic Review*. 40(2):473–485.

Slany A, Chérel-Robson M and Picard L (2020). Illicit financial flows and sustainable development: Panel-data evidence for Africa. Background paper for *Economic Development in Africa Report 2020*. UNCTAD.

Source Global Research (2019). *The Global Tax Market in 2019*. Available at https://reports.sourceglobalresearch.com/report/5004/the-global-tax-market-in-2019.

StAR (2019). *International Partnerships on Asset Recovery: Overview and Global Directory of Networks*. World Bank. Washington, D.C.

Stenberg K, Hanssen O, Edejer TT, Bertram , Brindley C, Meshreky A, Rosen JE, Stover J, Verboom P, Sanders R and Soucat A (2017). Financing transformative health systems towards achievement of the health Sustainable Development Goals: A model for projected resource needs in 67 low-income and middle-income countries. *Lancet Global Health*. 5(9):875–887.

Stoop N, Verpoorten M and van der Windt P (2018). More legislation, more violence? The impact of Dodd-Frank in the DRC[Democratic Republic of the Congo]. *Public Library of Science One*. 13(8).

Switzerland, Interdepartmental Coordinating Group on Combating Money-Laundering and the Financing of Terrorism (2015). Report on the national evaluation of the risks of money-laundering and terrorist financing in Switzerland.

Tax Justice Network (2020). Financial Secrecy Index 2020 reports progress on global transparency – but backsliding from US[United States], Cayman [Islands] and UK[United Kingdom] prompts call for sanctions. Available at https://www.taxjustice.net/2020/02/18/financial-secrecy-index-2020-reports-progress-on-global-transparency-but-backsliding-from-us-cayman-and-uk-prompts-call-for-sanctions/.

Thirtle C, Xavier I, Lin L, McKenzie-Hill V and Wiggins S (2001). Relationship between changes in agricultural productivity and the incidence of poverty in developing countries. Report No. 7946. Department for International Development.

Torgler B (2002). Speaking to theorists and searching for facts: Tax morale and tax compliance in experiments. *Journal of Economic Surveys*. 16(5):657–683.

Torgler B (2003). Tax morale in transition countries. *Post-Communist Economies*. 15(3):357–381.

Tørsløv TR, Wier LS and Zucman G (2018). The missing profits of nations. Working Paper No. 24701. National Bureau of Economic Research.

Trenczek J (2016). Promoting growth-enhancing structural change: Evidence from a panel of African, Asian and Latin American countries. Discussion Paper No. 207. Courant Research Centre. Göttingen, Germany.

Tropina T (2016). Do digital technologies facilitate illicit financial flows? Background paper for the *World Development Report 2016*. World Bank.

Uguru LC (2016). On the tax implications of capital flight: Evidence from Nigeria. *Journal of Research in Economics and International Finance*. 5(1):1–7.

UN-Women (2018). *Turning Promises into Action: Gender Equality in the 2030 Agenda for Sustainable Development*. Available at https://www.unwomen.org/digital-library/publications/2018/2/gender-equality-in-the-2030-agenda-for-sustainable-development-2018.

UN-Women (2019). The gender gap in agricultural productivity in sub-Saharan Africa: Causes, costs and solutions. Policy Brief No. 11.

UNCTAD (2003). Management of Capital Flows: Comparative Experiences and Implications for Africa (United Nations publication. Sales No. E.03.II.D.20. New York and Geneva).

UNCTAD (2013). Reform of investor–State dispute settlement: In search of a road map. International Investment Agreement Issues Note No. 2.

UNCTAD (2014a). *Trade and Development Report, 2014: Global Governance and Policy Space for Development* (United Nations publication. Sales No. E.14.II.D.4. New York and Geneva).

UNCTAD (2014b). *World Investment Report 2014: Investing in the SDGs[Sustainable Development Goals] – An Action Plan* (United Nations publication. Sales No. E.14.II.D.1. New York and Geneva).

UNCTAD (2015a). *World Investment Report 2015: Reforming International Investment Governance* (United Nations publication. Sales No. E.15.II.D.5. New York and Geneva).

UNCTAD (2015b). Investment policy framework for sustainable development. Available at https://unctad.org/en/pages/PublicationWebflyer.aspx?publicationid=1437.

UNCTAD (2016). *Trade Misinvoicing in Primary Commodities in Developing Countries: The Cases of Chile, Côte d'Ivoire, Nigeria, South Africa and Zambia* (united Nations publication. Geneva and New York).

UNCTAD (2017). *Commodities and Development Report 2017: Commodity Markets, Economic Growth and Development* (United Nations publication. Sales No. E.17.II.D.1. New York and Geneva).

UNCTAD (2018). UNCTAD's reform package for the international investment regime. Geneva and New York.

UNCTAD (2019a). *State of Commodity Dependence 2019* (United Nations publication. Sales No. E.19.II.D.8. New York and Geneva).

UNCTAD (2019b). *Trade and Development Report, 2019: Financing a Global Green New Deal* (United Nations publication. Sales No. E.19.II.D.15. New York and Geneva).

UNCTAD (2019c). Taking stock of international investment agreement reform: Recent developments. International Investment Agreement Issues Note No. 3.

UNCTAD (2019d). *Commodities and Development Report 2019 – Commodity Dependence, Climate Change and the Paris Agreement* (United Nations publication. Sales No. E.19.II.D.8. New York and Geneva).

UNCTAD and UNODC (forthcoming). Conceptual framework for the measurement of illicit financial flows.

UNDP (2017). *Income Inequality Trends in Sub-Saharan Africa: Divergence, Determinants and Consequences*. New York.

UNECA (2014). *A Country Mining Vision Guidebook: Domesticating the Africa Mining Vision*. Available at https://www.uneca.org/sites/default/files/PublicationFiles/country_mining_vision_guidebook.pdf.

UNECA (2015). *Illicit Financial Flows: Report of the High-Level Panel on Illicit Financial Flows from Africa*. Available at https://repository.uneca.org/bitstream/handle/10855/22695/b11524868.pdf.

UNECA (2016). *Greening Africa's Industrialization* (United Nations publication. Sales No. E.16.II.K.3. Addis Ababa).

UNECA (2019). *Fiscal Policy for Financing Sustainable Development in Africa: Economic Report on Africa*. Addis Ababa.

UNECA and African Minerals Development Centre. (2017). *Impact of Illicit Financial Flows on Domestic Resource Mobilization: Optimizing Revenues from the Mineral Sector in Africa*. Addis Ababa.

UNECA and African Union (2011). *Minerals and Africa's Development: The International Study Group Report on Africa's Mineral Regimes*. UNECA. Addis Ababa.

UNESCO (2015). *Education for All 2000–2015: Achievements and Challenges*. Paris.

UNESCO (2018). *Fighting the Illicit Trafficking of Cultural Property: A Toolkit for European Judiciary and Law Enforcement.* Paris.

UNFCCC (2015). Twenty-first Conference of the Parties Report Add.1 – Paris Agreement. FCCCP/CP/2015/10/Add.1. Paris.

UNFCCC (2019). Background note on the $100 billion goal in the context of UNFCCC process, in relation to advancing on SDG[Sustainable Development Goal] indicator 13.a.1. Available at https://unstats.un.org/sdgs/tierlll-indicators/files/13.a.1_Background.pdf.

United Nations (2017). *United Nations Handbook on Selected Issues for Taxation of the Extractive Industries by Developing Countries*. New York.

United Nations, General Assembly (2011). Twelfth United Nations Congress on Crime Prevention and Criminal Justice. A/RES/65/230. New York. 1 April.

United Nations, General Assembly (2017a). Promotion of international cooperation to combat illicit financial flows in order to foster sustainable development. A/RES/71/213. New York. 18 January.

United Nations, General Assembly (2017b). Research-based study on the impact of flow of funds of illicit origin and the non-repatriation thereof to the countries of origin on the enjoyment of human rights, including economic, social and cultural rights. A/HRC/36/52. New York. 9 August.

United Nations, General Assembly (2019). Promotion of international cooperation to combat illicit financial flows and strengthen good practices on assets return to foster sustainable development. A/RES/73/222. New York. 10 January.

United Nations, Security Council (2002). Final report of the Panel of Experts on the Illegal Exploitation of Natural Resources and Other Forms of Wealth of the Democratic Republic of the Congo. S/2002/1146. 16 October.

United Nations, Security Council (2016). Letter dated 22 January 2016 from the Panel of Experts on South Sudan established pursuant to Security Council resolution 2206 (2015) addressed to the President of the Security Council. S/2016/70. 22 January.

United Nations, Security Council (2019). Strengthening the partnership between the United Nations and the African Union on issues of peace and security in Africa, including on the work of the United Nations Office to the African Union Report of the Secretary-General. S/2019/759. 19 September.

United Nations Conference on Trade and Employment (1948). *The Havana Charter for an International Trade Organization*. Article 55.

United Nations Environment Programme (2016). *The Adaptation Gap Finance Report 2016*. Nairobi.

United Nations University Press (2007). *Multilateralism Under Challenge? Power, International Order and Structural Change*. Tokyo.

United States, Government Accountability Office (2015). Dodd-Frank regulations: Impacts on community banks, credit unions and systemically important institutions. Report to congressional addressees.

UNODC (2011). Estimating illicit financial flows resulting from drug trafficking and other transnational organized crimes. Research report.

UNODC (2018). *Global Study on Smuggling of Migrants* (United Nations publication. Sales No. E.18.IV.9. New York).

UNODC and OECD (2016). Coherent policies for combating illicit financial flows. Issue Brief. Inter-Agency Task Force on Financing for Development.

UNODC and World Bank (2007). Stolen Asset Recovery Initiative: Challenges, opportunities and action plan. Washington, D.C.

UNSD (2008). *International Merchandise Trade Statistics: Supplement to the Compilers Manual* (United Nations publication. Sales No. E.08.XVII.9. New York).

UNSD (2011). *International Merchandise Trade Statistics: Concepts and Definitions 2010*. Statistical Papers Series M No. 52.

UNSD (2019). International merchandise trade statistics bilateral asymmetries: How to measure, analyse, reduce and way forward. Available at unstats.un.org/unsd/tradekb/Attachment441.aspx?AttachmentType=1.

Usman FR and Arene CJ (2014). Effects of capital flight and its macroeconomic determinants in agricultural growth in Nigeria (1970–2013). *International Journal of Food and Agricultural Economics*. 2(4):107–126.

van der Does de Willebois E, Halter EM, Harrison RA, Park JW and Sharman JC (2011). *The Puppet Masters: How the Corrupt Use Legal Structures to Hide Stolen Assets and What to Do About It*. World Bank. Washington, D.C.

Vitola A and Senfelde M (2015). The role of institutions in economic performance. *Business: Theory and Practice*. 16(3):271–279.

von der Goltz J and Barnwal P (2019). Mines: The local wealth and health effects of mineral mining in developing countries. *Journal of Development Economics*. 139(C):1–16.

Waris A (2017). How Kenya has implemented and adjusted to the changes in international transfer pricing regulations: 1920–2016. Working Paper No. 69. ICTD.

Waris A and Latif LA (2015). Towards establishing fiscal legitimacy through settled fiscal principles in global health financing. *Health Care Analysis: Journal of Health Philosophy and Policy*. 23(4):376–390.

WCO (2018). Illicit financial flows via trade misinvoicing. Available at www.wcoomd. org/-/media/wco/public/global/pdf/media/newsroom/reports/2018/wco-study-report-on-iffs_tm.pdf?la=en

Wei C (2015). Taxation of non-residents' capital gains. In: Trepelkov A, Tonino H and Halka D, eds., *United Nations Handbook on Selected Issues in Protecting the Tax Base of Developing Countries* (United Nations publication, New York).

Wendling ZA, Emerson JW, Esty DC, Levy MA and de Sherbinin A (2018). *2018 Environmental Performance Index*. Yale Centre for Environmental Law and Policy. New Haven, United States.

Wijnen W and de Goede J (2013). *The UN[United Nations] Model in Practice 1997 – 2013*. Available at https://www.ibfd.org/sites/ibfd.org/files/content/pdf/UN-Model-in-Practice-%201997-2013-research-draft-by-IBFD.pdf.

Woodroffe N and Grice T (2019). *Beyond Revenues: Measuring and Valuing Environmental and Social Impacts in Extractive Sector Governance*. Natural Resource Governance Institute.

World Bank (2004). Corruption and money-laundering: Concepts and practical applications. Module 1. Available at http://pubdocs.worldbank.org/en/887011427730119189/AML-Module-1.pdf.

World Bank (2008). Democratic Republic of the Congo: Growth with governance in the mining sector. Report No. 43402-ZR.

World Bank (2016). The World Bank Group's response to illicit financial flows: A stocktaking.

World Bank (2017a). Illicit financial flows. Available at https://www.worldbank.org/en/topic/financialsector/brief/illicit-financial-flows-iffs.

World Bank (2017b). *The Growing Role of Minerals and Metals for a Low Carbon Future*. Washington, D.C.

World Bank (2018). *Poverty and Shared Prosperity 2018: Piecing Together the Poverty Puzzle*. Washington, D.C.

World Bank (2019). *Illegal Logging, Fishing and Wildlife Trade: The Costs and How to Combat It*. Washington, D.C.

World Bank (2020). *World Development Report 2020: Trading for Development in the Age of Global Value Chains*. Washington, D.C.

World Economic Forum (2011). *Water Security: The Water-Food-Energy-Climate Nexus*. Island Press. Washington, D.C.

World Economic Forum (2015). State of the illicit economy. Available at http://reports. weforum.org/state-of-the-illicit-economy-briefing-papers-info/.

World Food Programme, United States (2017). Winning the peace: Hunger and instability. Washington, D.C.

Yagboyaju DA and Akinola AO (2019). Nigerian State and the crisis of governance: A critical exposition. *SAGE Open*. 9(3).

Yikona SM, Slot B, Geller M, Hansen B and El Kadiri F, eds. (2011). Ill-*Gotten Money and the Economy: Experiences from Malawi and Namibia*. World Bank. Washington, D.C.

Yitzhaki S (1974). A note on income tax evasion. *Public Finance Quarterly*. 15(2):123–137.

Zharan K and Bongaerts JC (2018). Survey on integrating of renewable energy into the mining industry. *Journal of Environmental Accounting and Management*. 6(2):149–165.

Zucman G (2013). The missing wealth of nations: Are Europe and the US[United States] net debtors or net creditors? *Quarterly Journal of Economics*. 128(3):1321–1364.

Zucman G (2014). Taxing across borders: Tracking personal wealth and corporate profits. *Journal of Economic Perspectives*. 28(4):121–148.

Zucman G (2017). *La richesse cachée des nations : Enquête sur les paradis fiscaux*. La République des Idées. Paris.

Zucman G (2019). Taxing multinational corporations in the twenty-first century. Research Brief 10. Economists for Inclusive Prosperity.